. on or bef
.ed bel

ALTERNATIVE MEDI   IN

D1343432

ALTERNATIVE MEDICINE IN BRITAIN

Edited by

MIKE SAKS

CLARENDON PRESS · OXFORD
1992

Oxford University Press, Walton Street, Oxford OX2 6DP

Oxford New York Toronto
Delhi Bombay Calcutta Madras Karachi
Petaling Jaya Singapore Hong Kong Tokyo
Nairobi Dar es Salaam Cape Town
Melbourne Auckland
and associated companies in
Berlin Ibadan

Oxford is a trade mark of Oxford University Press

Published in the United States
by Oxford University Press, New York

British Library Cataloguing in Publication Data
Data available

Library of Congress Cataloging in Publication Data
Alternative medicine in Britain/edited by Mike Saks.
p.   cm.
Includes index.
1. Alternative medicine—Great Britain—History.   2. Alternative
medicine—Great Britain.   I. Saks, Mike.
[DNLM: 1. Alternative Medicine—Great Britain.   2. Therapeutics—
Great Britain.   WB 890 A4656]
R733.A47   1991   362.1'0941—dc20   91–3587
ISBN 0–19–827278–2 (Hbk.)
ISBN 0–19–827277–4 (Pbk.)

Typeset by Cambrian Typesetters, Frimley, Surrey
Printed and bound in
Great Britain by Bookcraft (Bath) Ltd,.
Midsomer Norton, Avon

This book is dedicated to
Maj-Lis, Jonathan, and Laura,
without whose support it would not have been possible.

ACKNOWLEDGEMENTS

Thanks are due to all the publishers and authors who co-operated with me in producing this volume. Formal acknowledgement of the copyright permissions given for the non-exclusive world rights in English to use the items reproduced in this collection is set out below:

1. Unpublished paper presented at the British Sociological Association Annual Conference, University of Manchester, 1976. Reprinted by permission of Professor J. Larner, principal executor of the estate of Professor C. J. Larner.
2. Reprinted from A. Oakley, 'Wisewoman and Medicine Man: Changes in the Management of Childbirth', in A. Oakley and J. Mitchell (eds.), *The Rights and Wrongs of Women* (Harmondsworth: Penguin, 1976), 17–58. Copyright © Ann Oakley 1976. Used by permission.
3. Original article © Dr P. W. G. Wright 1990, by permission of the author.
4. Reprinted from E. Maple, *Magic, Medicine and Quackery* (London: Robert Hale Ltd., 1968), 111–31, by permission of the author.
5. Reprinted from T. M. Parssinen, 'Professional Deviants and the History of Medicine: Medical Mesmerists in Victorian Britain', in R. Wallis (ed.), *On the Margins of Science: The Social Construction of Rejected Knowledge*, Sociological Review Monograph No. 27 (University of Keele, Keele, 1979), 103–20, by permission of Routledge and Kegan Paul plc.
6. Reprinted from P. A. Nicholls, *Homoeopathy and the Medical Profession* (London: Croom Helm, 1988), 133–64, by permission of Associated Book Publishers Ltd.
7. Reprinted from M. Chamberlain, *Old Wives Tales* (London: Virago Press, 1981), 94–138, by permission of Virago Press and the author. Copyright © Mary Chamberlain 1981.
8. Reprinted from P. Vaughan, *Doctors' Commons* (London: Heinemann, 1959), 89–105, by permission of the author.
9. Original article © Professor G. V. Larkin 1990, by permission of the author.

10. Reprinted from B. Inglis, *Natural Medicine* (London: Fontana/Collins, 1980), 95–115, by permission of Collins Publishers and Curtis Brown, London. Copyright © Martin Esslin.

11. Original article © Dr J. Vincent 1990, by permission of the author.

12. Reprinted from G. Allen and R. Wallis 'Pentecostalists as a Medical Minority', in R. Wallis and P. Morley (eds.), *Marginal Medicine* (London: Peter Owen, 1976), 110–37, by permission of Peter Owen Ltd.

13. Reprinted from S. J. Fulder, *The Handbook of Complementary Medicine* (Oxford: Oxford University Press, 2nd edn., 1988), 41–62, by permission of Jacintha Alexander Associates and Hodder and Stoughton Ltd.

14. Original article © Dr M. Saks 1990, by permission of the author.

15. Reprinted from R. West, 'Alternative Medicine: Prospects and Speculations', in N. Black, D. Boswell, A. Gray, S. Murphy and J. Popay (eds.), *Health and Disease: A Reader* (Milton Keynes: Open University Press, 1984), 341–47, by permission of the Open University. Copyright © The Open University Press.

16. Reprinted from British Medical Association, *Report of the Board of Science and Education on Alternative Therapy* (London, 1986), 61–75, by permission of the British Medical Association.

17. Reprinted from British Holistic Medical Association, *Report on the British Medical Association Board of Science Working Party on Alternative Therapy* (London, 1986), 64–74, by permission of the British Holistic Medical Association and the authors, Dr P. C. Pietroni and Dr. D. Aldridge.

18. Reprinted from T. Huggon, 'Brussels Post-1992: Protector or Persecutor?' *Journal of Alternative and Complementary Medicine* (Feb. 1990), 13–15, by permission of Tom Huggon and the *Journal of Alternative and Complementary Medicine*, Mariner House, 53A High Street, Bagshot, Surrey.

CONTENTS

Introduction

Mike Saks

This edited collection of readings on alternative medicine in Britain is intended to fill a major gap in the social scientific literature on alternative medicine, for while social scientists have written a good deal on this highly topical subject in the contemporary era, very little of their work is centred on British society. The comparison is particularly stark in relation to alternative therapies in the United States, where a much wider span of social scientific literature exists,[1] perhaps in part because of the stronger American tradition of frontier medicine and fee-for-service health care which has generated a more organized and extensive network of alternative practitioners in modern times.[2] There are signs that this anomalous situation is now slowly beginning to be addressed. However, with the primary exception of some stimulating discussions that have recently appeared in readers tracing the history of alternative medicine,[3] the landscape is still relatively bleak as far as Britain is concerned—with the subject rarely being mentioned or given significant coverage even in mainstream British social science texts relating to health care.[4]

This book helps to redress the balance in this area of growing

[1] This is apparent from the disproportionate emphasis given to the United States in the contents of two of the more highly regarded recent social scientific collections on alternative medicine published in Britain. See J. W. Salmon (ed.), *Alternative Medicines: Popular and Policy Perspectives* (London: Tavistock, 1985), and R. Wallis and P. Morley (eds.), *Marginal Medicine* (London: Peter Owen, 1976).

[2] R. Wallis and P. Morley, 'Introduction', ibid. 9–19.

[3] See, for instance, W. F. Bynum and R. Porter (eds.), *Medical Fringe and Medical Orthodoxy* (London: Croom Helm, 1987), and R. Cooter (ed.), *Studies in the History of Alternative Medicine* (London: Macmillan, 1988).

[4] This is well illustrated by C. Ham, *Health Policy in Britain* (London: Macmillan, 2nd edn., 1985); N. Hart, *The Sociology of Health and Medicine* (Ormskirk: Causeway Press, 1985); R. Klein, *The Politics of the National Health Service* (London: Longman, 2nd edn., 1989); and B. Turner, *Medical Power and Social Knowledge* (London: Sage, 1987).

academic interest by drawing together both previously published and original commissioned work on alternative medicine of relevance to social scientists in the British context. In so doing, it covers selected aspects of the past, present, and future of alternative practices in health care in this country. It is argued that the changing position of such therapies over time cannot be fully understood without reference to the socio-political process underpinning the professionalization of medicine which has had a major impact on both the conceptual boundaries, and the destiny, of alternative medicine in Britain. In consequence, the items included here will have particular—if not exclusive— relevance in the social sciences to students of sociology, politics, social policy, and social history.

The book, however, is targeted towards a broader readership than social scientists alone; it is also designed to appeal to practising health professionals and those taking vocational courses in the health field, as well as the interested lay reader. As such, while the unique collection of contributions gathered here is both challenging and scholarly, it remains highly accessible. The content of this volume is therefore to be distinguished from that of many books on alternative medicine which simply inform the reader about this area in a popular, and sometimes sensation- alist, style or serve as basic manuals for the would-be practitioner of unorthodox therapies.[5] At the same time, the various items contained in this collection have been selected in such a way that prior knowledge of the social sciences, and their associated theories, is not a necessary prerequisite for understanding its main themes.

THE CENTRAL CONCEPT OF ALTERNATIVE MEDICINE

The reader covers a range of unorthodox therapies—spanning from acupuncture, herbalism, and homoeopathy to chiropractic,

---

[5] On the popular tradition, see, for example, J. L. Fraser, *The Medicine Men: A Guide to Natural Medicine* (London: Thames/Methuen, 1981), and T. Kaptchuk and M. Croucher, *The Healing Arts: A Journey Through the Faces of Medicine* (London: British Broadcasting Corporation, 1986). The practical applications of alternative medicine are more thoroughly discussed in texts like G. Lewith (ed.), *Alternative Therapies: A Guide to Complementary Medicine for the Health Professional* (London: Heinemann, 1985), and D. Rankin-Box (ed.), *Complementary Health Therapies: A Guide for Nurses and the Caring Professions* (London: Croom Helm, 1988).

osteopathy, and spiritual healing—all of which are here defined as 'alternative medicine'. However, since the labels of 'traditional medicine', 'complementary medicine', and 'holistic medicine' are also extensively applied to such practices in the literature on this subject,[6] an explanation needs to be provided as to why the term 'alternative medicine' should be used as a central co-ordinating concept in the organization of this book.

One major rationale for employing the notion of 'alternative medicine' in this context is that the competing concepts outlined above are insufficiently comprehensive for the purposes intended. Thus the well-established notion of 'traditional medicine', for example, might well apply to the laying on of hands and classical acupuncture, but does not encompass chiropractic which is of more recent origin. Similarly, for all the ideological capital unorthodox practitioners may derive from co-operating with the medical establishment, the label of 'complementary medicine' excludes therapies like homoeopathy which in their purest form are based on philosophies that fundamentally conflict with medical orthodoxy. On the other hand, the much in vogue term 'holistic medicine'—which implies a concern to engage both the mind and body of the individual in diagnosis and treatment—fits homoeopathy well, yet rules out, amongst other things, the work of osteopaths who adopt a mechanistic approach to human disorders.

The concept of 'alternative medicine', in contrast, is not only more all-embracing in its coverage, but is also of greater analytical utility than the above definitions. The main problem with the other terms is that they are focused too heavily on identifying similarities in the actual nature of unorthodox practice itself in an extremely heterogeneous field—in which there are literally dozens of therapies available, based on a myriad of differing theories and techniques.[7] What their proponents fail to recognize is that the key distinguishing feature of such therapies is not their common content, but their socio-politically defined marginal standing in the health care system. In this sense,

---

[6] See R. Eagle, *A Guide to Alternative Medicine* (London: British Broadcasting Corporation, 1980), and J. Richman, *Medicine and Health* (London: Longman, 1987).

[7] For a useful review of the many different kinds of therapy that fall into the category 'alternative medicine' see A. Stanway, *Alternative Medicine: A Guide to Natural Therapies* (Harmondsworth: Penguin, 2nd edn., 1986).

the notion of 'alternative medicine' as employed in this reader can be taken to encompass all the health care practices that at any specific point in time generally do not receive support from the medical establishment in the British context, whether this be through such mechanisms as orthodox medical research funding, sympathetic coverage in the mainstream medical journals, or routine inclusion in the basic medical curriculum.

Having said this, alternative medicine—for all its diverse forms—is mainly holistically based in modern Britain in so far as it is most frequently underpinned by an emphasis on stimulating the life force of the individual in his or her total social environment, with the aim of promoting health and preventing illness. This stands in contrast to orthodox medicine which tends to be wedded to a biomedical approach in which the body is mechanistically viewed as analogous to a machine whose individual parts can be repaired through direct intervention when breakdown occurs.[8] The current broad-brush association in Britain of the biomedical and holistic approaches with orthodox and unorthodox provision of health care respectively cannot, however, be taken to represent a static picture. As the readings in this book demonstrate, much of the alternative medicine in this country today has links with mainstream health practices of centuries past and may well be on course to become at least part of the new orthodoxy of the future. This underlines the need for a relativistic notion of alternative medicine, the content of which may change over time in any single society, depending on socio-politically inspired definitions of dominance in the health care system. It also justifies the substantial balance of historical material that this book contains on alternative medicine—which is necessary to ensure that any consideration of the present standing and future of this area is imbued with an appropriate sense of perspective.

ALTERNATIVE MEDICINE AND THE MEDICAL
PROFESSION IN BRITAIN

This sense of historical perspective about alternative medicine in Britain can now be sharpened with special reference to the interrelationship between this field and the development of the

8   J. W. Salmon, 'Introduction', in id. (ed.), *Alternative Medicines*, 1–29.

medical profession. The period of two or three hundred years immediately preceding the nineteenth century forms an appropriate starting-point here. At this time, health care was a very diverse enterprise, with only relatively few 'official' medical practitioners in existence. These consisted of the lower-status surgeons and apothecaries whose training was based on the apprenticeship system and a very small number of university-educated physicians who served the social élite.[9] Most everyday health care was undertaken by a plurality of other groups including female midwives and empirics who had no formal training. Their work was supplemented by members of the lay public who practised healing without any direct economic reward for a variety of motives, such as neighbourliness and religious duty.[10] It was therefore difficult at this time to talk about a distinct medical orthodoxy and hence to define what constituted alternative medicine, particularly in an era in which a greater emphasis seems to have been placed on self-help in health care than in our own.[11]

All this was to change with the development of a centrally organized, unified, and exlusionary medical profession by the mid-nineteenth century. The long campaign involved in the creation of this profession gave the licensed practitioners it encompassed an important stake in differentiating themselves from their irregular counterparts.[12] The pivotal 1858 Medical Registration Act sealed the process of professional closure and set up a single register of legally recognized practitioners with self-regulatory powers and a monopoly over not only the title of 'doctor', but also state medical employment. Whilst it was still legal for non-registered practitioners to operate under the common law, this legislation for the first time formally defined, in a consolidated manner, the scope of alternative as well as orthodox medicine on a national basis. Alternative practice was

[9] R. Stevens, *Medical Practice in Modern England* (New Haven: Yale University Press, 1966).

[10] R. Porter, *Disease, Medicine and Society in England 1550–1860* (London: Macmillan, 1987).

[11] See, for example, G. Smith, 'Prescribing the Rules of Health: Self-Help and Advice in the Late Eighteenth Century', in R. Porter (ed.), *Patients and Practitioners: Lay Perceptions of Medicine in Pre-Industrial Society* (Cambridge: Cambridge University Press, 1985), 249–82.

[12] I. Waddington, *The Medical Profession in the Industrial Revolution* (London: Gill and Macmillan, 1984).

further delimited, moreover, by a series of additional legal enactments which extended into the twentieth century. Prominent amongst such provisions were those expanding the orthodox medical division of labour to include a number of other professions subordinated to medicine,[13] and the National Health Insurance Act of 1911 and the National Health Service Act of 1946 which gave mainstream practitioners, with their monopoly of government employment, a considerable market advantage over their unorthodox competitors.[14]

The success of the medical profession in attaining its dominant location at the heart of the health care division of labour had the effect of underwriting the historically novel position of biomedicine as the basis of medical orthodoxy in modern Britain. The biomedical approach was not central in the period immediately before the modern industrial era. At this stage, the therapies mainly in use were folk remedies reflecting several different systems of thought and even 'official' practitioners were typically engaged in such activities as purging, sweating, vomiting, and blood-letting, aimed at restoring the total body system to a state of balance.[15] The ascendance of the medical profession brought marked changes in this situation, however, as the nature of medical practice shifted away from eighteenth-century 'bedside medicine' in which higher class clients in particular played a major part in determining their own diagnosis and treatment.[16] This was transformed first into 'hospital medicine' where the disease rather than the sick person became the major focus in an essentially classificatory medical system, and then into 'laboratory medicine' which further objectified the patient through its biomedical emphasis on active intervention in human physiological processes, predicated on the conception of the body as a complex of cells.[17] It was against this dominant, mechanistic view of health and illness which developed in the nineteenth and

[13] See, for instance, G. V. Larkin, *Occupational Monopoly and Modern Medicine* (London: Tavistock, 1983), and R. Dingwall, A. M. Rafferty, and C. Webster (eds.), *An Introduction to the Social History of Nursing* (London: Routledge 1988).

[14] J. L. Berlant, *Profession and Monopoly: A Study of Medicine in the United States and Great Britain* (Berkeley, Calif.: University of California Press, 1975).

[15] Porter, *Disease, Medicine and Society in England*.

[16] N. D. Jewson, 'Medical Knowledge and the Patronage System in Eighteenth Century England', *Sociology*, 8:3 (1974), 369–85.

[17] N. D. Jewson, 'The Disappearance of the Sick-Man from Medical Cosmology 1770–1870', *Sociology*, 10:2 (1976), 225–44.

twentieth centuries in Britain that holistic therapies like homoeopathy and spiritual healing progressively came to be defined as alternatives.

The effect on health states of the rise to power of a unified medical profession primarily espousing a biomedical approach, together with the consequent marginalization of a wide range of alternative practices, is open to radically conflicting interpretations. On the one hand, the establishment of the monopolistic position of the medical profession might be welcomed for the contribution that drug treatment and surgical intervention ultimately made to health care, with alternative medicine being seen as justly confined to the periphery by the State because it is at best largely unproven and at worst a positive danger to the public.[18] On the other, emphasis might be placed on the increasingly evident counter-productive side-effects, and limited effectiveness, of contemporary medical orthodoxy,[19] as well as the apparent therapeutic benefits of many forms of alternative medicine[20]—all of which raises serious questions about the legitimacy of the legally enshrined monopolistic advantages of the medical profession over alternative practitioners. This is not a debate that is easily resolved, but the interpretation made will at least partially hinge on how far the protectionist strategy the medical profession has pursued in seeking and maintaining its currently dominant position in health care is viewed as being inspired by altruism or unconstrained self-interest.[21] This critical

[18] British Medical Association, *Report of the Board of Science and Education on Alternative Therapy* (London: British Medical Association, 1986). On the unproven and potentially dangerous effects of apparently harmless alternative treatment, see also the controversial study by F. S. Bagenal, D. F. Easton, E. Harris, C. E. D. Chilvers, and T. J. McElwain, 'Survival of Patients with Breast Cancer Attending the Bristol Cancer Help Centre', *Lancet* (8 Sept. 1990), 606–10.

[19] See I. Illich, *Limits to Medicine* (Harmondsworth: Penguin, 1977), and C. Medawar, *The Wrong Kind of Medicine?* (London: Consumers Association/ Hodder and Stoughton, 1984).

[20] This is well illustrated, amongst others, by T. W. Meade, S. Dyer, W. Browne, J. Townsend, and A. O. Frank 'Low Back Pain of Mechanical Origin: Randomised Comparison of Chiropractic and Hospital Outpatient Treatment', *British Medical Journal* (2 June 1990), 1431–6, and D. T. Reilly, M. A. Taylor, and C. McSharry, 'Is Homoeopathy a Placebo Response? Controlled Trial of Homoeopathic Potency, with Pollen in Hay Fever as a Model', *Lancet* (18 Oct. 1986), 881–6.

[21] See M. Saks, 'Sociology, Professions and the Public Interest: Professional Ideology and Public Responsibilty', paper presented at International Sociological Association Conference on Professions and Public Authority: Historical and Comparative Perspectives, Northeastern University, Boston, Mass., April 1990.

dialogue about the reasons for the demarcation of orthodox and alternative medicine is very clearly reflected in the tension between some of the readings in this collection, even though most were written in a climate that has become decidedly less willing to accept self-justificatory professional ideologies at face value.

THE EXPANSION OF INTEREST IN ALTERNATIVE MEDICINE

Irrespective of the position adopted on this issue, though, there can be no doubt about the dramatic expansion in interest in alternative approaches to health care in Britain since the early 1960s. At the beginning of the 1960s medical hegemony was rather more complete and a negative view tended to be reflexively taken of alternative practitioners by both the public and the medical establishment alike. Now there is evidence that, despite the ideological and structural disadvantages under which alternative therapists operate in relation to orthodox medicine, public consultations with them are rising sharply—to the extent that recent surveys estimate that as many as one in seven people currently visit unorthodox practitioners for treatment.[22] This has been paralleled by the development of strong popular support for the inclusion of alternative therapies within mainstream public sector medicine, so much so that a recent MORI poll showed that almost three-quarters of the population wished to have better established forms of alternative therapy, such as acupuncture, homoeopathy, and osteopathy, more widely available on the National Health Service.[23] In this light, it is not surprising to note that, although alternative medicine is still not receiving significant institutional support from the British medical establishment, growing numbers of orthodox health personnel, including many doctors, are showing an interest in alternative philosophies and techniques.[24]

[22] See, for instance, Consumers Association, 'Magic or Medicine?', *Which?* (Oct. 1986), 443–7.

[23] R. Thomas, 'Give Us More Alternatives on the NHS', *Journal of Alternative and Complementary Medicine* (Dec. 1989), 11.

[24] K. Thomas, 'Non-Orthodox Health Care in the UK', *Complementary Medical Research*, 4:2 (1990), 32–4.

This interest has also been politically manifested in so far as there are now two junior government ministers with specific responsibilities for alternative medicine in this country. The political profile of alternative medicine has been enhanced, moreover, by the fact that members of both of the main political parties in Britain over the past two decades have been more than ready to lend their support to this cause in the Houses of Commons and Lords respectively. This resulted in 1989 in the establishment of the re-formed Parliamentary Group for Alternative and Complementary Medicine which has since hosted a series of meetings on this subject and provides an important political focus for the alternative medicine lobby.[25]

The potential implications of the gathering political support in this area in the years ahead serve to underline the importance of looking to the future of alternative medicine in this reader, as well as reflecting on its historical and contemporary dimensions. This provides an appropriate cue for briefly reviewing, and highlighting the significance of, the whole range of selections on alternative medicine in Britain, which are grouped into the ensuing four parts of this book.

HEALTH CARE IN BRITAIN BEFORE THE MID-NINETEENTH CENTURY

The first part of the book focuses on health care in Britain in the era before the medical profession had risen to its position of ascendancy following the mid-nineteenth century. The readings included here, which begin in the sixteenth and seventeenth centuries, show just how open and diverse the health-care field was at this stage. As Larner affirms, there was no clearly delineated orthodoxy giving rise to any really meaningful conception of alternative medicine. However, the seeds for its development were sown with the founding of the Royal College of Physicians of London and the licensing of the apothecaries and surgeons early in the sixteenth century. The position of 'official' medicine, moreover, was later strengthened against folk practitioners by the Witchcraft Acts that could be used against those claiming special powers. Nevertheless, Larner suggests that a

[25] M. Saks, 'Power, Politics and Alternative Medicine', *Talking Politics*, 3:2 (Winter 1990/1), 68–72.

position of medical dominance could not yet be seen to have developed at this time because the number of officially licensed practitioners was so small, access to them was so variable, and their painful heroic therapies were so unattractive. Most people in fact relied on self-treatment and a disparate band of folk healers when illness struck, utilizing one or more of the heterogeneous cluster of treatments on offer—which ranged from charms and incantations at one end of the spectrum to herbal preparations at the other.

Oakley picks up a key theme underlying Larner's work—namely, that women played a central and highly valued part as healers in these early days amongst all social groups. She argues that they not only had a wide span of knowledge on which to base their activities, but also were generally trusted by the public more than their male counterparts. The focus of her contribution, though, is on the role of women healers in dealing with childbirth. Oakley notes that lay female midwives were particularly tainted by the association with witchcraft in the later stages of the pre-industrial era. Male doctors also increasingly closed ranks against them in the incipient process of professionalization that was occurring at this time. The outcome was that the traditional, empirically based authority of the female midwife–healer was progressively undermined in a rapidly changing, patriarchal society at the same time as the foundations of the modern professional medical monopoly were beginning to be laid. This was a trend that was to endure as the exclusion of women from the universities and the bodies of physicians and surgeons served to deny them access to the new medical knowledge that was developing in this field—which favoured the position of the male medical attendants (men midwives), who did not hesitate to vilify their female competitors whenever the opportunity arose.[26]

The growing demise of female authority in healing in the sixteenth and seventeenth centuries bears out the broader tenet that the mainstream practices of one age can soon become the alternative practices of another. Wright demonstrates this further in relation to astrology in seventeenth-century England. The notion that the planets affect health states may have a marginal

---

[26] M. Stacey, *The Sociology of Health and Healing: A Textbook* (London: Unwin Hyman, 1988).

medical status today, but this belief was most assuredly part of the 'official' medicine, as well as the folk traditions, of this earlier period—even being practised by members of the Royal College of Physicians at the apex of the medical hierarchy. This highlights the fact that there is a fine dividing-line between the 'orthodox' and 'unorthodox' in health care. Interestingly, Wright's analysis of the reasons for the decline of astrology in medicine following the seventeenth century suggests that the definition of the boundaries of alternative medicine is not simply based on the adequacy, or otherwise, of the knowledge involved. Rather, it is a social creation, contingent in large part on relationships of power. This power, for Wright, lay very much in the hands of the evolving medical profession from the seventeenth century onwards and was effectively employed in accordance with its own occupational self-interests within the socio-political context in which it operated in this period.

The contribution by Wright also throws into focus the problems of reading back from structures of professional dominance in medicine in the present to interpret the past. It is precisely this pitfall to which Maple might be seen as being prey in his colourful social history of the 'great age of quackery' in eighteenth-century Britain, in which such practices as bone-setting, healing by touch, and herbalism thrived. Maple cynically portrays the involvement of 'quacks' in the provision of these and other remedies in his depiction of some of the better known characters lying outside 'official' medicine at this time; with few exceptions, they are seen as being ignorant, avaricious, and dangerous, duping both the general public and royalty alike. Not so much attention is devoted to the shortcomings of the regular practitioners of the day who, far from being paragons of altruistic virtue, may well have been little different from the commercially oriented 'quacks' that they denounced.[27] For all this, however, Maple does provide an alternative perspective on the historical aspects of eighteenth-century health care that usefully underlines the debates which can arise in interpreting the relationship between orthodox and unorthodox medicine.

Leading figures in the medical profession, though, were in a far stronger position to impose their own distinctive notion of

[27] See R. Porter, *Health for Sale: Quackery in England 1660–1850* (Manchester: Manchester University Press, 1989).

orthodoxy by the first half of the nineteenth century. Parssinen charts the way in which their developing power base in Victorian Britain was used specifically against medical mesmerists, whose relative therapeutic success did not insulate them from heavy criticism from their colleagues. His main argument is that the accusations of fraudulent quackery to which they were exposed were heavily related to the challenge that mesmerism—and other heretic practices like homoeopathy and hydrotherapy—posed to both the esoteric knowledge claims and financial well-being of their medical contemporaries. Of particular importance here is the fact that the association of renegade medical practitioners with such disreputable practices as mesmerism threatened to undermine the drive to professionalize medicine through reforming legislation—with all the benefits that this process of collective social mobility was to entail.[28]

THE RISE OF MEDICAL ORTHODOXY AND THE DEVELOPMENT OF ALTERNATIVE MEDICINE

The second part of the collection—which covers the period from the mid-nineteenth century to the first two decades of the National Health Service—focuses on the rise of medical orthodoxy following the passing of the 1858 Medical Registration Act and the consequent fate of the increasingly clearly defined forms of alternative medicine that continued to be practised in the new era. Nicholls, writing on homoeopathy in Britain in the second half of the nineteenth century, describes how the small band of medical homoeopaths managed to sustain their growth into the 1850s and 1860s. He claims that this was achieved despite opposition from the reformed profession which was based on its interest in social advance and supported by an ideology of serving the public interest and maintaining standards of scientific integrity and honour. The immediate economic threat from the medical homoeopaths was eventually stemmed, however, by a number of measures taken by the developing medical establishment, including a ban on professional contact with homoeopathic practitioners and the strategic use of professional control over medical appointments, medical education, and medical

[28] N. Parry and J. Parry, *The Rise of Medical Profession: A Study of Collective Social Mobility* (London: Croom Helm, 1976).

journals. But, as Nicholls ironically indicates, the most effective weapon deployed against the homoeopaths at this time was probably the reactive change in orthodox medicine itself, away from the damaging heroic therapy which it had so favoured in the past.

Alternative medicine, though, continued to manifest itself after the mid-nineteenth century not only inside the profession itself, but also more extensively outside the ranks of the medically qualified.[29] This was certainly true of the local midwife who attended most of the childbirths of the urban poor, as described in the extract by Chamberlain. The appeal of the experienced 'old wife', in contrast to the more highly trained midwife, was only in part the lower cost; Chamberlain suggests that this form of care was frequently preferred too because of her more 'natural' approach and greater sensitivity to the local conditions encountered in her work. Moreover, the willingness of the old wives to assist in birth control—particularly in performing illegal abortions—helped to sustain the demand for their services amongst the working class, at the time when the medical profession was wary about being associated with this sensitive area lest it jeopardize its hard won professional status. But the role of the old wife, abortion apart, gradually declined as the twentieth century progressed, not least because of legislation establishing the state registered midwife and the provision of local authority midwifery services. It is a testimony to the growing dominance of the medical profession at this stage that the registered midwives who increasingly supplanted the old wives were themselves subordinated to doctors through legislative limitations imposed on the practice of midwifery by the profession.[30]

Yet if the first half of the twentieth century witnessed the growing subjugation of ever more areas of life to orthodox medical control and, conversely, the further demise of alternative health care practices, this was also a pattern that was apparent in relation to the 'secret remedies' that were sold to deal with 'female irregularities' and a host of other maladies in this period.

[29] See, for example, *Report as to the Practice of Medicine and Surgery by Unqualified Persons in the United Kingdom* (London: HMSO, 1910).

[30] J. Donnison, *Midwives and Medical Men: A History of the Struggle for the Control of Childbirth* (London: Historical Publications, 2nd edn., 1988).

These 'secret remedies', the composition of which was not disclosed, are discussed more fully by Vaughan. He notes how the British Medical Association conducted a sustained campaign against the marketing of such preparations which formed part of a highly lucrative industry with booming sales by the turn of the century. In consequence, proprietary manufacturing companies were progressively forced through legislation to limit their advertising claims and the scope of application of their remedies as well as to reveal their contents on the labels. While such activity could again be seen as protecting the interests of doctors against escalating external competition, Vaughan interprets the role of the medical profession in this area as being primarily public spirited—with the profession serving to protect gullible consumers against fraudulent and potentially harmful quacks.

Whether or not this interpretation is wholly accepted on the basis of the compelling illustrations presented, the State in Vaughan's account clearly has a crucial role as a gatekeeper, policing the frontiers of orthodox and unorthodox medicine. Larkin sees the body politic as having a similarly critical influence in the years between the First and Second World Wars in Britain, from the viewpoint of the relationship between state registration and the market position of health practitioners. Taking osteopathy as a case-study, he documents the unsuccessful attempt of osteopathic practitioners in the 1930s to gain a comparable legal status to that of doctors through parliamentary means. Larkin claims that the response of the medical profession to their efforts was as vigorous as it was negative given fears about encroachment from a group that not only offered treatment at variance with orthodox medicine for a wide range of complaints, but was also decidedly reluctant to take on a secondary status akin to that of the midwives earlier in the century. Leaving tactical ineptitude aside, it is argued that the major factor that, rightly or wrongly, condemned the osteopaths to failure in the inter-war period was the close connection that existed between the long-established medical corporations and the Ministry of Health. The resultant exclusion of the osteopaths, along with other non-medically qualified alternative therapists, from the public health services was to have very durable implications for their position, particularly with the coming of the National Health Service in 1948.

What is most striking about Larkin's account of the role of the State in relation to professional registration is just how little seems ultimately to have depended on the relative merits of the actual treatments offered by the medical profession and its osteopathic rivals. Inglis, in contrast, sees the pharmacological promise of medical orthodoxy in the period up to the 1940s as being central to the sidelining of alternative therapies after the founding of the National Health Service in Britain. He draws attention to the contradiction between the initial opposition of the medical profession to the National Health Service in face of an apparent challenge to its independence and the fact that, on implementation, the new system actually served to reinforce the profession's monopoly. This latter point is well exemplified by Inglis in relation to the herbalists, who faced major price and fee discrimination as a result of their exclusion from the service, at a stage when their only realistic possibility of entry was on subordinate terms to the medical profession. According to Inglis, moreover, the dominant position of the profession was further accentuated by the fact that the National Health Service was based from the outset on the mechanistic biomedical approach in which the growing profusion of specialists had a stake as a result of their training. This meant that the treatment offered by alternative practitioners like hypnotherapists and healers was not generally available to the public from the state medical system— as epitomized by the strong resistance of doctors to admitting spiritual healers into hospitals and establishing trials of spiritual healing, at a time when there was a continuing General Medical Council prohibition on co-operation with non-medically qualified alternative therapists.

ALTERNATIVE MEDICINE IN MODERN BRITAIN

Having completed the historical backcloth to this subject, discussion is then centred on alternative medicine in modern Britain in the third part of the book. Vincent initiates the proceedings here by intriguingly stretching the concept of alternative health care to include the contemporary resurgence of interest in self-help, which can and often does conflict with orthodox medical provision. After highlighting the discrepancy between the rhetoric and the reality surrounding the operation of self-help groups involved in health care in Britain, Vincent ties the current rise in self-help activity in the health sector primarily to the changing socio-political structure of British society and the shortcomings of existing health and welfare provision. Parallels in this respect are then drawn with the explanations that have been put forward to account for the increasing public demand for alternative therapies themselves—particularly dissatisfaction with orthodox medical care which is viewed as being based on a model that, amongst other things, is insufficiently oriented towards contemporary patterns of ill health, does not fit in with the popular emphasis on caring for the whole person, and generates significant iatrogenic effects. These are presented as part of a wider range of similarities between self-help groups and encounters in alternative medicine, which includes their common stress on equality and utilizing human capacities and experience, as well as their potential oppositional nature and the fact that both can be taken over by professionals for their own ends.

Allen and Wallis meanwhile focus on the analysis of the health beliefs and actions of Pentecostalists in Britain, who possess some characteristics of a health self-help group, while sharing differing views about the causation and cure of illness to those ordinarily espoused by medical orthodoxy in what has now become a predominantly secular society. Although medically based explanations of disease were broadly accepted at an immediate level by the small group of members of the Pentecostalist church that was studied, religious doctrines were influential in shaping the general theories held about the causation of illness. This religious influence was also evident in beliefs about the treatment of illness, not least amongst those who were strongly committed to the notion of miraculous 'divine healing' which contradicts dominant medical ideas in this area. However, divine healing in practice was mainly used as an alternative to mainstream medicine in the case of minor illnesses, with the doctor being visited as necessary if the desired results were not obtained. The health behaviour of the Pentecostalist minority, therefore, may be less distinct from conventional medicine than first meets the eye—which, as in the case of the self-help groups that act as an adjunct to medical orthodoxy, perhaps indicates the extent to which the medical profession still exercises a degree of control over even what appear to be genuinely alternative subcultures in lay health care.

None the less, as has been seen, increasing numbers of health care consumers are now seeking treatment from alternative therapists in modern Britain. Fulder charts the rapidly expanding and comparatively large numbers of such therapists now in existence both inside and outside the many organized associations in this field in the United Kingdom in general and Britain in particular. He also describes the main characteristics of the unorthodox practice in which they are engaged—including the form of consultations with clients, the organizational structures within which they work, and the kind of training on which the practice of most alternative therapists is based, together with the scale of fees charged in the private sector in which practitioners who are not qualified in medicine or a related profession are currently obliged to operate. As Fulder indicates, alternative medicine in Britain includes not only high-profile therapists like healers and osteopaths, but also a very diverse group of less well-known practitioners, such as those specifically serving ethnic minority populations in Britain—for instance, the hakim practising Unani or Ayurvedic medicine[31]—and the smaller numbers of exponents of radionics and reflexology. The availability of such a wide spectrum of unorthodox therapists, practising under the common law, confirms that alternative medicine in Britain today is not a monolithic phenomenon. Fulder concludes his contribution, though, by pointing to another aspect of this diversity—namely, the internal divisiveness which has cost alternative medicine dear in the political conflicts over its standing in relation to orthodox medicine.

However, divisions are not unique to the realm of the unorthodox. They also exist in the medical profession—as Fulder himself acknowledges when he refers to the substantial part some doctors themselves are now playing in the spread of alternative health care. According to Saks, the recent trend for increasing numbers of qualified medical practitioners and allied professionals to take up the practice of alternative medicine may be part of a move towards incorporation as a response to the growing threat that the expansion of the non-medically qualified in this field poses to the medical profession. This argument is illustrated with reference to acupuncture in which the stance of the medical

[31] C. G. Helman, *Culture, Health and Illness* (Bristol: John Wright and Sons, 1985).

profession has shifted sharply over the past twenty years from one of initial rejection to that of limited acceptance—on the profession's own terms. This could again be interpreted as a way of opening up new and beneficial knowledge developments to the public, whilst protecting them from the potentially deleterious consequences of quackery. But, as Saks suggests, the changes in the reception that British medicine has given to acupuncture are more compatible with an explanation based on professional self-interests in the ongoing struggle between the medical profession and its lay rivals.

ALTERNATIVE MEDICINE: THE FUTURE

The incorporationist trend in acupuncture raises crucial questions about the future of alternative medicine in Britain, an issue which is directly addressed in the fourth part of the reader. This final part begins with a contribution from West which highlights the dramatic improvement that has occurred in the standing of alternative medicine since the 1960s. At the same time, though, the response of the British medical establishment to this situation is regarded with a good deal of scepticism despite evidence of growing public disaffection with orthodox medical care and favourable international data on the results of treatment using alternative medicine. West notes that alternative therapists fear that their practice will be taken over by doctors who only have a short training in the therapies concerned; it is felt that this may simply lead to the reinforcement of the orthodox medical approach which divorces the techniques involved in alternative medicine from their holistic basis, rather than integrating them on an equal footing with those of orthodox medicine. West, however, emphasizes the unpredictability of the future and believes that it is still possible that alternative medicine will take up its place at the heart of the health care system in a transformed society. The growing interest in green politics in Britain in the lead-up to the 1990s gives added credibility to the prospects of this scenario emerging[32]—if resistance from the higher reaches of the medical profession can be overcome.

In this latter regard, West refers in her contribution to the decision of the British Medical Association to investigate altern-

[32] J. Porritt and D. Winner, *The Coming of the Greens* (London: Fontana, 1989).

ative medicine following the promptings of Prince Charles in his position as President of this body in the early 1980s. The outcome was the formation of a Working Party on alternative therapies, which was comprised of several eminent members of the medical profession, none of whom possessed direct experience of practising in this field. A key section of the Working Party's Report that was published in 1986 is reproduced at length in this reader. In general terms, this does not provide much reassurance for alternative therapists as to their future; it continues to define the heavily biomedically based practice of the medical profession as being both scientific and rational, whilst, in contrast, alternative medicine is largely seen as a maelstrom of pre-scientific quackery rooted in superstition and dogmatic metaphysics. Although the Working Party does not completely deny the value of some unorthodox practices, it argues that the sounder methodological base of orthodox medicine has resulted in a record of therapeutic success which far outweighs that of the alternatives. The Working Party also rejects the broader theories underpinning rival therapies and emphasizes the need for alternative practice to be kept under close medical supervision and control because of the dangers posed by the non-medically qualified—consultations with whom may either result in harmful delays in patients receiving effective orthodox medical care or directly cause damage in their own right.

Although the Report of the British Medical Association has been seen as constituting 'a fine example of the propensity of occupational groups for self justification and defence',[33] it should be stressed that the findings of the Working Party were highly contentious, even within the ranks of the medical profession itself. Accordingly, a response to the section of the Report included here follows from the British Holistic Medical Association—a minority group of doctors and medical students who favour a more holistic approach to medicine. Despite references in the Report to the need to increase the humanity of the medical encounter, these holistically oriented practitioners believe that the biomedical model of disease which underpins its conclusions crucially ignores the social and psychological aspects of illness behaviour, and berate the Working Party for further marginalizing

---

[33] P. Fairfoot, 'Alternative Therapies: The BMA Knows Best?', *Journal of Social Policy*, 16:3 (1987), 383–90.

legal standing (handwritten margin note)

alternative therapies which centrally address such issues. As part of its case, the British Holistic Medical Association challenges the narrow conception of 'objective' science on which the Report is based on the grounds that there are no universally accepted criteria for assessing scientific knowledge-claims. The extract concludes by charting a holistic future for health care in the twenty-first century, arguing, amongst other things, that primary health care focused on general practice should include alternative medicine. This is a very timely suggestion given the Government's 1989 White Paper, *Working for Patients*, which, while not specifically referring to the subject of alternative therapies, may make their adoption a more attractive proposition to medical practitioners in the light of the typically low costs involved and the cash constraints within which doctors will be working in the future.[34]

Further support is given to the view that the reform of the National Health Service represents an opportunity for the expansion of alternative medicine in the concluding contribution to the reader by Huggon and Trench. They emphasize, however, that members of the medical profession are currently at a considerable legal advantage as compared to the non-medically qualified in terms of the practice of alternative therapies in Britain—even though the extent of medical involvement in this area is restricted by the persisting biomedical domination of both the National Health Service and training in British medical schools. Having said this, Huggon and Trench observe that the common-law rights accorded to lay practitioners in Britain are exceptional in relation to many other European countries where only doctors are generally allowed to practise medicine. It is obviously possible, therefore, that the practice of alternative therapists without orthodox medical qualifications could be outlawed in the post-1992 single market of the European Community, if such therapists are not properly organized. It is pertinent to note that European legislation is already having the effect of substantially restricting the availability of herbal medicines in this country because they have not been shown to come up to the prescribed standard.[35]

[34] *Working for Patients* (London: HMSO, 1989).
[35] T. Huggon, 'Rule by Brussels—Liberation or Liquidation for Natural Medicines?', *Journal of Alternative and Complementary Medicine* (Jan. 1990), 13–16.

The real doubts that exist about the implications of the single market for unorthodox therapists highlight the difficulties faced by social scientists in moving from discussions about the past and present of alternative medicine to making firm judgements about what is inevitably an uncertain future in this field. As has been seen, there are a number of positive signs as regards the development of alternative medicine in Britain, especially the growing public interest in alternative therapies and the increasing political support that they have received in parliamentary circles. Against this, however, there are also many obstacles in the path of the full acceptance of such therapies, including the potentially damaging political effects of the continuing divisions between alternative practitioners themselves and, perhaps most centrally, the power and interests of the élite of the medical profession—as most recently manifested in the foundation of the Campaign Against Health Fraud which has zealously taken on the kind of 'quackbusting' mantle encouraged by the British Medical Association's Report.[36] Nor should the wider interests that impinge on the political process be forgotten, not only in relation to the European Community, but also in respect of the international corporations trading in pharmaceuticals and medical equipment which have a stake in keeping a watchful eye on the progress of unorthodox therapies, lest the sales of their products are adversely affected.[37] What is certain, though, is that the conjunction of these and other forces will shape, for better or worse, the future existence of the practices that currently make up alternative medicine in Britain and the role that they play in the health care system in the years ahead.

[36] S. Martin, 'Who's Protecting Who—and from What?', *Journal of Alternative and Complementary Medicine* (Aug. 1989), 21–2.

[37] M. Saks, 'The Politics of Health Care', in L. Robins (ed.), *Politics and Policy Making in Britain* (London: Longman, 1987), 52–69.

PART I

HEALTH CARE IN BRITAIN BEFORE THE MID-NINETEENTH CENTURY

1

Healing in Pre-Industrial Britain

Christina Larner

This paper examines the practice of healing and the prevailing attitudes to it in pre-industrial Britain[1] . . . Medical practice in the sixteenth and seventeenth centuries is particularly interesting . . . because of a number of factors. In the first place village life in both England and Scotland had at this time many of the features of simple societies. So far as healing was concerned there was a body of folk medicine culled from a variety of sources, and very little distinction, if any, was made between practical medicine: the use of plants, herbs, and minerals of varying degrees of proved efficacy, and ritual healing: the use of charms and incantations. At the same time the society, while pre-industrial, was not pre-literate. There was an educated class prepared to discuss and analyse the efficacy of different types of healing, and, as a result of two other factors, to debate their legitimacy. These other factors were the emergence of an official medical profession and the passing of Acts against witchcraft and sorcery in England in 1542 and Scotland in 1563. These Witchcraft Acts had the effect of making the practice of unofficial healing by local cunning men and women a somewhat dangerous activity, in that the claim to have special powers which were not sanctified by the Church could lead to witchcraft charges being laid. The claims of the emergent medical profession to special legitimacy were undoubtedly made stronger by the Witchcraft Acts, but the two factors were not strongly connected, since healing was only a peripheral problem in the witchcraft issue which was more directly about acts of *maleficium*.

It is the fact that not only were there at least two levels of medical practice then as now, but also an educated class interested in commenting on these and discriminating between them, that makes this period so valuable. Like us, many of the

[handwritten margin note: + Practical medicine]

[1] This anachronism is a convenient shorthand for England and Scotland before the Act of Union.

population thought that they could distinguish magic and superstition from science. What I hope to do is to look pragmatically at some of their attitudes and definitions in relation to ours ... without getting too enmeshed in the debate on rationality.

I would like to start then with a threefold distinction ... between different types of pre-industrial healing: official and scientific healing; practical or common-sense healing; and ritual healing. Official and scientific healing are classed together because they tend to overlap. Official healing was that sanctioned by the emergent professional associations and taught in the universities. That is its political or trade-union aspect; only those who were themselves official healers could say who might join them. To describe this type of healing as scientific is not to say that they had got their facts right in terms of twentieth-century positivist science; it is merely to say that 'scientific' healing in this period was based upon current physical knowledge and was susceptible to intellectual argument within the current paradigm. It was expected that diseases and their cures could be explained. It was this combination of political power plus a monopoly over the explanation of disease and healing which was the basis for all the future power of the profession. In the period under discussion today, their territory did not yet extend very far.

The other two types of healing which I want to distinguish were both unofficial, and together make up folk medicine. Practical or common-sense healing concerned the use of particular herbs and minerals of established utility. No one here was in the least interested in reasons. These could be used without the intervention of any professed healer, but very often recourse would be had to a local healer who would be known to have special knowledge of how to mix these herbs. Practical healing cannot therefore be totally separated from ritual healing of which the essence is the spell, the charm, and the power of the cunning man or woman.

There are of course quite a lot of difficulties about overlap intrinsic in any attempt to sort healing or diagnosis into categories. Take, for example, the wearing of an amulet as a cure for colic. It would seem reasonable to classify this under unofficial, practical medicine, but for the seventeenth-century wearer it was based on contemporary scientific assumptions about the physical properties of certain substances and their effects on the functioning of human bodies. It was an entirely different sort of action from getting Goodwife Thomson to mutter a few charms. And today we wear copper bracelets against rheumatism.

Take again the example of the distinction between the scientific–official and the practical approach in the explanation of venereal disease, which hit European ports in the latter half of the fifteenth century. According to the doctors of the University of Ferrara, which was the . . . most up-to-date school of medicine in the civilized world at the time, syphilis descended on a community at a particular astrological conjuction. The area of debate, which was argued out in great detail, was which planets, and when. The Town Council of Aberdeen, on the other hand, unversed in contemporary medical theory, in 1499 declared that the disease in Aberdeen could be associated with the presence in the town of 'whoorish women' who ought to be sent packing. We may overlook the sexist package here and refrain from debating the relative culpability of lecherous sailors, for it was part of received Christianity until about the eighteenth century that women were more sensual and wicked than men. The point here is that we have in essence the difference between scientific and practical knowledge at this time. And the type of knowledge I am calling scientific—the opinions about physical properties held by leading thinkers (high magic)—impinged very little at the level of folk medicine which was an amalgam of practical knowledge and low magic.

There is an additional problem of definition here in the use of the word magic. Magic has at least two aspects: it relates to special powers, and to the inexplicability of its effectiveness. Magic is not available equally to the population; it is only available to special people. It cannot therefore be fully understood. Official scientific healing, while open to explanation within its contemporary paradigm, in fact retains aspects of the magical as it is experienced by the general population—it is too esoteric for them to follow the explanation. In so far as magic is concerned with healing I would like to add one further dimension. For the patient there must be effort and arduousness of experience. This arduousness is an acknowledgement by the patient in the face of something not comprehended, of the power of the healer and of his medicine.

The disgust of Na'aman when told by Elisha to go and bathe in Jordan to cure his leprosy was a reaction to an inadequacy of arduousness. The river was too small and too conveniently local. The magical element in the healing relationship is a dynamic one depending on the recognition by the patient of the power of the healer and his medicine. This is present almost as much in a relationship with an official healer who may or may not be willing to explain his medicine to his patient.

In looking at the practice of folk medicine in Scotland and England in this period, I shall be drawing on my own research for the Scottish material and on secondary sources, notably Keith Thomas,[2] for the English.

It was observed by the sixteenth-century puritan writer, Perkins, that 'Charmers were more sought than physicians in time of need'. There were of course at least two good reasons for that, and one of them was that there were far more of them around. In the sixteenth century in England, official medicine was just beginning to get going. The Royal College of Physicians was set up in 1518 to license physicians in the city of London. The then greatly inferior surgeons were licensed four years earlier and the apothecaries about the same time. There were severe demarcation disputes. Apothecaries were not allowed to diagnose complaints. That would be overstepping the mark. But in any case they covered only a small area. Most of the population were out of range of official medicine, and even when they were not they preferred not to use it. For the other good reason for turning to the charmer was that official medicine when available tended to be painful. It was about purging, blood-letting, and cauterizing, and left a trail of early iatrogenic disease in its wake. In one real sense the urban rich suffered most in the sixteenth century, but theirs was very much a minority experience. The suggestion that most people positively avoided official medicine for its unpleasantness may appear to contradict my theory about arduousness, but there are many forms of this, and it does not necessarily have to involve physical pain. The careful performance of certain rituals also falls into this category.

Keith Thomas detects three basic assumptions behind folk medicine of this period. The first is that disease is a foreign

---

[2] K. Thomas, *Religion and the Decline of Magic* (London: Weidenfeld & Nicholson, 1971).

presence, and this assumption was to a certain extent shared by official healers as well. The second is that religious language possessed a mystical power which could be deployed for practical purposes. The third was that other charms and certain potions owed their power to the healer himself. One might add that there were some potions, herbs, and other remedies which the individual could simply use for himself—a type of sixteenth-century aspirin.

As Thomas rightly says, 'In the sixteenth century these practices did not reflect a single coherent cosmology or scheme of classification, but were made out of the debris of many different systems of thought.' Despite this these separate assumptions all hang together pretty well. In Scotland in the witchcraft trials it was common to accuse the witch of 'putting on' and 'taking off' a disease with a charm. This charm was the agent whereby this external evil was either imposed or removed. The witch or healer was the active force by which the charm was applied, whether or not the particular charm was one which could be thought to stand on its own. But where the spell was the effective agent the important thing was the words themselves. Anyone could chant them. They could be written down and worn round the neck, and whether the wearer could read the words or not was irrelevant.

These charms were indeed made out of the debris of different systems of thought, though undoubtedly the largest ingredient was the prayers of the pre-Reformation Church. This was true in both England and Scotland. Paternosters, Aves, and Creeds, either straight or adulterated, loomed large. Others were more remote and mysterious: Janet Brown in Scotland was accused in December 1643 of charming with the following:

> Our Lord forth raide;
> His foal's foot slade;
> Our Lord down lighted;
> His foal's foot righted;
> Saying: Flesh to Flesh, blood to blood,
>   and bane to bane
> In our Lord his name.

It is impossible to interpret or date anything like this other than stating that a witness quoted it in court in 1643. Believers in an organized witch cult would no doubt want to interpret the reference to Our Lord as being a reference to the Devil, but there is no evidence that it had meaning for Janet Brown, or indeed that the words had meaning as opposed to efficacy at all.

A Devonshire charm of the same period quoted by Keith Thomas was specifically to cure scalds and burns, and much more obviously to the point:

> Two angels came from the west,
> The one brought fire, the other frost,
> Out fire, out frost
> In the name of the Father, Son, and the Holy Ghost.

Even more direct is the one for toothache:

> Jesus Christ, for mercy sake
> Take away this toothache.

The sufferer was supposed to write this three times on a piece of paper; say it aloud, and then burn the paper. The burning of papers on which charms had been written was a very common ritual. The victim of the disease did not need to be able to read the words. The words stood on their own.

If we turn to the role of the healer himself—who could be variously cunning man, cunning woman, charmer, sorcerer, or witch—there were assorted other performances at his or her disposal. Cutting girdles on the afflicted was very common, the purpose being to let the disease out; burning and burying animals was another device. And all sorts of performances were gone through with the patient's urine. Sometimes activities like the boiling up of urine and adding plants and minerals might be regarded as curative in itself. On other occasions it was a diagnostic or prophetic substance. If the urine remained cloudy overnight the patient would die. If it cleared up he would recover. Urine featured in official medicine too. From the patient's point of view we may note in passing that little seems to have changed here. There are a remarkably varied number of conditions today from pregnancy to drunken driving for which the production of a specimen is regarded as the appropriate response.

Most of the healers clearly believed in their powers. They were after all part of the community; they shared in its culture. Yet at the same time there were varying degrees of conscious manipulation. Secrecy was important. The patient was often not told what his treatment had been, what it was about, and what it was supposed to do. (Here I hardly need to labour the contemporary parallel.) Most were also, by extension, familiar with the principles of the placebo. The importance of impressive procedures was not lost on them. The contemporary giant red pill to be taken three times a day before meals—looking as different as possible from aspirin—had its parallel in highly coloured noxious potions, long-lasting rituals, arduousness of performance.

The next question is really, what did they think their own limitations were? And what did their clients think their limitations were? What could they cure? And what could they not cure?

There were some diseases, notably the plague, which no local healer was foolish enough to pretend to cure. The best things they could offer were prophylactics against plague. There was no suggestion either of being able to cope with very severe physical injuries other than by bone-setting and ointments. But one serious disease for which some cures were claimed over a long period, related to the belief in the King's touch. Of all the magical healers the King was the most magical. Closely related to this was the belief in the supernatural origins and divine nature of kingship, and some indeed connected their power with the sacred oils poured at coronations. Kings and Queens touched the sick in England. This was begun as early as Edward the Confessor but its heyday was in the sixteenth and seventeenth centuries. It does not seem to have been employed in Scotland so far as I know, and James VI when he came to England—despite having done a great deal personally to promote the divine origins of kingship—was *most* reluctant to go through with what he thought was a highly superstitious procedure. He was, however, prevailed upon to do so on the grounds of tradition. Later seventeenth-century monarchs such as Charles II and James II were at it frequently. King William refused to have anything to do with it, and the rite was performed for the last time by Queen Anne.

The principal disease which the King's touch was supposed to be able to cure was scrofula or King's Evil, an inflammation of the glands of the neck. Many other diseases of the head, neck, and eyes were often lumped together under these terms. For the ordinary healer, however, who was more dependent on results or attributed results, it was necessary to be careful about their claims. Some specialized in particular diseases, but once a general power was conceded to the healer it was difficult to refuse to attempt a particular cure. No doubt a great many instances of organic disease went undiagnosed other than as a wasting sickness of some sort. The healers, however, did of course extremely well, as healers of all sorts do, on the kind of affliction that time heals anyway. They did best of all in the whole area of psychosomatic disease. In this field, Thomas observes that the seventeenth-century charmers, believing in their own methods, were ideally equipped to achieve results.

Healers in this period were for the most part highly aware of the effect of mind over matter. Effect on the mind was the first rather than last thing they looked for. Closely connected with this they were extremely ready to diagnose a supernatural cause. *Someone* had overlooked them, *someone* had it in for them, *someone* had bewitched them. The remedy was the right incantation—or the identification of the source of witchcraft.

Now it is in this murky area of the relationship between healing and witchcraft that the curing man or woman in both England and Scotland in the sixteenth and seventeenth centuries was likely to fall foul of the law. The new laws against witchcraft generated a new awareness of the sinister side of healing power. They represented at one level a new attempt by the Church and the State to control all unofficial sources of power.

For the power to heal was two-edged. Power to heal could be withheld; it could be deployed in the whole ambiguous area of love potions, aphrodisiacs, or prophesying the sex of unborn children, and so on. In fact very few healers confined themselves to healing. Special powers were special powers. The healer could be persuaded to become a killer or harmer, even more likely he or she could initiate curses and vengeances on his or her *own* behalf if crossed or refused payment. The actual tendency of the person of reputation to be ambiguously balanced between good and evil powers, between white and black magic, was greatly increased by the hostility of the authorities to anyone claiming special powers at all, and by the authorities declaring them all to be equally demonic or at least of dubious origin. Anyone in this category was likely to fall foul of the witchcraft laws. Nearly all seventeenth-century prosecutions in England and Scotland began with acts of *maleficium*: powers used to harm; to harm individuals or their sheep, pigs, or cattle.

There was a difference between England and Scotland here. In England the prosecution was likely to begin and end with a particular charge, *maleficium*, for which a particular penalty might be exacted. In Scotland in the seventeenth century the High Court of Judiciary required evidence of a pact with the Devil— *maleficium* was simply one of the preliminary signs.

Defence lawyers tended to concentrate hard on disputing *maleficium* for if that could be dealt with there was little likelihood of the case being pursued. In one case in which a witch was accused of laying on a disease by threatening and charming, the lawyer argued that for this to stick then the threatenings must be specific and the specific misfortune immediately follow; also there had to be a necessary contingency between what the witch did and what followed. And in this connection defence lawyers had detailed lists of types of diseases which might be caused by witchcraft and those which were clearly natural. These of course tended to alter from case to case, but fevers, distractions (described as the most malignant and burning of all feverish distempers), swoonings, and swellings were more readily attributed to witchcraft than other afflictions. There was also a curious and useful idea current among the lawyers that one witch could not put on and take off the same disease—that was regarded as being too much power for the Devil to hand out to one servant. If then a witch was accused both of laying on and taking off the disease this in the hands of a competent lawyer might get her off. In this, official opinion was in conflict with local wisdom.

A typical Scottish case was that laid against Janet Mackmuldroch in Dumfriesshire in 1671. She was accused of a number of *maleficia* as a result of which both people and animals died, but three of the accusations were that she caused and then removed a disease. In one instance when she was reproved by one Robert Cairns for stealing a tail of corn on the Sabbath she 'bad the divill pyk out his eyn'. The Friday after at midnight he contracted a sudden disease and sent for Janet. She refused to come, and he therefore left his death upon her and ordained his friends to pursue her as a witch and necromancer. On other occasions she was said to have visited those she had afflicted and offered them a potion, after drinking which they recovered.

The confusion in the minds of lawyers and others about magical power and disease was recognized by Sir George Mackenzie, who published an account of his defence of an accused witch in 1672.[3] Mackenzie, while justifying to the last the belief in witchcraft, even to providing a scientific explanation as to how the Devil may copulate with humans—'by taking on him a body of condensed air'—was also one of those most worried about miscarriages of justice. When discussing the possibility of a particular disease being caused by nature rather than by witchcraft he says,

Nature is very subtile in its operations, and we are very ignorant in our inquiries: from the conjunction of which two, arises the many errors and mistakes we commit in our reflections upon the productions of nature; to differ then from one another because of these errors, is sufferable, though to be regreted; but to kill one another, because we cannot comprehend the reason of what each other do, is the effect of a terrible distraction.

[3] G. Mackenzie, *Pleadings in Some Remarkable Cases* (Edinburgh, 1672).

2

The Wisewoman and the Doctor

Ann Oakley

Women have a long history as community healers in pre-industrial Europe and colonial America. The 'good woman', 'cunning woman', or 'wisewoman' was the person to whom people turned in times of illness; she represented the chief medical practitioner available to a community living in constant poverty and disease. In the literature of the period male healers are not mentioned nearly so frequently as female healers; the bulk of lay healing was done by women.[1] There is good reason for this. The role of housewife in pre-industrial society encompassed a much wider range of functions than it does today. Healing the sick was work that devolved not only upon the upper-class ladies of households, but also upon the lower-class wives of the community.[2] In their role as healers these women had knowledge of anatomy, astronomy, psychotherapy, and pharmacology. They knew and used pain-killers, digestive aids, anti-inflammatory agents, ergot (an important midwifery drug), belladonna, and digitalis (today still used in the treatment of heart disease).[3] Moreover, their work was highly valued. In pre-industrial England the female practitioner was widely trusted above her male counterpart, whose main treatment consisted of letting

[1] Judging by the contemporary sources quoted by historians; for example in Keith Thomas's *Religion and the Decline of Magic* (London: Weidenfeld & Nicholson, 1971). In the witchcraft literature, women are more often mentioned than men in connection with a healing role. See e.g. C. Hole, *A Mirror of Witchcraft* (London: Chatto and Windus, 1957), and A. Macfarlane, *Witchcraft in Tudor and Stuart England* (London: Routledge & Kegan Paul, 1970). Richard H. Shyrock has some information about lay medicine in colonial America and later periods in his *Medicine in America: Historical Essays* (Baltimore: Johns Hopkins Press, 1966). See also J. F. Kett, *The Formation of the American Medical Profession* (New Haven, Conn., 1968), ch. 1, 'The Weak Arm of The Law'.

[2] A. Clark, *Working Life of Women in the Seventeenth Century* (London: Frank Cass, 1968).

[3] Almost all the herbs which composed the typical medieval garden have been found to contain some property of value to modern medicine. See M. J. Hughes, *Women Healers in Medieval Life and Literature* (Morningside Heights, NY, 1943).

blood. 'Also for Goddys sake be war what medesyns ye take of any fysissyans at London; I shal never trust to hem', wrote Margaret Paston to her husband. Sir Ralph Verney gave his wife similar advice, telling her to 'give the child no phisick but such as midwives and old women . . . doe prescribe; for assure yourself they by experience know better than any physition how to treate such infants'.[4] Such references to lay female healers occur frequently in letters and diaries of the period. Doubtless this attitude favouring the female healer also made sound economic sense; the services of male doctors were more expensive.

The care of infants and of women in childbirth was an integral part of the female healing role. As Alice Clark, in her account of seventeenth-century working women, describes the rural English practice:

It was customary, when travail began, to send for all the neighbours who were responsible women, partly with the object of securing enough witnesses to the child's birth, partly because it was important to spread the understanding of midwifery as widely as possible because any woman might be called upon to render assistance in an emergency.[5]

Women of all classes depended upon the lay midwife to see them safely through childbirth. Midwifery skills were acquired by experience and informal apprenticeship in much the same way as general medical skills. In some cases the occupation was passed on from mother to daughter. Although there were those midwives who lacked any systematic instruction, some entered long apprenticeships (among London midwives, a seven-year training was sometimes undertaken). In these instances payment would be made to the instructing midwife—in the 1690s a three-year apprenticeship cost £5.

Practising wisewomen–midwives had a generally respectable, and sometimes high, status among the people they served.[6] The negative appellation 'witch' was fostered by the medieval Church, to whom disease was a God-given affliction, and thus a

---

[4] Both these quotes are taken from Hughes, *Women Healers*, 50.

[5] Clark, *Working Life of Women*, 269.

[6] '. . . midwifery existed on a professional basis from immemorial days . . . The midwife held a recognized position in society and was sometimes well educated and well paid . . . it is certain that women of a high level of intelligence and possessing considerable skill belonged to the profession', ibid. 265, 268.

phenomenon which had to be under strict religious control. Also, of course, the female healer challenged the male hegemony of the Church. There are two problems here. The first concerns how and why the association between witchcraft and the female healing–midwifery function came to be established. The second problem is a statistical one: to what extent *were* women healer–midwives suspected, accused, and punished as witches? Neither of these issues seems to be tackled directly in existing studies. Sociological and anthropological interpretations of witchcraft and its persecution cite sexual hostility (of the community), economic marginality (of the accused) in a period torn by the opposed forces of charity and individualism, and the conservative position and social power of village women in a rapidly segmenting society.[7] Most European witches *were* women. In the series of Essex witch-accusations studied by Macfarlane, for example, 268 (92 per cent) of a total of 291 accused witches were women (and eleven of the men were either married to an accused witch or appeared in a joint indictment with a woman). A similar pattern emerges in a re-analysis of data on the Salem witch trials in New England, where 120 (74 per cent) of 162 accused witches were female, the typical witch was a married or widowed woman aged between 41 and 60, and most of the males accused of witchcraft were either the children or husbands of female witches.[8] The women accused of witchcraft in England and elsewhere tended to be married or widowed, to be middle-aged or old, and to be of low socio-economic status.

Three hierarchies corresponded; Church over laity, man over woman, landlord over peasant. The existence of the woman–midwife–witch–healer challenged all three of these hierarchies.

[7] Barbara Ehrenreich and Deidre English's pamphlet, *Witches, Midwives and Nurses* (Glass Mountain Pamphlets) makes the connection between healing, midwifery, and witchcraft roles, but does not present precise evidence about the degree of overlap. Thomas Forbes's *The Midwife and the Witch* (New Haven, Conn.: Yale University Press, 1966), asks the question whether midwives were witches but fails to provide an answer. Keith Thomas (*Religion and the Decline of Magic*, 178) simply says that 'popular magicians' went under a variety of names, including 'wisewoman', 'sorcerer', and 'witch'. The sexual hostility interpretation of witchcraft is offered for Continental witchcraft especially; see M. Douglas (ed.), *Witchcraft Confessions and Accusations* (London: Tavistock, 1970). Accusations of sexual perversions and orgies with the Devil are not found very often in English witchcraft material.

[8] J. Demos, 'Underlying Themes in the Witchcraft of Seventeenth-Century New England', *American Historical Review* (1970), 1311–26.

She undermined the supremacy of the Church, men, and the landed classes. She represented a lay peasant subculture and she symbolized the actual or potential power that a minority group possesses: it is a threat to the established order. Women and peasants posed this kind of threat. The Church's claim was not that witches or wisewomen were unable to cure illness (or that curing illness was itself wrong) but rather that their success was a consequence of an alliance with the Devil, a temptation to which the feminine temperament was held to be peculiarly suspect. In practice neither the lay practitioners of medicine nor their clients distinguished clearly between 'natural' remedies (herbal ointments, potions, etc.), and supernatural or symbolic ones. The Church frowned on magic, but the people believed in it. The assumption of control by the Church in the sixteenth century over the licensing of midwives followed from ecclesiastical anxiety about the popular belief in magic (although other motives were involved, including a desire to clamp down on incompetent medical practice, and the aim of raising money). Until about the middle of the sixteenth century, a distinction was maintained between the 'good' or 'white' witch and the 'bad' or 'black' witch. In 1548, an English Witchcraft Act specifically listed the 'good' witch as an unlicensed practitioner of medicine, and distinguished between her activities and the necessarily evil acts of the 'bad' witch. A later Act (of 1563) abolished this distinction and declared that 'witchness' was a condition of the accused person.

The midwife's role in childbirth came in for particular attack. Any midwife was liable to be accused of being a witch, but particularly the unsuccessful among them. The *Malleus Maleficarium*, a famous medieval witch-hunting text, charged the witch–midwife with various reproductive crimes, including destroying the unborn child and causing an abortion. 'No one', said the authors 'does more harm to the Catholic Faith than midwives.' Witches were thought not only to kill and eat children (the idea of the Black Mass) but also to cause barrenness, abortion, and lactation failure; according to Henry Boguet, writing in 1590:

Those midwives and wisewomen who are witches are in the habit of offering to Satan the little children which they deliver, and then of killing them, before they have been baptised, by thrusting a large pin into their brains. There have been those who have confessed to having killed more than forty children in this way. They do even worse; for they kill them while they are still in their mothers' wombs.[9]

Behind these dramatic accusations lies a germ of truth. The medieval wisewoman in her role as lay healer and obstetrician almost certainly tried to help women carrying unwanted babies. Midwives in small-scale societies perform the same role today, and in our modern industrialized culture, it is still common for women to offer other women advice on how to bring about the miscarriage of an unwanted baby. The illegal backstreet abortionist, operating with her knitting needles or soap-and-water, can be seen as a direct descendant of the medieval midwife–witch. Professional opinion has done its best to label as evil the untrained woman who performs any reproductive care activity (one sign of this is the low opinion of untrained midwives which is reflected in much of the medical–historical literature). But in a sex-divided society, an ethic of 'we women must help each other' often flourishes, and may be as applicable to reproductive care as to those other essentially feminine activities—housework and childcare—where its existence has been established.[10]

Witch–healers and midwives were the practitioners and experts of a female-controlled reproductive care system—a system which had probably been in existence for a very long time. The force of the initial attack upon it was very great; integral to the Church's hostility to lay healing was a misogyny which led easily into an alliance with sexism and capitalism. The fifteenth and sixteenth centuries were a period when the position of women *via-à-vis* men was in a state of flux. In a growing commercialistic society, women had proved their independence and business efficiency. This practical equality challenged the law which was sex-discriminatory. Much popular discussion and pamphleteering concerned the breakdown in old conventions of masculine and feminine behaviour and what should be done about it: the independent woman evoked fear and a backlash of patriarchal assertiveness. The anti-feminism of the Church,

---

[9] Quoted in G. Parinder, *Witchcraft: European and African* (London: Faber, 1958).
[10] See, for example, N. Dennis, F. Henriques, and C. Slaughter, *Coal Is Our Life* (London: Eyre and Spottiswoode, 1956); M. Young and P. Willmott, *Family and Kinship in East London* (Harmondsworth: Pelican, 1962).

symbolic of, and connected with, patriarchal authority generally, had a particular alliance with the oppressive power of the landed classes.

Behind this attitude lay a double standard. Whilst the poor had to endure their suffering, medical care for the upper classes was acceptable, and this was male medical care. Between the eleventh and thirteenth centuries European medicine began its career as a secular science and a profession, with an impetus gained from contact with the Arab world. Until the thirteenth century medical practice was open to all; the only formal qualification available was a licence gained from a university education. But almost without exception women were barred from the universities, and with the development of barber–surgeons' guilds during the thirteenth century, medicine began to close its doors to those without a university licence.[11] Other groups, including the apothecaries, also created professional associations and demanded exclusive rights to practise. Through this kind of monopolistic procedure, the male doctor discredited and disadvantaged the urban literate woman healer.

The early 'professionalization' of medicine was strictly controlled by the Church. In England an Act of 1512—the first attempt by the State to regulate medical practice—left the responsibility for surveying the competence of medical practitioners to the Church authorities. University-trained physicians could, in theory, only practise with the advice of a priest, and were not supposed to treat patients who refused confession. In the medieval witch trials the male doctor was the 'expert' called in by the Church: it was he who determined who should be burnt as a witch. The *Malleus Maleficarium* (whose authors were appointed by Pope Innocent VIII to root out witchcraft in Germany) explicitly defined the role of the doctor in the witch-hunts and associated the status of doctor with the possession of formal training: 'If a woman dare to cure without having studied', they pronounced, 'she is a witch and must die.' A corollary to the 1512 Act included midwives in the Church licensing system, and a condition of the licence was that the midwife agree not to practise any form of witchcraft. (Many

[11] See Hughes, *Women Healers*, ch. 4, 'Academic Medicine'. On the exceptions to the rule banning women from the universities see K. C. Hurt-Mead, *A History of Women in Medicine* (London, 1938).

midwives, particularly in isolated rural areas, remained unlicensed; a licence was expensive and a woman could still practise
as a midwife's 'deputy' without a licence.) The attempted
suppression of women healers followed directly from the association between Church doctrine, university-trained medical men,
and the ruling classes. Male medicine became a fashionable habit.
Female medicine was stereotyped as evil magic. A pamphleteer,
writing about London in the seventeenth century, noted that
there was 'scarce a pissing place about the City' which was not
decorated with advertisements by lay healers; but the constant
barrage of anti-women legislation and pronouncements from
Church and State undoubtedly had an effect. The popular status
and authority of the female healer was gradually eroded.

The practice of the early male doctors was very different from
the practice of the traditional female healer. Superstition and
irrational beliefs played a far greater part in male medicine than
in female medicine. Medical students, like other scholarly young
gentlemen, devoted a large part of their study to Plato, Aristotle,
and Christian theology. Medical theory was almost wholly
restricted to the work of Galen, the ancient Roman physician,
who maintained the theory of 'complexions' or 'temperaments'
of men. While wisewomen operated empirically, trusting the
evidence of their senses, using trial and error, and believing in
cause and effect, male medicine was highly theological and anti-
empirical: hence its acceptability to the Church.

Chaucer characterizes the fourteenth-century 'Doctour of
Phisyk' as a pretentious charlatan in *The Canterbury Tales:*

> In all this world ne was ther noon him lyk
> To speke of phisyk and of surgerye;
> For he was grounded in astronomye . . .
> He knew the cause of everich maladye
> Were it of hoot, or cold, or moyste, or drye
> And where engendred and of what humour;
> He was a verray parfit practisour.

A broad hint of irony is dropped in this last line. As well as his
book-learning, Chaucer's Doctor was rather fond of money: he
made a small fortune during plague epidemics. The portrait
compares unfavourably with the empirical approach to illness
adopted by Pertelote in *The Nun's Priest's Tale*; Pertelote represents

the good housewife whose domestic skills included a comprehensive knowledge of herbal medicine.

Not surprisingly, modern histories of medicine do not acknowledge its female beginnings. Instead, they trace a direct descent from the Hippocratic physicians of ancient Greece. The witch–healer is dismissed as an undiagnosed hysteric.[12] No doubt once witch-hunting was under way, witchcraft did acquire the function of feminine protest (although of course the label 'hysteric' remains highly political). But the witch's healing role did not in the first instance evolve as feminist rebellion. Interestingly, the so-called Hippocratic oath, which is part of the official code of medicine today, probably itself contains a reference to the woman healer–midwife. The clause 'I will not give to a woman an abortive remedy' has always puzzled historians because it contradicts the liberal abortion policy prevailing in Greece at that time (the fourth century BC). The alternative explanation is suggested by one medical historian, Noel Poynter; he suggests that the abortion clause is in fact an admission of a restrictive practice aimed at avoiding demarcation disputes. Obstetrics and gynaecology was the province of female midwives in Greek society, and some of these midwives were highly trained physicians and surgeons. Literary evidence indicates that they were skilled abortionists and also knowledgeable about effective contraception.[13]

---

[12] See I. Galdstone (ed.), *Historic Derivations of Modern Psychiatry* (New York: McGraw Hill, 1967), 50.

[13] N. Poynter, *Medicine and Man* (London: C. A. Watts and Co., 1971).

3

Astrology in Seventeenth-Century England

Peter Wright

To modern eyes, few things seem further from our conventional image of medicine than astrology. Yet this has not always been so. From the earliest times until at least the end of the seventeenth century—if not later—astrology formed a major strand within medicine; not simply in the folk-healing carried on by 'wisewomen' and other informal healers active among the common people, but also in licensed, 'orthodox' medical practice—including even that of the tiny élite of university-trained physicians.

We would be wrong, however, to assume that seventeenth-century astrology was simply a survival from earlier, more medieval styles of thinking, which might have lingered on in the minds of the most unself-critical, backward-looking doctors. On the contrary, as the Middle Ages drew to a close the notion that the stars influenced human health almost certainly became stronger—not weaker. Indeed, it appeared to gain plausibility from several aspects of the new scientific knowledge. Parallels could be found between astrological theory and certain elements of the new astronomy and physics, and this encouraged some of the most advanced thinkers of the day, including Kepler and, possibly, Newton, to believe that it might be feasible to reform astrology by purifying it of error and rebuilding it from a foundation of unchallengeable, experimental knowledge.[1] The existence of attitudes such as these perhaps helps to explain why astrological allusions crop up repeatedly even in the writings of the greatest medical innovators of the period, such as Thomas Sydenham or William Harvey, discoverer of the circulation of the

[1] See K. Thomas, *Religion and the Decline of Magic* (London: Weidenfeld & Nicholson, 1971), 346 and 1414–18; P. W. G. Wright, Astrology in Mid-Seventeenth-Century England: A Sociological Analysis, unpublished Ph.D. thesis, University of London, 1983, 154–60; and P. Curry (ed.), *Astrology, Science and Society* (Woodbridge, Suffolk: Boydell, 1987).

blood. To take but one example, the latter recommended that certain medicines should be administered 'every new and full moon'.[2]

Some of the most eminent members of the medical profession were supporters of astrology. During the late seventeenth century they included no less than six physicians to the British Royal Family, one of whom, William Ramesey, was the author of several works extolling the importance of astrology in medical practice. In a publication of 1661, for instance, he insisted that no one could deny '. . . that *Astrology* is necessary to be known by all such as practice physick'.[3]

Other prominent physician astrologers included Sir Francis Prujean, President of the Royal College of Physicians from 1650 to 1654, and Richard Mead, one of the most sought-after doctors of his day, who held an MD from the University of Padua, had also studied at Leyden (then, probably, the most prestigious medical school in Europe) and had been elected a Fellow, both of the Royal Society and of the Royal College of Physicians. As late as 1704, Mead published a Latin monograph whose title translates as *The Rule of the Sun and Moon over the Human Body.*

In folk-healing too, astrological ideas were central especially when this involved herbal remedies—as it often did. While it is undoubtedly true that herbs were pressed into service for pragmatic reasons—because they were readily available, cheap, and seemed to work—there was more to it than that. Both herbalists and their patients lived within a culture which shared a network of assumptions about causation and modes of cure, although these assumptions might sometimes be vague, inexplicit, or even partially contradictory. When the sick needed treatment, herbs and other medications were not simply used at random: they were chosen on the basis of taken-for-granted presuppositions about what might cure what. Astrological theory was a major force in shaping these assumptions; it provided a guide to how heavenly bodies could exert influence over particular aspects of the world, control specific parts of the human body, and govern whether they functioned healthily.

---

[2] Quoted in B. S. Capp, *Astrology and the Popular Press: English Almanacs 1500–1800* (London: Faber and Faber, 1979), 207.

[3] W. Ramesey, *Tractatus de Veneris; or, a Treatise on Poysons* . . . (London, 1661), in the Epistle Dedicatory (no pagination).

One way of explaining these beliefs was by means of the concept of microcosm–macrocosm.[4] This was the notion that there existed a chain of interaction and causation which stretched back and forth from the tiniest portion of matter on the earth or the most trivial everyday event up to the vastness of the cosmos, the grandeur of the sun and moon's movements, or such awe-inspiring events as eclipses or the passage of comets. All formed part of a succession of interlocking hierarchical levels—rather like nests of Russian dolls. Each level, it was believed, paralleled and harmonized with the others in innumerable respects. Events in one were thought to precipitate events in others—just as the plucking of one string on a musical instrument could evoke from other strings a series of sympathetic resonances both up and down the musical scale.

This way of conceptualizing and explaining the world was deeply rooted in the minds of both educated and uneducated in Stuart England, and meshed tightly with contemporary ideas on many other topics including political power and art. This is shown by the frequency with which, for instance, notions of the microcosmic–macrocosmic link crop up in the imagery of Shakespeare or the Metaphysical poets.

Such ideas provided a framework of interpretation within which to make sense of herbalism and other techniques for healing. Thus, for example, the planet Saturn was believed to govern the metal lead with which it was thought to share qualities like coldness, earthiness, and masculinity.[5] In consequence Saturn was believed to produce personal characteristics such as gloominess, sluggishness, and suspiciousness; bodily features such as 'great ears' and 'hanging, lowering eyebrows'; and the illnesses of leprosy, dropsy, and excessive loss of blood from piles. It was supposed that these conditions could be treated by herbs which were antipathetic, or as the case required, sympathetic, to the qualities controlled by Saturn. Barley, for instance, was recommended as a poultice to soothe the pains of leprosy as it was a plant under the influence of Saturn.[6]

---

[4] See A. O. Lovejoy, *The Great Chain of Living* (Cambridge, Mass.: Harvard University Press, 1936).

[5] W. Lilly, *Christian Astrology* (London, 1647), 577–61. Also available in facsimile (London: Regulus, 1985).

[6] N. Culpeper, *The English Physician . . .* (London, 1733), enlarged edn., 57–61.

Although these notions of sympathy and harmony may appear strange to modern eyes we must remember that, three hundred years ago, they furnished the conceptual grid through which people were accustomed to apprehend and experience illness and to try to make sense of it. Just as nowadays it has come to seem obvious to us that germs can cause disease, or that exposure to something called radiation can lead to death, even many years later—essentially ideas that most of us take on trust—so then, it seemed obvious that planets and stars exercised influence over human bodies, illness, and even the course of human lives. Once we accept that there exist such major contrasts between the background assumptions of seventeenth-century medicine and those of our own time we are under an obligation to begin to reconsider completely the terms and categories we use for describing healing in the seventeenth century.

Obviously, we should not glibly assume that medicine and astrology were then distinct and separable bodies of knowledge and practice simply because that is how they now seem to be. Instead, we must acknowledge that—then—many, if not most, orthodox physicians worked with notions which we would now regard as astrological; and that numerous astrologers practised healing. Lucinda Beier has recently observed that '. . . rigid demarcations between academic, popular and magical healing techniques are anachronistic in a discussion of seventeenth-century English medicine'.[7] In other words, we have to question and rethink seemingly obvious distinctions between medicine and astrology and, indeed, between 'orthodox' medicine and 'quackery'.

This can be illustrated with reference to the use of astrological herbal remedies which was one of the techniques practised in what was termed 'natural' astrology—the study of the influence of astral forces on natural objects such as the earth, the weather, plants, animals, and even human bodies. This was generally accepted up until the end of the seventeenth century as a wholly legitimate and potentially fruitful field of knowledge.

But astrology also had a far more controversial and contested side: 'judicial' astrology. That was the branch which set out to

---

[7] L. M. Beier, *Sufferers and Healers: The Experience of Illness in Seventeenth-Century England* (London: Routledge & Kegan Paul, 1987), 108.

explain *human actions* in terms of the influence of the stars. What made it particularly contentious was its potential incompatibility with two aspects of Christian belief: individual free will and the omnipotence of God. An explanation of human conduct in astrological terms could be seen as challenging both.

Not surprisingly, some of the fiercest opponents of judicial astrology were clergymen, especially strict predestinarians (those who believed that God, at Creation, had predestined in detail the whole course of human history). However hard astrologers might try to cover themselves—as they often did, by insisting that the stars only inclined individuals to behave in certain ways but did not compel them, or by arguing that astral influence was one of the mechanisms by which God exerted his will—there was no escaping the latent tension between judicial astrology and Christianity. When the power of the Church over the behaviour of lay people was in the ascendant, or there were shifts in the dominance of particular theological currents within it, so this tension tended to flare up and lead to astrological almanacs being banned or to astrologers being prosecuted for practising magic.

Despite this, judicial astrologers were numerous in seventeenth-century England.[8] Evidence shows that they ranged from village amateurs (for whom astrology was no more than a sideline to supplement an income from healing, magic, or various village crafts), through more highly educated individuals (such as apothecaries, priests, and land surveyors who might be inclined to see astrology as a natural extension of their occupational expertise), right up to the astrological élite—the leading consultants who were to be found in London and some other large cities. These sometimes amassed considerable wealth both from the consultations themselves and from writing the almanacs which sold in vast numbers in this period.

Essentially, judicial astrology aimed to answer three related types of question: first, to explain why certain things had happened (why, for instance, had someone been persistently unsuccessful in trade?); secondly, to make predictions about the future which often bordered on counselling (for example, advising a client on what career to adopt, or whether to marry); and, thirdly, to determine questions of fact (such as whether a

---

[8] Thomas, *Religion and the Decline of Magic*, 359–60.

missing spouse was dead or where a stolen horse might be found).

The surviving casebooks of astrologers show that the questions which clients brought to them spanned the whole range of human insecurity, uncertainty, discomfort, distress, and, indeed, physical pain. By today's standards, many were medical in nature—one of the commonest being that of women who wanted to know whether they were pregnant. Other clients presented physical and psychological ill health or even sent a sample of urine with a request for diagnosis by post.[9]

While we know little about precisely why people chose to consult astrologers, rather than, say, priests or apothecaries—and it is hard to judge how sceptical they were of the services they received—what is clear is that clients seem to have gone to them for almost every conceivable kind of problem, not least for those which we now classify as medical. Astrologers were clearly perceived as general practitioners in the fullest possible sense.

In this respect, it is vital to reiterate that three hundred years ago the boundaries of medicine were very different from today. If we do not grasp this we risk distorting utterly our conceptual understanding of the past and of misconstruing its relevance to the present. This is well exemplified by the concept of a doctor. It is true that then, as now, there were official, licensed, medical practitioners (the physicians, surgeons, and apothecaries whose practice was regulated in various ways and was based on some kind of training or apprenticeship) who, at first sight, bear some resemblance to modern doctors.[10] Many, indeed, would have claimed the title of 'doctor'. As noted earlier, however, some of these orthodox practitioners certainly made use of astrological techniques. It may be revealing to point out that the best-known consultant astrologer of his day, William Lilly (1602–81), obtained an official license in 1670 to practise medicine, despite having no formal medical training.

Unlike today, moreover, licensed practitioners were relatively few especially in rural areas; and, in general, the mass of the

---

[9] Thomas, *Religion and the Decline of Magic*, 339–40.

[10] See M. Pelling and C. Webster, 'Medical Practitioners', in C. Webster (ed.), *Health, Medicine and Mortality in the Sixteenth Century* (Cambridge: Cambridge University Press, 1979); G. Homes, *Augustan England: Professions, State and Society* (London: Allen and Unwin, 1982); and Beier, *Sufferers and Healers*.

population was unable to consult them, because of their high fees or inaccessibility. Today, in contrast, 'doctors' are comparatively far more numerous and are consulted by all sections of the population as the professional healers of first resort. Today, too, medical knowledge is highly distinct from everyday under-standings of sickness and suffering and is rooted in a body of esoteric, highly technical medical science which provides power-ful and effective forms of therapy. Although licensed practitioners in the seventeenth century also laid claim to esoteric, technical knowledge—above all the inheritance of classical Latin and Greek texts—this knowledge could not be separated sharply from other elements of classical learning (such as that, for example, of clergymen), nor was it rooted in experimental practice.

In this earlier period the ill sought help from a diversity of practitioners, many of whom would not, to our eyes, seem to be medical in orientation.[11] Some of the sick, but probably only a very small minority, consulted the licensed practitioners; others went to semi-professional healers of various kinds such as bone-setters, astrologers, midwives, wisewomen, or white witches, many of whom would have drawn on astrological knowledge to a greater or lesser degree. The very poorest, and perhaps a majority, probably turned to the informal help of kin and neighbours, or to clergymen and the wives of country gentlemen—who tended to see healing as one of the duties which their social position obliged them to discharge.

What marked out licensed practitioners from the rest was essentially the fact that they were accredited members of organized professional groups with the legal authority (some-times rather hard to enforce) to exclude others. In the last analysis, it was this social power, not the special character of the knowledge that they possessed, nor the therapies that they practised, which distinguished them from the unlicensed.[12] They were occupational groups, that is, which had succeeded in

---

[11] It is still the case, of course, that today the sick seek help from many sources other than licensed medical practitioners. For a survey of some of the literature on 'lay referral systems' see D. Tuckett (ed.), *An Introduction to Medical Sociology* (London: Tavistock, 1976), 23 ff. None the less, medical dominance ensures that unlicensed practice is subordinate and generally occupies the lower levels of the 'hierarchy of resort', especially in the case of acute illnesses.

[12] This notion of professional power develops out of that put forward by T. J. Johnson, *Professions and Power* (London: Macmillan, 1972).

establishing themselves in privileged positions in the labour-market with the power to discredit their competitors.

Although even today professional power is still important in maintaining the definition of who is to be regarded as a licensed medical practitioner, other crucial factors have come into play which did not exist in the same way in the seventeenth century— above all the requirement that practitioners be trained in modern science-based medical knowledge.

To recognize the marked differences between the meaning of the category of doctor in the seventeenth century and today has profound implications. It removes any justification for trans-ferring the present prestige of medicine back to the licensed practitioners of three centuries ago (something which is all too common in the history of medicine). From this it follows too that we have every reason to question the notion of quackery in use then: from the perspective which is being presented, the 'quacks' were simply the competitors whom the licensed practitioners were trying to put out of business—there is no necessary reason to assume their practice was deceptive nor their remedies harmful.

This should not surprise us. Although today we may feel confident that we know how to distinguish medical from non-medical problems, dispassionate reflection soon shows that the distinction which we use is inseparable from the particular circumstances of the societies in which we live; it is fashioned by numerous factors amongst which are the nature of medical technology, the forms of organization of medical practice, and more general social values such as conceptions of health and images of the body. Our definition of a healer, for example, is likely to be very different if we think of the body as a machine whose parts can fail and be replaced, as opposed to conceptualizing it as a link between personal existence and social experience.[13]

Indeed, the boundary between medical and non-medical can shift quite rapidly. Only recently have psychiatrists ceased to regard homosexuality as a disease; there is still debate over whether the menopause is a medical problem; and hyperactive behaviour has come to be defined as a medical condition. Thus,

---

[13] See B. S. Turner, *Medical Power and Social Knowledge* (London: Sage, 1987), 212–26.

during the closing years of the seventeenth century and the first decades of that which followed, the relative positions of astrological practice and licensed medical practice began to change quite strikingly. Although astrological elements endured within medicine for some time, astrological practice as a distinct field rapidly began to lose support in educated circles, while licensed medicine maintained its status, or even increased it.

Like all fundamental evolutions of opinion, this change is not easy to chart; its course seems to have been essentially incremental rather than revolutionary. Perhaps this is not surprising given that, for a protracted period, ways of reconciling astrology with the new scientific knowledge could still be found by those with sufficient persistence and ingenuity. As Keith Thomas observes, 'scarcely anyone attempted a serious refutation of astrology in the light of the new principles'.[14]

What seems to have happened was that astrology gradually came to appear as both less interesting and less plausible than previously. For example, the enthusiasts for astrology, who had been present among the founding members of the Royal Society in 1660, found little opportunity to establish connections between the subject and the interests of their fellows; their astrological ideas were ignored rather than attacked. As their generation died out it was replaced by one amongst whom support for astrology as a legitimate branch of knowledge was almost non-existent. Astrology was left a stagnant and diminishing backwater cut off from the main flow of authoritative and fashionable ideas.

But astrological elements in medicine did not simply disappear. They rather became progressively less explicit as astrological rhetoric was abandoned and orthodox medical practice distanced itself from astrological consultation. Some can even be traced in modified form through the nineteenth, and into the early twentieth, centuries—as, for example, in late nineteenth-century debates over the character of seasonally linked conditions such as 'Summer Diarrhoea'.[15]

How, then, are we to explain why astrology lost its hold

---

[14] K. Thomas, *Religion and the Decline of Magic*, 418.
[15] See, for example, P. W. G. Wright, 'Babyhood: The Social Construction of the Care of Infants as a Medical Problem', in M. Lock and D. Gordon (eds.), *Bio-Medicine Observed: Social/Cultural and Historical Approaches* (Dordrecht: Reidel, 1988).

amongst the educated, yet orthodox medical practice did not? This cannot be done by pointing to unproblematic differences in the 'truth' or 'effectiveness' of their two bodies of knowledge. From today's standpoint most of the medical knowledge of the late seventeenth-century period appears mistaken and the majority of the therapies employed inefficacious, if not actually damaging. Astrology too appears mistaken, but in these years was, none the less, not easy to refute beyond challenge.

But, of course, to judge the truth and potency of knowledge from other periods in terms drawn from our own is sociologically and historically naïve. The difference in the fortunes of the two practices can only be explained adequately if we examine changes in the ideological and political power of their practitioners, and in the conditions under which they practised. We have to think of medicine and astrology not as two naturally distinct fields springing from two separate bodies of knowledge (the first 'true' and the second 'false'), but as two different, yet overlapping, forms of professional practice which happened to evolve in different ways and to attain different social positions. We have to consider why these had different degrees of success in marking out and promoting their particular sets of activities, and in convincing others of their legitimacy.

As I have suggested in more detail elsewhere,[16] for a variety of reasons astrologers failed to erect clear boundaries around their practice and were unable to establish any form of professional control over their clientele. More importantly, perhaps, they found themselves excluded from the main sources of cultural authority and legitimacy in Restoration England—above all the Crown, the Church, and the universities.

The reasons for this are complex but certainly include the fact that astrology carried radical connotations both because of its ready accessibility to the masses (its rudiments could be mastered from a textbook in a few weeks) and, relatedly, because of the support for it among the most radical elements of the parliamentary forces during the Civil War.

[16] See P. W. G. Wright, 'A Study in the Legitimisation of Knowledge: The "Success" of Medicine and the "Failure" of Astrology', in R. Wallis (ed.), *On the Margins of Science: The Social Construction of Rejected Knowledge*, Sociological Review Monograph No. 27 (University of Keele, Keele, 1979), and Wright, Astrology in Mid-Seventeenth-Century England, 296–325.

Astrology had been one element in the struggles over professional power which had taken place during the 1650s—struggles in which Levellers, radicals, and some astrologers had combined to attack the learned professions for monopolizing learning in their own interests and keeping it away from the mass of the people by locking it up in Greek, Latin, or Norman French (as university-educated clergymen, physicians, and lawyers were accused of doing).[17]

Nicholas Culpeper (1616–54) an astrologer, apothecary, and ex-Cromwellian soldier, exemplifies this position; he translated into English the Latin Pharmacopoeia of the Royal College of Physicians with the express aim of making available its contents (much of which had a strong astrological flavour) to the widest possible audience. For this, he was subject to scurrilous attacks from the Royalist press including the revealing accusation that his action led both to 'rebellion and atheism'.[18]

Although there were also patrons of astrology who were strongly Royalist, and they continued to patronize and support astrologers after the restoration of the Stuart monarchy in 1660, they never found an effective way of inserting astrology securely within the social institutions from which flowed cultural legitimacy. The relationship of astrology with the Church was ambiguous and uneasy, as was that with Oxford and Cambridge, where the influence of the Church was dominant. And astrologers were not only unable to obtain a royal charter to establish their own professional monopoly, but also found themselves increasingly constricted by the monopoly of the Royal College of Physicians; from being virtually unenforceable during the 1650s, this monopoly was applied with greater vigour and success under the restored monarchy.

In contrast to astrology, therefore, licensed medicine advanced its position: the Restoration renewed the power of the royal prerogative on which its monopoly depended; the political climate which was permeated by fear of action by the common

---

[17] This conflict is discussed in C. Webster, *The Great Instauration: Science, Medicine and Reform, 1626–1660* (London: Duckworth, 1975), and A. G. Debus, *Science and Education in the Seventeenth Century: The Webster-Ward Debate* (London: Macdonald; New York: Elsevier, 1970).

[18] This accusation was included in the Royalist paper, *Mercurius Pragmaticus* (1649), quoted in F. N. L. Poynter, 'Nicolas Culpeper and his Books', *Journal of the History of Medicine*, 17 (1962), 152–67.

people strengthened acceptance of its privileges; and the association of some of its leading members with the newly established Royal Society enabled it to tap some of the growing prestige of its new, institutionalized natural philosophy, which was also shrewdly, if cynically, adopted by Charles II.[19]

The point of considering the contrast between the fates of astrology and orthodox medicine in these years is to highlight that what we consider to be orthodox medicine or alternative medicine at a given time is not the result of intrinsic differences in the kinds of knowledge on which they are based. It is, instead, the result of social mechanisms which lead to certain kinds of healing being regarded as legitimate or orthodox, and others not. These mechanisms may be shaped to a great extent by factors which have little, if anything, to do with the 'truth' of the knowledge employed or the 'proven effectiveness' of the treatments concerned.

One major factor which affects what practices are defined as orthodox and what as unorthodox, or alternative, is professional power—namely, the capacity of the different professional groups which practise a treatment to link their activities and themselves to symbols of authority and legitimacy; to maintain links with the powerful; and even to determine the very language and conceptual framework which is employed to describe and compare different modes of treatment. This power ensures that such modes of treatment incorporate their own socially constructed view of the world and reflect their own occupational interests.[20]

[19] For a discussion of the part played by political and ideological factors in the demarcation of natural knowledge see P. W. G. Wright, 'On the Boundaries of Science in Seventeenth-Century England', in E. Mendelsohn and Y. Elkana (eds.), *Sciences and Cultures: Anthropological and Historical Studies of the Sciences* (Dordrecht: Reidel, 1981).

[20] The insight that professional power involves the power to prescribe the terms and language of debate has recently become a prominent theme in several different kinds of literature. See, for example, E. Freidson, *Professional Powers: A Study in the Institutionalization of Formal Knowledge* (London: University of Chicago Press, 1986), 1–20; P. Day and R. Klein, *Accountabilities: Five Public Services* (London: Tavistock, 1987), 55–75; and L. Haskell (ed.), *The Authority of Experts* (Bloomington, Ind.: University of Indiana Press, 1984).

4

The Great Age of Quackery

Eric Maple

The Glorious Revolution of 1688 had the honour of inaugurating the era of mammon who was destined to replace the Deity as the central symbol of British life. It also ushered in what might well be described as the Great Age of Quackery.

The quack began to occupy some of the highest positions in the social order. The King of France was rescued from the lethal clutches of his physicians by a violent remedy administered by an empiric, and at home Queen Anne, the last British monarch to perform the ceremony of touching for the King's Evil, permitted herself to be 'touched' financially by a number of spectacular charlatans.

Among the best known of these was William Read, an illiterate ex-tailor who, in the words of his critics: 'Having failed as a mender of garments set up as a mender of eyes', and who received the honour of an appointment as oculist to Queen Anne and George I and a knighthood into the bargain. He had a fashionable establishment in the Strand where he treated not only bad eyes but wry necks and wens and was on terms of intimacy with such men of eminence as Swift and Steele. At his death his widow attempted to carry on his lucrative profession but with little success.

Another enterprising oculist was Dr Grant, first a tinker and then a Baptist minister who, like Read, received the appointment as oculist to the Queen, as well as a knighthood. The poets, who were unsparing with their satire, summed up popular opinion in the Grub Street Journal:

> Her Majesty sure was in a surprise
> Or else was very short sighted
> When a tinker was sworn to look after her eyes
> And the mountebank tailor was knighted.

The reaction of the medical profession to these adroit manipulators can be imagined but their combined hostility failed to affect in any way the status of the quacks in polite society. Seemingly undisturbed by the accusation that they were no more than 'sow gelders, shady apothecaries, unfrocked priests, French shampooers, corn cutters, bath house keepers, urinarians, mystics, presumptuous midwives, itinerant abortionists, sleight-of-hand men, mechanic fellows, shiftless craftsmen and runaway husbands turned satyr', the quacks continued to hold the aristocratic community in thrall for the elementary reason that the orthodox physician could offer nothing better.

The oculist quack dominated his own particular department of medicine and his remedies were in great demand. These consisted of magical eye lotions, curative waters, and Lisbon snuff then selling at 23s. a pound and ideally suited to the purse of the wealthy patient. For those who could not afford this treatment there remained self-medication—the application of a gold ring, and in extreme cases goose dung, to the affected eye.

The most notorious of the oculist quacks of the eighteenth century was without doubt the self-styled 'Chevalier' John Taylor, a qualified physician who has been described as 'the prototype of all the modern medical fakers'. He moved within royal circles, for he had skilfully insinuated himself into the services of King George II, and he described himself as 'Opthalminator Pontifical, Imperial and Royal'. It was his boast that he had visited 'every Court, Kingdom, province, state city and town in Europe' and that he had at his command secret remedies which must never under any circumstances be allowed to fall into profane hands. There was perhaps an element of truth in this wild claim for there is no doubt that he had developed considerable skill in the treatment of opthalmic disorders. In his pursuit of the secrets of the oculist's art Taylor was said to have blinded no less than five of his horses. Finally, he himself went blind, dying in obscurity in a hospital at Prague. Dr Johnson described Taylor as the most ignorant man he had ever met and 'an instance of how far impudence will carry ignorance'.

Literary men always took savage joy in harrying the quacks and again and again exposed their pretensions with acid pens. Poor John Partridge, a genuine physician and astronomer who augmented his income by boot repairs and almanack making, was cruelly satirized by Swift in perhaps the most devastating of all quack epitaphs:

> Here five foot deep lies on his back
> A cobbler, starmonger and quack
> Who to the stars in pure good will
> Does to his best, look upward still.
> Weep all ye customers who use
> His pills, his almanacks, his shoes.

It was in fact a pill which established the reputation of Joshua
Ward (generally known as 'Spot' Ward from a birthmark on his
face) the most flamboyant pill-maker of all time. 'Ward's drop' or
pill, which was extensively advertised as 'a remedy for all
distempers' and consisted in the main of antimony, was no
novelty having been manufactured a half-century earlier by a
charlatan named Russell. Ward, an ex-footman, was called in to
examine King George II's injured thumb and replaced the
dislocated digit with such a violent wrench that the King's first
reaction was to kick his shins. On discovering himself cured,
however, he was so overwhelmed with delight that he rewarded
the quack with an apartment in Whitehall, presented him with a
carriage and horses, and granted him the privilege of driving
through St James's Park. Ward's famous pill became the standby
of high society, and Princess Caroline was persuaded to take one
for her rheumatism. There were minor set-backs, of course, when
one or two of Ward's patients died, but society readily accepted
his explanation that such deaths were caused by the physical
state of the patient and most certainly not by the pill.

By a travesty of justice, both human and divine, Ward was
honoured by the Apothecaries Act of 1748, which sought to
eliminate unqualified pill-makers from medicine but which
specifically excluded his pill from its provisions. Once again the
poets summed up the situation in caustic lines. Wrote Pope:

> Of late, without the least pretence to skill
> Ward's grown a famed physician, by a pill.

Such barbs fell harmlessly from the armour of this quack who
could claim a monarch as his patron, Lord Chesterfield, Horace
Walpole, and Henry Fielding as his patients, and who was
destined to be buried in Westminister Abbey . . . .

Defoe in his 'Description of a Quack Doctor' confessed himself
overwhelmed by the brazen audacity of the quacks and accused
them of using 'the most vulgar phrases imaginable, traversing the

spacious realms of fustian and bombast'. Of one such quack he wrote: 'for hard word and terms which he, nor you, nor I, nor anybody else could understand, he poured them out in such abundance that you'd have sworn that he had been rehearsing some of the occult philosophy of Agrippa and reading extracts from the Cabala.'

This type of appeal still had considerable effect upon a community that was separated by only a mere half-century or so from the age of magic.

During the eighteenth century the burlesquing of quackery reached new heights and even found a place in the cult of satirical heraldry. This had originated in seventeenth-century Germany and had inspired Horace Walpole's design of the coat of arms for the Old and Young Club, a gambling hall in St James's Street, and the motto, *'cogit, amor, nummi'*, an oblique reference to cheating at dice. Far better known was Hogarth's *Undertakers' Arms*, which incorporated the features of Mrs Mapp, the bone-setter, bearing a bone in her hand between 'Chevalier' Taylor and 'Spot' Ward . . .

Crazy Sally Mapp, the bone-setter of Epsom whose prominence upon this coat of arms was no more than her due, was a forceful practitioner whose strength of arm was only equalled by her powers of vituperation, most of the terms passing her lips being quite unprintable, yet such was her prowess as a healer that she was consulted by leading physicians and men and women of the best society. She appears to have been a typical folk-healer and descended from a long line of bone-setters whose skills had been handed down from generation to generation. Her violence of demeanour earned her the reputation of being half-crazed without diminishing her popularity in the least. The mob loved her, and this in eighteenth-century England was the hallmark of success. On one occasion Sal, who always travelled in a resplendent coach, was mistaken by the mob for one of the King's unpopular German mistresses and well and truly hooted. Sal had only to lean out of the coach and shout 'Damn your bloods, don't you know me? I am Mrs Mapp the bone-setter', for the mood of the mob to change at once, and she received a mighty cheer.

Her skill as a manipulator of bones was phenomenal and it is possible that she represents a true link between the folk medical practitioner of the past and the modern orthopaedic specialist and as such she might be considered one of the pioneers of 'fringe medicine'. Sal Mapp's fame led to the social enfranchisement of her whole family, her sister becoming the famous 'Polly Peachum' who married the Duke of Bolton. Alas, like so many of her kind, Sal was doomed to suffer the inevitable eclipse. She died, utterly destitute, at Seven Dials and was given a pauper's funeral . . . .

Healing by touch had been discontinued by George I, but in the lower reaches of society it long remained sound medicine and attracted considerable attention whenever practised. A toucher of the name of Tunis became quite famous for his cures of the King's Evil in Scotland. He is described in a contemporary account as a seventh son of a seventh son and . . . 'he touches or rubs over the sore with his hand two Thursdays and two Sundays successively in the name of the Trinity. When asked the secret of his power he answered "It is God that cures".' Right down to the end of the eighteenth century and beyond, the power of touch continued to exercise its magical hold over the popular mind. As a possible last example of this ancient rite many scrofulous persons continued to make pilgrimage to Ashburnham Church, Sussex, for the purpose of touching a pair of drawers and a shirt once worn by Charles I in the hope of a miraculous cure.

No better example of the interrelationship between folk medicine and medical quackery exists than that provided by the handbill issued by James Hallett, a well-known Sussex quack of the 1790s. Headed 'Great News to the Afflicted' it was addressed 'To all who are afflicted with Diseases let them be ever so stubborn or long standing or if given up by Physicians, or turned out of hospitals incurable: with the help of God, to be radically cured by James Hallett, the original curer of all diseases.' There appears to have been no physical disability which the remarkable Hallett would not tackle with confidence—King's Evil, scorbutic eruptions, sore heads, deafness, roaring noises in the head, cancers, blindness, apoplexy, disorders of the lungs and liver, wens; in short, to continue in his own words, every imaginable 'tedious tormentation' including 'nativities for the cure of witchcraft and other diseases that are hard to be cured'. Hallett, in common with many other tradesmen of his day, issued his token coins, one side bearing the words 'James Hallett curer of all disease 1795' and the other 'Mathematician and Astrologer', followed by the injunction 'Know thyself'. A firm believer in regular surgery hours, Hallett advertised himself as available 'at his new house three doors from the Waggon and Lamb, West Gate, Chichester, every Wednesday and Thursday morning until 10, and Saturday until 3 o'clock. To be seen at No. 8 Half Way House on Saturday evening, Sunday, Monday and Tuesday until 11 o'clock and Thursday evening and Friday till 11 o'clock'.

Incorporated in his omnibus list was a treatment for what was euphemistically described as 'a certain disease, whether fresh or thirty years' standing—cured by herbs only'.

magic

Herbal lore remained the basis of most medicines, particularly those of the poor, for the ancient Doctrine of Signatures was far from dead. A dramatic reversal in the whole approach to the subject was now in process, however. In its original form the philosophy of herbalism had been based upon the principle that a remedy was valueless without its accompanying incantation. Its development upon scientific lines could only take place when the element of magic had been discarded. This was now taking place, although eighteenth-century herbalism was still enmeshed in a web of ancient symbolism going back to the Quack's Charter of the reign of Henry VIII. Every type of practitioner whether orthodox or unorthodox has at some period or other subscribed to herbalism. Even at the turn of the century quacks were to be found distilling aphrodisiacs and vegetable perfumes from road-side stills, but it is comforting to learn that their other sinister sideline, the concoction of vegetable poisons and their antidotes, had been abandoned.

A relic of this grim aspect of old-time quackery has survived in the term 'toady'. This was the nickname given to the Toad Eater, an obsequious parasite of the medical quack and 'an allusion to the practice of the assistants of conjurors and quacks of eating toads, popularly supposed to be poisonous, in order to make their employers effect seemingly miraculous cures'. As the poet put it:

> Be the most scorned toad eater of the pack
> And turn toad eater to some foreign quack

Magic still retained its hold on the imaginations of the rural poor but since money had to be sought where it was most likely to be found, old-fashioned forms of therapy tended to be discarded by quacks in favour of fashionable, money-making recipes. Some of the older prescriptions make disturbing reading today. For asthma one drank wine in which woodlice had been steeped, and for loss of memory rubbed the forehead with castor oil. Cramp could be cured by a garter made from rosemary leaves or eel-skin, and sore eyes healed by powdered hens' dung. These fantastic remedies belong properly to mythology but occasionally one proved its worth. It was the investigation of the secret remedy of a Shropshire healer in 1775 that led to the discovery of the medicinal value of digitalis.

It seems paradoxical that absolutely opposing medical philosophies should exist side by side, yet in spite of every advance into new speculative and scientific fields, the old faith-healing techniques survived the ordeal of progress quite unscathed. John Atkins discussed in his *Navy Surgeon* published in 1737 the application of faith-healing techniques to the psychology of life at sea and the means necessary to adapt amulets 'to the patient's imaginations'. Ashore, a Lincolnshire charm for ague demonstrated the power of faith-healing rites that had originated in pre-Reformation times: 'When Jesus came to Pilate he trembled like a leaf and the Judge asked him if he had the ague. He answered that he neither had the ague nor was he afraid, and whosoever bears these words in mind shall never fear the ague or anything else.'

Eighteenth-century folk medicine [therefore] consisted of three main elements: faith healing, empiricism-cum-magic, and empiricism without magic. Upon this broad basis of popular belief medical quackery had rested for centuries.

5
Medical Mesmerists in Victorian Britain

Terry Parssinen

... Animal magnetism, or mesmerism, as it was called after its founder, first flourished in France in the 1770s and 1780s. Anton Mesmer believed that he had discovered the existence of an invisible, rarefied liquid that permeated all bodies in the universe, animate and inanimate. He claimed that a person's state of health depended upon a proper ebb and flow of the liquid throughout his body. Certain individuals have the power to alter a person's bodily fluids by moving their hands in patterns around the person's body—rather like a magnet that can change the configuration of iron filings—and thus restore him to health.[1]

Mesmer's theories proved to be extremely popular, at least in part because he combined in a single system particular elements that resonated with older traditions. His idea of an invisible but powerful liquid was not unlike the theory of aether, which had long been a staple of Western natural philosophy; his theory of disease, based on the idea of bodily fluids, resembled humoural pathology; and his therapies were reminiscent of 'touch-healing', which still enjoyed a strong popular following. Thus Mesmer drew on existing intellectual and social traditions, and welded them into a unified system that had great appeal.

After a long controversial life as a medical and scientific doctrine on the Continent, mesmerism was finally introduced into England in 1837 by one of the most formidable medical men of the age, Dr John Elliotson (1791–1868).[2] He was Professor of Medicine at the young but prestigious University of London, one of the founders of University College Hospital, and the translator

---

[1] R. Darnton, *Mesmer and the End of the Enlightenment in France* (Cambridge, Mass.: Harvard University Press, 1968).

[2] F. Kaplan, ' "The Mesmeric Mania": The Early Victorians and Animal Magnetism', *Journal of the History of Ideas*, 35:4 (1974), 691–702; G. Rosen, 'John Elliotson, Physician and Hypnotist', *Bulletin of the Institute of the History of Medicine*, 4 (1936), 600–3; J. H. Harley, *Doctors Differ* (London, 1946).

of Blumenbach. In addition to his academic qualifications, he was known as an innovator who had been one of the earliest English proponents of the stethoscope, and had experimented boldly and successfully by using large doses of drugs on his patients. Elliotson became the leader of a small group of medical mesmerists, only some of whom had received medical training. Under Elliotson's leadership, they flourished throughout the 1840s and early 1850s.

Elliotson did not claim that mesmerism was a medical panacea that would invalidate all existing therapies. However, he did claim that the discovery of the power of mesmerism was akin to Harvey's discovery of the circulation of the blood, both in terms of the irrational resistance which it encountered among medical men, and in terms of its potential for furthering medical knowledge. In addition, mesmerism had two immediate applications: as a therapy for patients suffering from neurological disorders, and as an anaesthetic for surgical patients.

In his own journal, *Zoist*, begun in 1843, Elliotson cited scores of cases of patients suffering from hysteria, epilepsy, tic doloreaux, and other nervous disorders, who had been treated unsuccessfully by traditional therapies, but who had recovered when they were treated mesmerically. A typical example was the case of a woman, aged 30, who had been deeply affected by the business reverses suffered by her father eleven years before. She was subject to fits of jumping up and down and clapping her hands together until they bled. For the past five years, she had been in and out of various London hospitals, and had been treated by forty practitioners.

Dr Watson shaved her head and electrified her. Under the others she was bled in the arm TWENTY-FIVE times; *cupped* SEVENTEEN *times;* had TWO setons, THREE issues, leeches and blisters WITHOUT NUMBER, and was in bed for SEVENTEEN days in a state of salivation. One practitioner attended her for a year and gave her carbonate of iron largely, and made her wear bags of steel filings on her back and feet, silk stockings and gloves: but the filings increased her sufferings when she jumped. She was mesmerised daily for periods of two weeks or a month when she felt the fits coming on. After a year of such treatment, the fits ceased entirely, and have not returned in the three years since she was treated.[3]

[3] 'Cures of Epileptic and Other Fits with Mesmerism', *Zoist*, 1:4 (1844), 407–69.

If the use of mesmerism as a therapy was promising, its use as an anaesthetic was startling. Before the introduction of ether into Britain in 1847, British surgeons either drugged their patients with alcohol or opium, or gave them nothing at all. Especially after 1842, mesmerists began to report large numbers of cases in which their patients underwent major surgery—for example, the removal of a tumour or a limb—completely insensible to pain while in a mesmeric trance.[4]

One might expect that the new science, which enjoyed the support of one of the leading medical men of the day, and which seemed to counter important weaknesses in contemporary medicine, would have aroused considerable interest and even support among Victorian medical men. Quite the contrary. Elliotson was forced to resign from his position at the University of London, his experiments were denounced or ignored, his followers were ridiculed, and medical men went to great lengths to castigate mesmerically induced insensibility to pain as either a fraud, or a perversion of God's will. Why did mesmerism evoke such impassioned negative response?

From early Victorian medical journals and pamphlets, one can cull hundreds of denunciations of mesmerism as quackery, fraud, and chicanery usually punctuated by the choicest expletives of the day: 'Humbug!', 'Errant Nonsense!', and so on. But these are mere shell explosions. What one would like to have is a detailed plan of battle, or even better, a Thucydidean explanation of why the war was being fought. But these do not exist; they can only be inferred from the odd outbursts.

We can understand the motivation behind this reaction if we go beyond the stated denunciations to an appreciation of the mentality of medical men, and of the social standing of their profession. I wish to argue that mesmerism was considered professionally illegitimate in mid-Victorian Britain because on one level, it contradicted so completely the contemporary theory and practice of medicine, and because on a second, and more significant level, it threatened the social and professional aspirations of medical men during a critical period in their history.

In what way did mesmerism challenge contemporary medical

---

[4] J. Elliotson, *Numerous Cases of Surgical Operations without Pain in the Mesmeric State* (London, 1843); J. Esdaile, *The Introduction of Mesmerism as an Anaesthetic and Curative Agent, into the Hospitals of India* (Perth, 1852).

theory? Elliotson and his followers endorsed the classic 'fluidist' interpretation of mesmeric phenomena. Mesmerism was, according to Elliotson, a scientific discovery of great human power, whose medical potential was undeniable, but as yet only partially understood. Nineteenth-century medical men denounced most of the quacks of their day as 'empirics'; that is, as mere opportunists who claimed that a specific remedy 'worked' without understanding why.[5] The dangers of this kind of medicine were clear. An empiric lacked the comprehensive knowledge to deal effectively with the whole health needs of the patient. Seen from another perspective, however, the denunciation of empirics underscored an important and timeless claim by medical men that they, and they alone, have access to an esoteric body of knowledge which is essential to professional practice. While empirics annoyed orthodox medical men—and often drained away a part of their livelihood—they did not challenge them theoretically. But mesmerists did, by claiming that the orthodox theory of the origin of disease was incorrect, or at best woefully incomplete. Mesmerism thus threatened the legitimacy of medicine by disputing its claim to possess exclusive, esoteric knowledge about the nature of disease and health.

Occasionally, a medical man would admit that the success of mesmerism, and other medical heresies of the 1840s, was a commentary on the lack of public confidence in heroic medical practice and the prevailing localized theory of disease. J. Evans Riadore noted that the popularity of 'new fangled systems' could be attributed to

the want of success attending the old practice, arising from the too generally contracted opinion, that diseases originate either in the stomach, liver, or the brain, and that the remedial means consist in administering mercury, purgatives, starving diet, and employing bleeding and cupping, and afterwards some preparation of iron, with or without bitters, and walking exercise; without sufficiently regarding other sources of disease, particularly the constitutional predisposition to certain diseases.[6]

[5] E. H. Ackerknecht, *Therapeutics from the Primitives to the Twentieth Century* (New York, 1973); A. Berman, 'The Heroic Approach in 19th Century Therapeutics', *Bulletin of the American Society of Hospital Pharmacists*, 11:5 (1954), 321–7.

[6] J. Evans Riadore, *On the Remedial Influence of Oxygen or Vital Air . . .* (London: Churchill, 1845).

But most medical men regarded mesmerism, along with homoeopathy and hydropathy, as fraudulent systems, reminiscent of eighteenth-century medical panaceas. Samuel Flood, a surgeon of Leeds, called them 'little truths run mad', and compared them to astrology and alchemy. For Flood, as well as other medical men, it was sufficient to be convinced that mesmeric phenomena could be explained by 'the force of imagination, and the influence exerted by the mind upon the body' to label mesmerism 'a delusion'.[7] It is a measure of the commitment of orthodox medical men to a purely somatic explanation of disease that they could consider mesmerism a hoax if they were convinced that it worked through the imagination, regardless of its efficacy.

But mesmerism's challenge to medical theory was indirect, and only dimly perceived; its threat to contemporary medical practice was much more obvious. Except for Elliotson and few others, most mesmerists who practised as healers were not professionally trained seekers after truth. It required no special training or formal education to acquire, and it could be practised by anyone who believed that he was in possession of that knowledge. In 1844, the *London Medical Gazette* sputtered that mesmerism 'admits the humblest and most insignificant, unrestrictedly for a time, into the society of the proud and lofty; it enables the veriest dunderheads to go hand in hand, as "philosophical inquirers" (forsooth!) with men of the highest scientific repute!'[8]

In addition, mesmerism was an economic challenge to orthodox medical practice. Unlike many of the more traditional medical quackeries, the medical heresies of the 1840s—mesmerism, homoeopathy, and hydropathy—were patronized by an affluent, urban clientele. Even the *Dublin Medical Press*, in an antagonistic editorial on the subject, admitted that mesmerism's patrons included 'successful lawyers, good generals, wealthy merchants, and great politicians'.[9] Since medical fees were generally high, and those who could afford them relatively scarce, this competition was a source of considerable discomfort to medical men.

---

[7] S. Flood, 'On the Power, Nature, and Evil, of Popular Medical Superstition', *Lancet* (16 Aug. 1885), 179–81, and (23 Aug. 1845), 201–4.

[8] 'On the Absurdities of Mesmerism', *London Medical Gazette* (23 Aug. 1844), 704–6.

[9] 'Who Are the Quack Fanciers', *Lancet* (20 Sept. 1845), 328.

They were particularly vexed by licensed practitioners who began to practise one of the 'new systems' of medicine. Medical men castigated such renegades as unprincipled mercenaries and saw the process as being the result of 'the difficulty in the present overcrowded state of [medical] society of gaining an honest livelihood'.[10]

Another aspect of mesmeric healers which particularly rankled medical men was their resemblance to magico-religious healers of the recent past who cured their patients by touching them. Valentine Greatrakes, a seventeenth-century Irishman, who was widely known for his healing power throughout the British Isles, was the best-known practitioner in this tradition. And, as recently as the early eighteenth century, English monarchs have treated scrofula by the 'royal touch'. Naturally physicians had striven to differentiate their form of scientific medicine from what they characterized as superstitious magic. They greeted mesmerism with a flurry of articles claiming that it was only the most recent example of this spurious form of healing.[11] Mesmerists, meanwhile, welcomed the comparisons, claiming on their part that touch-healing was simply an unselfconscious form of mesmerism.[12]

Yet it was only in part because of its challenges to contemporary medical theory and practice that medical men considered mesmerism illegitimate. Of greater importance was the fact that mesmerism threatened to taint it at the very time when the leaders of the profession felt it extremely important to maintain a spotless reputation.

In the 1840s, the institutions and legal boundaries of the medical profession were changing. The tripartite division of the British medical profession into physicians, surgeons, and apothecaries, derived from a late medieval distinction among functions which no longer corresponded to medical practice. Physicians were limited to practice among the very wealthy in large cities, and the number of 'pure' surgeons was very small indeed. The overwhelming majority of medical men were general practitioners

[10] 'Mesmerism Exposed', *London Medical Gazette* (26 July 1844), 575.

[11] 'Mesmerism', *Lancet* (8 Sept. 1838), 834–6; 'Letter to the Editor', *Provincial Medical and Surgical Journal* (12 Aug. 1843), 417.

[12] J. Elliotson, 'On Valentine Greatrakes and Local Mesmerisation', *Zoist*, 3 (1845), 98–102.

(the term became widely used in the early nineteenth century) who had qualified as surgeon–apothecaries, but who usually practised all forms of medicine. Yet politically the general practitioners were virtually powerless, as the profession was dominated by the Fellows of the élitist Royal Colleges of Physicians and Surgeons in London, Edinburgh, and Dublin. There were no common standards in medical education, the quality of which varied widely, and there were nineteen different bodies which had the power to license medical practitioners according to their respective regulations. While the Royal Colleges and the Society of Apothecaries had the power to sue unlicensed practitioners who operated within their jurisdictions, they were usually unwilling to do so because of the expense involved, and the reluctance of the juries to find for the plaintiffs in such cases.[13]

Moreover, medical men had a poor reputation with the general public, for a variety of reasons. Medicine was often characterized as a profession filled with marginal men: drunken, randy medical students; half-caste army and navy surgeons; impecunious Scots with dubious medical degrees in their kits; and irreligious professors of anatomy who furtively purchased exhumed corpses from grave-robbers. But if some medical men were marginal because they lacked respectability, most were marginal simply because they seemed to be tradesmen rather than gentlemen. Particularly in small towns and rural areas, where medical men dispensed drugs as well as medical advice, and were paid for the former but not the latter, the line between the 'doctor' and the shopkeeper, at least in the eyes of the lay public, was very thin indeed.[14]

These unsettled conditions spawned a reform movement which had grown to considerable strength by the late 1830s. The movement had three principal foci: the firebrand Thomas

---

[13] W. J. Bishop, 'The Evolution of the General Practitioner in England', in E. Underwood (ed.), *Science, Medicine and History*, ii (London: Oxford University Press, 1953), 351–7; C. Newman, *The Evolution of Medical Education in the Nineteenth Century* (London: Oxford University Press, 1957); P. Vaughan, *Doctors' Commons: A Short History of the British Medical Association* (London: Heinemann, 1959).

[14] 'Remuneration of General Practitioners', *Lancet* (1 June 1839), 382–3; 'On the Present Mode of Remuneration in the Medical Profession', *Lancet* (13 May 1843), 235.

Wakley, surgeon, radical Member of Parliament from Finsbury, and editor of the popular medical weekly, *Lancet*; the Provincial Medical and Surgical Association (later the British Medical Association), an organization whose strength lay in its broad base among provincial general practitioners; and John Forbes, publisher and editor of *British and Foreign Medical Review*, a scholarly and respected spokesman for reform.

From the late 1830s until the early 1850s, reformers petitioned Parliament in support of a succession of bills to reform the profession. Although the specific provisions varied from one bill to another, the reform programme consisted of the following essential demands: (1) the supersession of existing bodies by a single medical organization which would register all medical practitioners, and administer a qualifying examination to all candidates; (2) the standardization of medical education; and (3) criminal sanctions against unlicensed practitioners.[15]

This programme stressed what Eliot Freidson has identified as the core of 'the profession of medicine'; namely, an autonomous body which sets standards for education and licensing, and which may enlist the police power of the State to suppress unlicensed practitioners.[16] These demands, however, were not easily won. It was first necessary to convince the lay public, and their representatives in Parliament, that medical men were sufficiently knowledgeable and selfless to deserve the power of autonomous decision-making.[17]

To the dismay of the reformers, their lay opponents continued to insist on the right of every Englishman to select his own brand of medical treatment, without the interference of laws and licensing bodies. Thus Wakley, Forbes, and the Provincial Association saw the necessity of changing public opinion by trying to enhance the public image of medical men. For example, one of the reformers' burning causes of the late 1830s and 1840s was their campaign to force the repeal of a provision of the New Poor Law of 1834 which established a competitive bidding system for the appointment of medical officers of Poor Law Unions. Although this system harmed medical men economically, its most deleterious effect was on the image of the profession. The

---

[15] 'State of the Medical Profession', *Lancet* (5 Feb. 1841), 655–6.
[16] E. Freidson, *Profession of Medicine* (New York: Dodd Mead, 1970).
[17] 'Progress of Medical Reform', *Lancet* (4 Jan. 1840), 539.

public was treated to the squalid sight of impoverished country surgeons, scrambling to underbid one another for a contract from a union, often at £11 or £12 per year, like purveyors of potatoes or bread. By reinforcing the unprofessional image of medical men as tradesmen, this practice sharply undercut the reformers' attempts to raise the social status of the profession.[18]

Still another aspect of the reformers' campaign to enhance the public image of the profession was their attempt to expose, to discredit, and, if possible, to prosecute quacks. According to contemporary medical literature, the kingdom abounded with quacks in the early nineteenth century as never before.[19] Thomas Wakley felt especially impelled to protect the public's health and the reputation of the profession by exposing some of the more blatant of these practitioners in London. In the 1830s he attacked them recklessly, risking libel suits in order to expose them. The public, he reasoned, could not be expected to empower the profession to regulate itself if it allowed medical quacks to practise unchecked. His campaign against them was a demonstration of his power, and his good faith with the public, which was intimately tied up with his overriding campaign for professionalization. In one of his many editorial denunciations of quackery, Wakley specifically linked it to the issue of the profession's image:

We propose to extirpate unsparingly everything that openly or secretly lowers the dignity or rank of medical science and its professors. The IDEA of a Profession, of a Faculty, in the maintenance of which all, the highest and lowest, are alike interested, and which the elder medical men held in such reverence, has well nigh disappeared from us. This must be restored. Every offence, every injury done to the profession thus embodied, whether by members of the profession or by interlopers, is *quackery* to our code.[20]

Wakley's attack on mesmerism was of a piece with his ongoing struggle against medical quackery. In the summer of 1838, John Elliotson began to give public demonstrations of his mesmeric manipulations of two teenaged sisters, Elizabeth and Jane O'Key. Elliotson did not limit his demonstration to the so-called 'lower'

[18] 'Medical Officers Under the Poor Law', *Lancet* (9 July 1842), 524–5.

[19] 'Mesmerism', *Institute* (7 Dec. 1850), 228–9; 'Quackery and Its Pretensions', *Provincial Medical and Surgical Journal* (9 Sept. 1843), 490–2.

[20] 'The Lancet in 1846', *Lancet* (4 July 1846), 16.

phenomena: somnambulism, cataleptic rigidity, and insensibility to pain. Instead he seemed to endorse the much more controversial belief that mesmeric entrancement raises certain individuals to a higher plane of knowledge. For example, after becoming convinced that the O'Key sisters had the power of medical diagnosis while entranced, he took them to the men's ward of the Hospital late one night, where they caused complete disruption by not only 'diagnosing' certain cases, but by loudly prophesying the imminent deaths of several patients. As a result of his experiments with the O'Key sisters, Elliotson was savagely attacked by his former friend Wakley, and forced to resign his professorship at the University of London.[21] Wakley's attack on Elliotson was the first and most important, although not the only, medical denunciation of mesmerism. The attacks came continuously from all quarters of the reforming party in the 1840s.[22] Why did they feel so compelled to denounce the mesmerists?

In the 1830s and 1840s, mesmerism became a popular culture phenomenon. Self-proclaimed 'professors' of the subject swarmed throughout the kingdom, demonstrating their subjects' clairvoyant powers through 'experiments' in which the entranced subjects would read from a book or paper while blindfolded and the like.[23] Often these itinerant performers also claimed to practise medical mesmerism in private consultations. In the eyes of orthodox medical men, this was a reincarnation of the seventeenth- and eighteenth-century tradition of medical mountebanks, who performed a short entertainment before hawking their patent medicines at fairs and carnivals.[24] It was bad enough that the public equated medical men with tradesmen; would they now equate them with showmen as well?

Moreover, mesmerism was not taken seriously by the great Victorian quarterly reviews, the pace-setters of upper middle-class opinion. Indeed, the quarterlies treated mesmerism as an

---

[21] 'Animal Magnetism; or Mesmerism', *Lancet* (1 Sept. 1838), 805–14; 'Mesmerism', *Lancet* (8 Sept. 1838), 834–6; J. F. Clarke, *Autobiographical Recollections of the Medical Profession* (London, 1874), 155–94.

[22] G. Sandby, *Mesmerism and Its Opponents* (London, 1848).

[23] T. M. Parssinen, 'Mesmeric Performers', *Victorian Studies*, 21:1 (1977), 87–104.

[24] 'Animal Magnetism', *Medico-Chirurgical Review* (1839), 630–1; 'On Mesmerism', *Medical Times* (13 July 1844), 311; 'The Early Irish Mesmerists', *Dublin Journal of Medical Science* (1847), 254–71.

object of ridicule. Those who dabbled in it were either tricksters or fools. J. F. Ferrier, writing in *Blackwood's*, echoed the majority opinion when he explained the apparent success of mesmerism:

Imbecility of the nervous system, a ready abandonment of the will, a facility in relinquishing every endowment which makes man *human*— these intelligible causes, eked out by a vanity and cunning which are always inherent in natures of an inferior type, are quite sufficient to account for the effects of the mesmeric manipulations on subjects of peculiar softness and pliancy.[25]

Finally, mesmerism was suspect because it seemed to place one person so totally in the power of another. While that idea in the abstract was unsettling enough for ordinary Victorians, it assumed an even more sinister meaning when the operator was an older man, and the subject, as was usually the case, a young girl. While this sexual tension in mesmeric performances made for good entertainment, it did nothing to enhance the public image of the science. Furthermore, the power of mesmerism was transportable. What a gentleman had seen performed on the stage one night he might try in his own home the next. As mesmerism spread across the breadth of the kingdom, outraged Victorians railed against it, as though an army of seducers had been set loose to prey on the unsuspecting virgins of the land. Wakley's editorial in the *Lancet* of 15 December 1838 reflected this fear:

Mesmerism, according to its advocates, acts most intensely on nervous and impressionable females. What father of a family, then, would admit even the shadow of a mesmeriser within his threshold? Who would expose his wife, or his sister, his daughter, or his orphan ward, to contact of an animal magnetiser? If the *volition* of an ill-intentioned person be sufficient to prostrate his victim at his feet, should we not shun such pretenders more than lepers, or the uncleanest of the unclean? Assuredly the powers claimed by MESMER will eventually prove their own ruin. In endeavouring to raise themselves above ordinary mortals, they lay claim to attributes and powers which must place them, forever, beyond the pale of civilized society.[26]

Mesmerism was regarded as disreputable, for all of these reasons, by important segments of middle-class opinion. To alienate that

---

[25] J. F. Ferrier, 'Postscript to Eagles's Article, "What is Mesmerism?" ', *Blackwood's* 70 (1851), 84.

[26] 'Animal Magnetism', *Lancet* (15 Dec. 1838), 450.

opinion would be damaging to the goals of Wakley and the reform party. Their struggle to upgrade the status of the medical profession would be badly, perhaps irretrievably, damaged, if Elliotson and his followers were allowed to continue their experiments without reproach by the profession. Mesmerism was moral leprosy which contaminated the persons and institutions it touched.

Nowhere was this attitude better shown than in the debate amongst the medical students of University College on 4 January 1839, over whether or not to support Elliotson in his dispute with the Council. The discussion centred on a single issue: irrespective of the truth or falsity of mesmerism, how badly had the reputation of the institution been damaged by Elliotson's experiments? A speaker named Mr George summed up the case against Elliotson:

Carried on as mesmerism had been, in defiance of the whole profession, it must be injurious to the institution. Mesmerism was so disgraceful to the character of a public institution—so derogatory to the dignity of a physician—so opposite to everything that should have been expected from Dr Elliotson—that he blamed the Council for not having stopped it before.[27]

Confronted with the potential damage to their College, and possibly to their careers, a number of Elliotson's devoted students apparently had second thoughts about his work. While the pro-Elliotson organizers of the meeting had expected the students to vote three or four to one for his retention, in fact they split just about evenly.

Both because of their challenge to medical theory and practice, and also because of their threat to the social and political goals of the reformers, medical mesmerists were regarded by orthodox practitioners as deviants, who were outside the boundaries of professional respectability in the 1840s . . .

[27] 'University College and Hospital', *Lancet* (12 Jan. 1839), 594.

PART II

THE RISE OF MEDICAL ORTHODOXY AND THE DEVELOPMENT OF ALTERNATIVE MEDICINE

6

Homoeopathy in Britain after the Mid-Nineteenth Century

Phillip Nicholls

Homoeopathy continued to win converts among doctors and patients [after the mid-nineteeth century]. By 1853, 178 doctors in Britain and Ireland had publicly declared their allegiance to the new school, six veterinary surgeons had done so, fifty-seven dispensaries and three hospitals had been opened, and nine societies formed. In-patients and out-patients at hospitals and dispensaries had numbered in excess of 150,000 by 1852.[1] Fourteen years later, in 1867, the number of self-confessed homoeopaths had grown to 251, veterinary surgeons to twelve, and the number of hopitals (five) and dispensaries (fifty-nine) to sixty-four. Readership for homoeopathic literature was sufficient to sustain two quarterly journals and three monthly publications, and practitioners could give their adherence to any of four major medical societies. Extant books on homoeopathy numbered 198, tracts and pamphlets 192.[2] By the end of 1866, the London Homoeopathic Hospital alone had received 59,138 in- and out-patients.[3] . . .

The 1850s and 1860s, then, were a period of optimism and confidence for homoeopaths. The number of practitioners was growing, new hospitals and dispensaries for the poor were opening, and the system enjoyed a wide spectrum of public confidence, clerical sympathy, and aristocratic patronage. Of those able to pay for medical services, probably only the lower middle class had little contact with homoeopaths. Demand meant

[1] For these details see G. Atkin (ed.), *The British and Foreign Homoeopathic Medical Directory and Record* (London: Aylott and Co., 1853).

[2] See *The Homoeopathic Directory of Great Britain and Ireland* (London: Henry Turner and Co., 1867).

[3] 'London Homoeopathic Hospital', *Annals and Transactions of the British Homoeopathic Society and of the London Homoeopathic Hospital*, 5 (n.d.), 272.

that their fees were high enough to be prohibitive.[4] Dr Russell, addressing the Second Congress of Homoeopathic Practitioners in London (23–4 July 1851) was so convinced that homoeopathy had laid a firm 'hold of the practical English and American mind that nothing', he believed, 'can now check its steady and rapid advance'.[5]

Regular practitioners shared this prognosis. The absolute number of professed homoeopaths may never have actually been very large in Britain, but the regular profession was certainly alarmed at the rate of increase in its medical adherents, and the growing volume of popular support which the system had enjoyed since the 1840s. At the time, as Forbes had observed, it appeared to the orthodox that homoeopathy 'comes before us . . . as a conquerer, powerful, famous and triumphant'. And by 1851, Dr Cormack was sure that the advance of homoeopathy in the profession had reached the point at which 'it is time for us to be stirring, lest these apostates, when actually sheltered by [the Provincial Medical and Surgical Association], damage its respectability, and ultimately endanger its very existence'.[6]

The terms which the regular profession used to legitimate its action against homoeopaths—the preservation of the integrity of medical science, the defence of professional honour in the face of charlatanry, and a high-minded concern for public welfare— were really the public form in which deeper occupational interests about the collective social advance of medical practitioners found expression. The success of 'professionalism' as a strategy of group mobility depended on control over medical personnel and institutions, over the content of practice itself, and over the remuneration merited by professional status. Homoeopathy struck at all three concerns, but most immediately at that of finance. To the extent that patients dosed themselves homoeopathically, or sought the services of homoeopaths, so the livelihoods of regular practitioners were threatened. The overcrowded nature of the profession exacerbated the situation.

---

[4] See Dr Capper, 'The Progress of Homoeopathy in England', *Annals and Transactions of the British Homoeopathic Society and of the London Homoeopathic Hospital*, 5 (n.d.), 63.

[5] J. R. Russell, 'Address at the Second Congress of Homoeopathic Practitioners', *British Journal of Homoeopathy*, 9 (1851), 562.

[6] *Homoeopathy—Report of the Speeches on Irregular Practice* (London: John Churchill, 1851), 8–9.

Certainly, the financial temptation to practise homoeopathically was considerable. Homoeopaths themselves were open enough about this. As Dudgeon remarked 'any practitioner who declared himself a follower of Hahnemann was sure of getting rapidly into large practice. The mere material inducements to avow oneself a homoeopathist were of the most tempting character.'[7] Occasionally, too, these financial sentiments surfaced in allopathic literature. As the editor of the *London Medical Review* remarked, 'I venture to say, there is scarcely a medical man in the kingdom who has not felt the influence of this "delusion" on his professional income'—a situation which, he felt, was bound to worsen since 'I fear that the "delusion" is rather increasing than otherwise'.[8]

At bottom this financial threat orginated in the parlous condition of regular practice. Public confidence in medical practitioners was low, and would not improve until, as Dr Jenks candidly admitted 'An earnest and truthful endeavour [was made] to improve our professional knowledge.'[9] This improvement ultimately had to await the scientific revolution in medicine in the later decades of the century, and in the general imposition of more exacting educational standards. But one step forward which could have been taken immediately was for the profession to absorb the homoeopathic lessons which Forbes had spelt out in the 1840s. More than anything else, this would have stemmed the haemorrhage of converts to the system, both among doctors and patients. In fact, this is precisely what happened. The free market in medical services saw to that. While this was the most effective of responses to the homoeopathic challenge, it was also, however, a covert one. The public stance of the profession was to fight with the tactics of ostracism, exclusion, dismissal, and defamation. The campaign started in 1851.

At its nineteenth annual meeting, held at Brighton (13–14 August), the Provincial Medical and Surgical Association decided to act against irregular practice. A Committee, consisting of Drs Cormack, Tunstall, and Ranking, was appointed to consider what

[7] R. E. Dudgeon, *The Influence of Homoeopathy on General Medicine Since the Death of Hahnemann* (London: Henry Turner and Co., 1874), 34.

[8] Quoted by W. Bayes, *Medical Terrorism in 1862* (London: Henry Turner and Co., 1862), 12.

[9] *Homoeopathy—Report of the Speeches on Irregular Practice*, 5.

action might be taken. It reported on 14 August with a series of resolutions, all of which were adopted. The most important of these were, first, that homoeopathy was absurd, and that no reputable medical practitioner could or should have anything to do with it; secondly, that homoeopaths stood guilty of heaping abuse on the regular profession; thirdly, that therefore no member of the Association should entertain professional contact with homoeopaths; fourthly, that pure or eclectic homoeopaths, or practitioners who consulted with them, should cease to be members of the Association; and fifthly, 'That a Committee of seven be appointed to frame laws in accordance with these resolutions, to be submitted to the next annual meeting . . .'.[10]

The by-laws proposed by this Committee were read before the Association at Oxford the following year. These required that candidates for admission to the Provincial Medical and Surgical Association must give a written statement that they were not practising homoeopathy, and never intended to do so, and that any current member suspected of using the system or dealing professionally with those who did so should, in the absence of a satisfactory defence, be excluded from the Association, provided a two-thirds majority of those present supported the decision. These measures were also adopted.[11] At the 1858 meeting in Edinburgh, it was resolved to instruct the General Council of the British Medical Association (which the Provincial Medical and Surgical Association had become in 1856) to incorporate these strictures into its established legal framework.[12] In 1861, at Canterbury, the British Medical Association reaffirmed its general support for all these policies.[13]

The consultation ban—since loss of fees would be involved in refusing to meet homoeopaths—could only be motivated, so the profession told itself, by a well-developed sense of professional honour. Actually, one of the principal supports of this policy, the ostracism of those who broke the ban, depended for its force on an equally well-developed sense of material security. The potential loss of income from referrals by, and consultations with, regular colleagues was much greater than that risked from refusing to meet homoeopaths. In short, the threat of economic terrorism was the British Medical Association's favoured weapon in ensuring the solidarity of its members.

A huge volume of correspondence in the *Lancet* and the *British Medical Journal* was generated as a result of the British Medical Association's action. Surgeons wrote enquiring whether consultation was permitted in non-medical cases; accusations of practising or consorting with homoeopathy were made, defences written, and editorial comment elicited; and local societies usually endorsed, and sometimes argued about, the policies of exclusion and non-consultation. Regular medical journals of the period are rich in such cases. . . . But this did not prevent the fight from being carried to other quarters. Parliament was one of them.

The 1858 Medical Act had originally contained a provision which would have forbidden doctors from pursuing any therapeutic system other than that legitimated by the various teaching and licensing institutions. As the *British Journal of Homoeopathy* noted, 'anyone who will peruse the original draft, composed by an obscure clique of conspirators, will at once perceive that one of the main objects of the legislative scheme there disclosed was to extinguish completely and forever the homoeopathic heresy'.[14] Lord Grosvenor's long established support for homoeopathic institutions, however, meant that he could hardly remain silent. He tackled the offending clause in the House of Lords. He not merely succeeded in securing its deletion, but managed to obtain the addition of an amendment to the Bill—Clause 23—which forbad licensing bodies from insisting on guarantees of therapeutic purity as a condition of graduation. A repetition of action already taken along these lines by universities such as those of Edinburgh and St Andrew's was thus no longer to be feared. Homoeopaths were in celebratory mood at the news:

. . . thanks to the powerful influence of our parliamentary friends, . . . all the fangs of this serpent that threatened death and destruction to homoeopathy have been effectively drawn, and no ingenuity can pervert the Act into an instrument for our suppression or annoyance . . . for in place of anything like this taking place, the Act expressly forbids any of the small powers it confers being employed against us on account of our adoption of a particular medical theory.[15]

[14] 'The Medical Act', *British Journal of Homoeopathy*, 16 (1858), 530.
[15] Ibid. 534–5.

This, in fact, was the second time Grosvenor had fought in Parliament on behalf of homoeopathy. The first had involved a struggle to gain official recognition of the London Homoeopathic Hospital's record of success in treating cholera patients. After the epidemic of 1855 in London had subsided, the President of the General Board of Health contacted all metropolitan hospitals which had been involved in receiving patients who had contracted the disease. The intention was to compile a parliamentary report detailing the recovery rate achieved by different institutions, in the hope of identifying any superior plan of treatment which could be followed in future outbreaks.

In total 1,104 patients had received regular treatment; 573 (51.9 per cent) had died. Treatment had consisted of one of the following regimens: small or large doses of calomel, calomel and opium, other mercurials, salines, sulphuric acid, chalk and opium, iron, alum and alum mixture, acetate of lead and opium, cinchona and quinine, gallic acid (from the oakgall), ammonia, brandy, ether, camphor (*cinnamomum camphora*) and chloroform, cordial tonic mixture, cajeput (*melaleuca cajuputi*) oil, internal stimulants, castor (*ricinus communis*) oil, emetics, or olive (*olea europaea*) oil.[16] When the Board of Health presented its report, however, the statistics relating to the London Homoeopathic Hospital (ten deaths from sixty-one cases, all treated by spirit of camphor, given in the first to sixth centesimal potency), although supplied as requested, were omitted. The Management Committee of the Hospital wrote to the President of the Board of Health requesting an explanation, especially in view of the fact that:

... the returns of this hospital prove that in an institution ill adapted from its want of space and the arrangements of its wards for the purposes of a cholera hospital that the deaths *do not exceed* 16.4 per cent in an epidemic in which, as the Report issued by you shows, the deaths in severe cases under the *most successful* treatment pursued in other metropolitan hospitals were at the rate of 36.2 per cent ...[17]

There was no excuse for the omission of the homoeopathic statistics on the grounds of unreliable diagnosis. One of the metropolitan hospital inspectors—Dr MacLoughlin, a regular

---

[16] R. E. Dudgeon, 'Cholera', *British Journal of Homoeopathy*, 41 (1883), 326–7.

[17] See the reprinted correspondence under the heading 'Parliamentary Return of the Homoeopathic Treatment of Cholera', *British Journal of Homoeopathy*, 13 (1855), 679. Original emphasis.

practitioner—had confirmed that all the cholera cases he had observed at the London Homoeopathic Hospital were genuine.[18] Lord Grosvenor, vice-president of the Hospital, raised the issue in Parliament. Eventually, a separate parliamentary paper was published, in which the missing data were supplied.[19] Neverthe-less, the view of the Board of Health remained that the statistics had originally been omitted because they would 'compromise the value and utility of their averages of cure' and 'give an unjustifiable sanction to an empirical practice alike opposed to the maintenance of truth and to the progress of science'.[20] ...

Grosvenor's campaigns stuck long in the memory of the regular profession. On standing for re-election as the represent-ative of Westminster in 1865, the *British Medical Journal* advised readers that 'A man who is a quack in one thing is, in our opinion, likely to be a quack in all ....'.[21] Mr Hughes—author of *Tom Brown's Schooldays*—who was standing for Lambeth, received the same compliment. Dr Tweedie withdrew his name from the Committee appointed to further Grosvenor's election, and the journal hoped that medical practitioners in these constituencies would express their disapprobation in the appropriate manner at the polls.

Although the 1858 Act had prevented the imposition of therapeutic uniformity by licensing bodies, it did not stop claims from being lodged against homoeopaths in coroners' courts. Cases occurred both before and after the legislation was passed. If juries could be convinced that regular treatment, knowingly withheld in favour of homoeopathy, would have meant a good chance of saving the patient, verdicts of manslaughter became a possibility. ...

Generally, public sympathy for the medical underdog seems to have prevented juries from returning verdicts which most doctors would have liked in these cases. But where more direct action could be taken by the profession, over such issues as hospital and public appointments, and medical education, results were more tangible. Henderson and Newman [were] ... early victims. Dr Horner was a third. Ironically, Horner had spoken at the 1851 meeting of the Provincial Medical and Surgical Association—but

---

[18] Dudgeon, 'Cholera', 327.   [19] Ibid. 325.
[20] 'Parliamentary Return of the Homoeopathic Treatment of Cholera', 681.
[21] 'Editorial Comment', *British Medical Journal*, 1 (1865), 568.

afterwards, he had decided to enquire more closely into the system which both he and his colleagues had roundly condemned. His best-selling pamphlet, *Reasons for Adopting the Rational System of Medicine*—actually written as an explanatory letter to the Governors of the Hull General Infirmary where he worked—was the result.[22] It was to no avail. Soon after, he was removed from his post.[23] . . .

The dismissal of homoeopaths from hospital and other posts was matched by attempts to impede progress in terms of basic certification and higher professional honours. At one end of the scale, allopathic opposition ensured that Dr Black was refused the Fellowship of the Edinburgh College of Physicians;[24] at the other, the Universities of Edinburgh and St Andrew's refused to grant diplomas to practitioners of homoeopathy.[25] The Court of Examiners of the Society of Apothecaries of England stated identical intentions. King's College, Aberdeen, went so far as to examine one candidate, recommend him to the senate for graduation and then, despite having established his medical competence, reversed their decision to recommend graduation on discovering the man's homoeopathic inclinations.[26] . . .

Attempts to ostracize homoeopaths from all forms of normal professional intercourse extended, quite naturally, to the field of publication. Only very rarely were homoeopaths allowed to defend themselves or their system in regular medical journals. Indeed as Dr Drysdale, at the British Homoeopathic Congress in Birmingham (28 September 1870) put it, 'The editors and publishers of the medical periodicals were given to understand that the slightest sign of favour, or even the commonest fairness, towards the new doctrine, was to be the signal for stopping the sale of the publication.'[27]

---

[22] A fifth edition of 20,000 copies is listed in *The Homoeopathic Directory of Great Britain and Ireland*, 119. F. R. Horner, *Homoeopathy. Reasons for Adopting the Rational System of Medicine* (5th ed. (printed for the author?), Manchester, 1858).

[23] J. J. Drysdale, *Modern Medicine and Homoeopathy* (London: Henry Turner and Co., 1870), 9.

[24] See the editorial remarks in W. Ameke, *History of Homoeopathy: Its Origin; Its Conflicts*, trans. A. Drysdale and ed. R. E. Dudgeon (London: E. Gould and Son, 1885), 375.

[25] 'Historical Sketch of the British Medical Association', 859.

[26] A. Fyfe, 'University and King's College, Aberdeen, and the Homoeopathic Fraud', *Lancet*, 1 (1853), 123.

[27] Drysdale, *Modern Medicine and Homoeopathy*, 5.

Pressure was even brought to bear on booksellers. One German periodical of the regular school found this action not only unnecessarily extreme but also, for the British, hypocritical. The *Berliner Medicinische Central Zeitung* commented:

The agitation against homoeopathy has given rise to the excesses which are more than laughable—they are utterly contemptible. At the instigation of some fanatical medical men, a large publishing house (Highley and Son) have announced that henceforward they will neither publish nor sell any homoeopathic works, and it is expected that other publishers will follow their example. This mode of attempting to stop the child's mouth is absolutely revolting, and all the more barbarous as occurring in a land where the right to give expression is sacred.[28]

Patients, too, were pressurized. When the Provincial Medical and Surgical Association passed its resolutions against consultation with homoeopaths, it went to some length to ensure that the public was advised of its action. The meeting agreed to insert its 1851 strictures in *The Times*, the *Morning Post*, the *North British Advertiser*, *Saunder's News Letter*, and, 'in such other journals as the Council may sanction upon the recommendations of the BRANCH ASSOCIATIONS'.[29] Clearly, the intention was to deter potential patients from seeking homoeopathic assistance with the threat that regular help would not be forthcoming if they did. . . .

Accompanying attempts to frighten the public away from homoeopaths, and isolate them professionally, was a concerted effort to lampoon the system and its practitioners. This occurred at three levels: first, an attack on the character of homoeopaths themselves; secondly, to publicize and cheer instances where homoeopathy had failed to produce results; and thirdly, to demolish the system through theoretical critique.

The favourite double bind which the profession used to assail the intelligence and integrity of homoeopaths . . . [was put by] one correspondent in 1877 like this: 'I have known homoeopathic practitioners personally and I have always taken them to be honourable gentlemen, who were subject, as I thought, to a sort of craze . . .'.[30] Thus honourable homoeopaths, practising what they preached, were fools, and unworthy of professional recognition. On the other hand, the rescue of intelligence and sanity

[28] Quoted by Drysdale, ibid. 6.
[29] 'Historical Sketch of the British Medical Association', 859.
[30] L., 'The Recognition of Homoeopathists', *British Medical Journal*, 1 (1877), 400.

meant the sacrifice of honour: 'I for one protest . . . against the recognition of any men, whether homoeopathists or anything else, on the confessed ground that they do not really practise according to the system they profess.'[31] . . .

Fools, then, or knaves: either way, homoeopaths could not be fit associates. The argument was repeated *ad nauseam* in the literature of the period. What made its self-righteousness even worse was the fact that, by the time the correspondent quoted above was writing—the 1870s—the same argument could be made against the regular profession. Students were being introduced to an allopathic *materia medica* which bore the imprint of homoeopathic research. If on graduation, they ignored in practice what they had been taught, they were fools; if they did not, and failed to acknowledge their homoeopathic debts, they were undoubtedly knaves. . . .

One manifestation of the double-bind argument was the publication of accounts which showed both the harmlessness of swallowing whole vials of homoeopathic pills, and of poisoning by homoeopathic medication. Anecdotes regarding the former were frequent. One enthusiast was:

. . . exhibiting his medicine chest, and his globules, and expatiating largely on their wonderful properties, when a gentleman, who happened to be present, in order to convince him of his folly, emptied the contents of *every* bottle into his hand, and swallowed them all one after another! I saw him repeatedly for days together afterwards, and I can state positively that he received no damage whatever from his supper.[32]

In the 1870s, however, allopathic journals also reported cases where patients had been poisoned by homoeopathic medication. At the meeting of the Clinical Society of London (14 November 1873), Dr George Johnson related three instances, all involving 'Epp's Concentrated Solution of Camphor'. In the first, a young woman:

. . . having a cold and sore-throat, took in water twenty-five drops . . . She went to bed, and in a short time was found foaming at the mouth, black in the face, and violently convulsed . . . For several hours she was unconscious. She vomited blood-tinged fluid, smelling strongly of

[31] L., 'The Recognition of Homoeopathists', 400.

[32] J. Milner, 'Homoeopathy', *Lancet*, 1 (1860), 256–7. Original emphasis.

camphor, and had severe gastric pain. For several days she was partially paralysed, and six months afterwards she was still suffering from symptoms of nervous derangement. The preparation which caused these serious results is a saturated solution of camphor in alcohol, the preparation being an ounce of camphor to an ounce and a quarter of spirit.[33]

In the same year, Dr Clifford Allbutt reported another case,[34] and in 1875 three more were forthcoming.[35] Though all involved camphor, the implication was that homoeopaths were generally resorting to small doses of the highly concentrated mother tinctures in order to produce dramatic effects—thus risking iatrogenic damage—while claiming the credit (if due) for the infinitesimal principle, and for homoeopathy. Homoeopathic medication was thus either innocuous or dangerous. What else, after all, could be expected from fools or knaves?

The argument was specious. To begin with, the regular profession in the first half of the century had itself *defended* the need for vigorous medication. Moreover, as a reading of the camphor cases reveals, the bottles were generally labelled clearly, and the doses were often taken on patient initiative, rather than on medical advice. The problem was therefore one which could be solved by increasing public awareness of the difference between potentized remedies and mother tinctures, and by ensuring that chemists labelled their products clearly. But this was not the conclusion which the *British Medical Journal* wished to draw. The public, instead, should be advised 'that modern homoeopaths have gone from the harmless extreme of infinitesimal dilution to the dangerous extreme of the greatest possible concentration of active and poisonous drugs'.[36] . . .

The third level of attack consisted of theoretical rubbishing of homoeopathic principles. That homoeopathy was 'a monstrous lie,

[33] 'Clinical Society of London', *British Medical Journal*, 2 (1873), 617.

[34] T. C. Allbutt, 'Poisoning by Homoeopathic Camphor', *British Medical Journal*, 2 (1873), 679–80.

[35] G. Johnson, 'Another Case of Poisoning by Homoeopathic Solution of Camphor', *British Medical Journal*, 1 (1875), 171; A. Legat, 'A Case of Poisoning by Homoeopathic Solution of Camphor', *British Medical Journal*, 1 (1875), 243; G. Johnson, 'Another Case of Poisoning by Homoeopathic Camphor', *British Medical Journal*, 1 (1875), 272.

[36] 'Poisoning by Homoeopathic Solution of Camphor', *British Medical Journal*, 1 (1875), 351.

obnoxious to truth, opposed to science, and incompatible with reason' is a fair representation of the views often expressed in editorial comment.[37] But these arguments all tended to be *a priori*. The profession had *not* shown definitively that the system was innocuous. And even if it had, the fact remained that in many cases it was still superior to active drugging. . . .

Other critical exercises from the regular school came from Drs Gairdner, Braithwaite, Barr Meadows, and Sir Benjamin Brodie. Most drew forth response from the homoeopathic side— Henderson to Gairdner, Drs Bayes and Craig to Braithwaite, and Dr Sharp to Brodie.[38]

These statistical and theoretical examinations of homoeopathy covered much the same ground. As far as the latter were concerned, arguments were repeatedly but forward which strove to undermine the principles of proving, diagnosis, dosage, dynamization, and the similar remedy. Particular scorn was reserved for the records produced by homoeopathic provers. Braithwaite, for example, doubted whether anyone 'could believe that such minute . . . doses could produce the huge number of symptoms recorded, and that the effects of the medicines were working some forty days or so after being taken', for example, ' "1090 symptoms as the effects of . . . oyster shell; 1242 as the effects of the ink of cuttle fish; 1143 as the effects of . . . quinine; 930 . . . by doses of charcoal . . ." '[39] The simile was

---

[37] 'Editorial', *Lancet*, 1 (1860), 98.

[38] For the work of Gairdner, with Henderson's response, see W. T. Gairdner, *A Few Words on Homoeopathy and Homoeopathic Hospitals* (Edinburgh: Adam and Charles Black, 1857), and W. Henderson, 'A Note on Dr. W. T. Gairdner's Essay on Homoeopathy', *British Journal of Homoeopathy*, 15 (1857), 299–320. For the text by Barr Meadows, see Barr Meadows, *The Errors of Homoeopathy* (London: G. Hill, 3rd edn., 1876). Other critical examinations in the series were W. Braithwaite, *A Temperate Examination of Homoeopathy No. 1, The Doses and Provings* (London: Simpkin, Marshall, and Co., 2nd edn., 1859), and *A Temperate Examination of Homoeopathy No. 2, The Principles of Homoeopathy, with a Few Hints on the Nature and Cure of Disease* (London: Simpkin, Marshall, and Co., 1860). The homoeopathic responses were W. Bayes, 'Two Sides to a Question', *A Few Observations on Mr Braithwaite's Temperate Examination of Homoeopathy* (Manchester: Turner and Co., 1860), and W. S. Craig, *Homoeopathy. A Letter in Answer to Mr Braithwaite's Temperate Examination of Homoeopathy* (Manchester: Turner and Co., 1860). Brodie's original article and Sharp's rejoinder were subsequently put together anonymously as *Remarks on Sir Benjamin Brodie's Letter on Homoeopathy* (London: Henry Turner and Co., 1861).

[39] Braithwaite, *A Temperate Examination of Homoeopathy No. 1, The Doses and Provings*, 10. The number of symptoms referred to by Braithwaite within the inset

also attacked as a rule of strictly limited, therapeutic application. Moreover, it was argued, dynamizing medicines would dynamize the supposedly inert medium, similar symptoms could indicate different diseases, and homoeopaths themselves, some felt, were also inconsistent in the application of the simile principle.

Homoeopaths such as Henderson, Bayes, and Craig generally responded to these allopathic critiques by pointing out, as far as statistics were concerned, that the large number of cases involved in comparative examinations would mean that errors of diagnosis on both sides would be self-cancelling, and that deliberate falsification of returns was hardly something that professional honour would allow. And as regards the theoretical attacks, homoeopaths claimed that they missed the mark. Hahnemann, they conceded, had overstated his case. In practice, homoeopathy had changed, and criticism of Hahnemannianism did not therefore discredit the neo-homoeopathy favoured by British doctors.

. . . Crucially, however, regular medicine had changed too. No conception of the real difference between the two schools—even by the late 1850s—can be gained from an acquaintance with the allopathic literature which attacked the new school. In response to the presence of homoeopathy, and its popularity, regular practitioners had abandoned heroic therapy, and covertly turned to the *materia medica,* and even principles, of their rivals. This, much more than the forms of professional and institutional reactions to homoeopathy which have been detailed here, was responsible for its decline.

quotation marks are those quoted from homoeopathic sources by J. Y. Simpson, *Homoeopathy: Its Tenets and Tendencies, Theoretical, Theological and Therapeutical* (Edinburgh: Sutherland and Cox, 3rd edn., 1853).

7

The Old Wife, Pregnancy, and Birth Control

Mary Chamberlain

PREGNANCY AND POVERTY: OLD WIVES AND MIDWIVES

For the majority of poor women in the nineteenth century assistance at childbirth was provided by the midwives. Occasionally druggists would be called in to help, though they were notorious for their use of instruments. They were also expensive—the average fee in the mid-1860s was a guinea. Most deliveries therefore took place in the home, with the local midwife in attendance. The more highly trained midwives for the most part practised among a middle- and upper-class clientele. Most working-class women relied on the 'local woman', whose training was essentially empirical. Yet mortality rates—20–25 per 1,000—were considerably lower than those of hospitals, lying-in wards, and Poor Law infirmaries. The local midwife did not use instruments and required that the woman herself provide the necessary dressings and cloths. The risk of cross-infection was thereby substantially reduced.

The most obvious reason for choosing the local midwife lay in the fees she charged. The average fee in the 1840s was 2s. 6d., and in the 1870s 7s. (The doctor's fee in the 1860s was a minimum of 21s. for delivery alone, with extra charges for subsequent visits and mileage travelled. It often rose to 100 guineas and more for wealthier families.) Even after the 1902 Midwives Act, the fee for a registered midwife was between 7s. 6d. and 21s., and that for an unregistered midwife 5s. Most unregistered midwives also included other services—they expected to rest with the family for at least nine days after confinement, taking care not only of the mother and child but also of most, if not all the other household services. Mrs C., an 'unregistered' midwife who practised in Suffolk at the turn of the century, recalls:

You got to be there ten days. And I'd look after the father and the mother, and the baby and the other children—sometimes there'd be one and two and three and four and five and six (years). Very seldom would there be two years in between. There weren't nothing in my time to spread them . . . When I lived in I'd often sleep in a chair, to be truthful. And you took the things along with you that you wanted, that you knew the people hadn't got.[1]

This form of care was a valuable support and one which doctors and registered midwives would not undertake. Indeed, even those who might have been able to afford a trained midwife (though a midwife's fee was often equivalent to a week's wages) often preferred an untrained one for the extra help which she provided. The wife of an engine driver in Upton-upon-Severn, for instance, explained in 1892 that she

always had the 'woman who goes about nursing' [because] she did not see the good of paying a doctor a guinea just for the time, and looking after her and the baby for a few days afterwards, when she could get a woman who would do all that was needful at the time, and wash the child when it was born, and then attend her and the child for nine or ten days, all for 5/-.[2]

In times of distress, the local woman would often waive her fee or give credit, Mrs C. recalls again:

they give you five shillings. That was an expensive item. And how they afforded it I can't tell you. They hadn't always got the money. Where they got the money? So you'd do it free. But even then they had to give you extra, food you see. But bread was tuppence a loaf, and you could get a good loaf the next day for three ha'pence, which we often did. The ladies I went to were very nice, very kind, very grateful for what I done . . . The royalty, they had a different life. They had people to see after them. Whereas we hadn't. Who had you got? Nobody, only what you could pay for. And if you couldn't afford it, you got to do the best you could yourself.[3]

Mrs C., the daughter of a London 'woman', recalled:

once my sister was furious because she went out to help a girl what wasn't married. Her parents had come and said she was due and my

---

[1] Interview with Mrs C. (who wishes to remain anonymous), Suffolk, May 1977.
[2] Quoted in F. B. Smith, *The People's Health 1830–1910* (London: Croom Helm, 1979), 46.   [3] Mrs C., Suffolk.

sister said 'You won't get any money there'. And my mother said 'It
doesn't matter. If she's in trouble I'm going to help.' Yes, she did and my
sister was furious.[4]

Since the woman was invariably part of the local community
she was much better able to recognize genuine hardship than was
a system of rigid rules for determining destitution as applied by
the Poor Law or the charitable institutions.

Some midwives, like Ernest Bevin's mother, did occasional
work attending the childbirths of their neighbours. Others made
a regular living out of the practice, often supplementing it with
other medical services not available elsewhere, such as laying out
the dead, advising on sick children, and treating minor ailments.
The midwife was also known, and understood the conditions and
customs of her own community. Moreover, compared to the
doctors, her success rate in midwifery was high. Home deliveries
were infinitely safer than hospital deliveries. With uncomplicated
deliveries there was, in any case, little problem; with long
labours, often due to poor nutrition and physical weakness
(among other things), she was more patient in her attendance.
She was also less likely to interfere: midwives did not use
instruments and rarely inserted their hand inside a labouring
woman, unlike many of the doctors and the male accoucheurs.
The 'naturalness' of her technique often meant fewer complications and, unlike some of the doctors, she did not inspire fear. In
this area, experience was a far more efficient training than the
largely theoretical education of doctors.

I learnt with Mrs Soames, a dear old lady. She's dead now. We were
called out night and day . . . First of all, when we were called, we'd see
that the mother was alright. We had iron bedsteads, then, so we'd make
a pulley. I'd see they were ready for being delivered. We used to turn
them on their right side and they'd push against the bottom of the bed.
We'd manoeuvre the pulley so they could reach the bottom of the bed
and push. She had to do the work—sometimes it was a long time. We
didn't like a lot of straining, not on the last go. But as soon as we could
see the head we knew that things were alright.
    If it was lazy baby that wouldn't work and made his mother work, Mrs
Soames had a little bottle that she carried about with her, and she'd give

[4] Interview with Mrs Coker, Lambeth, Feb. 1980.

the mother 4 or 5 drops. It had no name on it. It was only a little tiny bottle, about an inch and a half. And it would force the pains down if the pains were slow and didn't follow as they ought to. And if they hadn't started labour, Mrs Soames would give them that. But other times, some labours would only give you four lots of pain and then the baby was there. And the child worked for me. And when we knew the waters had broken—we used to call them silver water—then we knew that the baby was on its way, and we also knew, when the baby was pitched right for birth, whether it was going to be long or short.

And when we saw the baby's head, we'd ease it out, and then I got the towel ready to receive it. And we'd tie the cord with white thread, we'd leave it a length, and then tie it up. And if it fell off clean, then the baby was clean and didn't have any diseases. Same with the afterbirth. If it came out cleanly and quickly and all bloody and not clotting, then we'd love to see it because we knew all was going well. Then we'd put it in a piece of old rag and burn it—it'd crackle like anything! Or if they didn't have a fire, bury it deep so the dogs didn't scratch it out.

We'd clean the baby's eyes and nose and we'd give it a real butter ball in its mouth, to help dissolve the saliva stuff that they had in their mouth. Only just a small ball, and it had to be real butter. And we'd clean the mother, and breast them. It was all breast feeding then, and much healthier. But if they didn't have any milk, which was very seldom, it would generally flow through at the beginning, if, after the second day, if it didn't come, we'd give the baby Jersey milk, with a little cream and tepid water and a little sugar. And as it got stronger, we used to give it a thin porridge. And porridge was porridge in those days, fine oatmeal and cooked so well there were no lumps or anything.

And we never lost any children. We fed the mothers up as best we could. And always after the birth we'd give the mothers porridge and then a piece of toast, and that cleared all the little hard pieces that had formed or clotted together.[5]

Difficult births posed a problem, but the success rate of doctors at such times was little better. 'The doctors', as Mrs C. remarked, 'needed us. They didn't use to come, only if it was a bad case.' The only baby Mrs C. ever lost was in fact due to the incompetence of the doctor after birth. (The baby bled to death after the doctor had circumcised him.) Doctors were called in emergencies, though not always paid. (Doctors who were summoned to such cases but refused to turn up for fear of not being paid were often acquitted at subsequent coroner's inquests.) 'The doctor', recalled

---

[5] Mrs C., Suffolk.

Flora Thompson in *Larkrise to Candleford*, 'was only seen there when . . . some difficult first confinement baffled the skill of the old woman who, as she said, saw the beginning and end of everybody.'

The Midwives Act of 1902 laid down that no person might use the title of midwife unless registered with the Central Midwives Board and that no woman 'habitually and for gain' might attend a woman in confinement except under the supervision of a doctor, unless registered. Well after the Act, many women continued to prefer the services of the unregistered and 'un-trained' midwife with her wide experience and knowledge of the social circumstances of her patients, to those of the new registered midwives. It was widely accepted that women 'knew' instinctively what was best for women in labour and for the subsequent care of mother and child. In Rotherham, for instance, 25 per cent of births in 1907 and 1908 were attended by 'old unqualified women'. One such woman, Granny Redman, dis-missed the 'new fangled certified midwives' on the grounds that they 'didn't known much, how could they with only three months training'.[6]

OLD WIVES AND BIRTH CONTROL

But if need and popularity ensured her survival, there were other, politically more potent, reasons why the old wife was often preferred. Midwives were not, until 1902, recognized by the State. Working-class midwives feared little competition from doctors or others who wished to enter their field. They were, therefore, somewhat immune to the charges of illegality which sometimes faced the male accoucheur.

This immunity also placed the old wife in a favourable position within her local community. Coming from the community and therefore from the same social and economic class as the women they treated, old wives recognized well the hardships caused by large families and poverty and shared, for the most part, their patients' beliefs regarding the morality of family limitation.

Knowledge of, and access to, effective birth control methods was virtually denied the working class until the 1930s. Abortion

---

[6] A. Mitchell, 'Now We Have an Act', unpublished thesis, 1974.

was a major form of birth control and infanticide a close second.[7] Although it had been made a statutory offence in 1803 and successive legislation culminating in the Offences Against the Person Act of 1861 tightened up laws against it, most working women did not consider it either illegal or immoral to attempt abortion before 'quickening' (the time at which the movements of the foetus are first felt—around 16–18 weeks)—the point at which life was believed to enter the unborn child—or, indeed, to fail to revive a sickly child at birth. With infant mortality so high in the nineteenth and early twentieth centuries, few working-class women could afford to feel sentimental about a child who, even if born, might not survive anyway. Untrained midwives were therefore often preferred because they had 'graveyard luck'—the euphemistic term used to describe those midwives skilled at saving the mother but losing the child. In addition, what limited (traditional) birth control advice was available would also have been given by her, as would advice about how to abort early in pregnancy. The vast majority of abortionists were untrained midwives—a fact which did not escape the notice either of the authorities or of the medical profession.

Lack of state or professional interest in working-class midwifery meant that the role of old wives as abortionists was on the whole disguised by their other functions. Only occasionally were women prosecuted, and then usually only if they were caught red-handed, for the local community had an interest in their protection. Abortion remained one of the few methods by which women in the nineteenth and early twentieth centuries had some control over their bodies and their lives.

The reluctance of the medical profession to enter into the debate on birth control was based largely on the fear that any sympathy for the birth control cause would have laid them open to accusations of, at best, quackery and, at worst, association with the old wives. For throughout the nineteenth century the medical profession was trying to improve its image in the public eye, partly by attempts to eliminate competition from unqualified sources and partly by making sure that only 'gentlemen' were

---

[7] See, for instance, the article by R. Sauer, 'Infanticide and Abortion in Nineteenth-Century Britain', *Population Studies*, 32 (1978), and by P. Knight, 'Women and Abortion in Victorian and Edwardian England', *History Workshop Journal*, 4 (Autumn 1977).

permitted to enter the profession and, once entered, were treated and paid accordingly.

The image-building attempts of doctors were aimed essentially at the bourgeoisie. The 1858 Medical Act, which established a medical register and made provision for the supervision of the education and qualifications of medical practitioners, only guaranteed the doctors a monopoly of practice in the limited area of public and commercial employment (the Poor Law and Friendly Societies). The reluctance to outlaw unqualified practitioners reflected in part middle- and upper-class doubts as to the doctor's professional competence; legislators and administrators shared these doubts. Anything, therefore, that cast a slur on the delicate position of the doctors was carefully eschewed by them. Work in all controversial areas was treated with the utmost caution: even public health and the temperance movement were initially viewed with scepticism. Indeed, the definition of what legitimately constituted medical practice was carefully controlled by the General Medical Council in order to create and retain a sharp professional distinction between themselves and all unqualified practitioners.

The definition of legitimate medical practice was based on a position of extreme conservatism. Any new movement was dismissed as being 'in our judgement, scepticism' as James Mackness noted in his *Moral Aspects of Medical Life* of 1846. Even new scientific discoveries made within the field of orthodox medical science were often greeted with as much hostility as praise, particularly within the area of childbirth (for example, the fierce debate over the use of chloroform in childbirth or the controversy over the causes of puerperal fever and the theories of Semmelweiss on this).

The position of the medical profession on birth control must be seen in this light. The main protagonists of birth control for much of the nineteenth century were regarded mostly by the middle classes as dangerous and immoral radicals in that they undermined the fundamentals of nineteenth-century bourgeois life—the family, the role of women, and the position of the working class. Doctors' responses to birth control issues varied from silence to outright condemnation—condemnation which was couched in moral as well as medical terms, and which also singled out for particular approbation the most emotive technique of birth control, namely abortion. Abortion was associated with the working classes and their heinous practices, and the old wife was singled out among them as being responsible for perpetrating this practice. The 1861 legislation was partly the result of lobbying by the medical profession. In the debate on birth control (synonymous with abortion in the doctors' eyes), the law placed the doctors firmly on the side of the righteous.

Doctors' repugnance for dealing with birth control was also based on their limited concept of medical practice. Their conservatism in defining medical areas meant that innovations which were not firmly under their control must necessarily be regarded as quackery. Purveyors of birth control information were therefore quacks and old wives. They were also reluctant to enter into issues which directly affected the working classes. (The doctors' support for public health measures was based as much on the fear that infection might spread to the middle classes as on humanitarian grounds.)

Midwifery, too, was a problem for doctors. They eschewed the study of midwifery itself as being 'an occupation degrading to gentlemen'. A qualification in midwifery was not considered necessary to obtain a doctor's qualification, and to have conceded that there was a valid field of study in midwifery would have conceded to the midwives that their occupation required special skills and knowledge. Association with midwifery was professionally dangerous. Where the working class was concerned, midwifery, abortion, and the 'still-birth' business were one and the same in the public image. To have sanctioned the training of midwives would have exposed doctors to the implicit charge of condoning other practices.

Although many doctors had little or no knowledge of obstetrics, they were prepared to attend deliveries among the middle classes and in the charitable hospitals and Poor Law infirmaries where control and the integrity of their position were assured. The 1902 Midwives Act, which required that only midwives registered with the Central Midwives Board could use the title, was only passed after concessions had been made to the British Medical Association and by persuading the Association that registration was more likely to eliminate the midwife–abortionist than non-registration. Of course, it did no such thing. Legal loopholes in the Act enabled unregistered midwives to continue in practice until 1926. . . .

Moreover, although the law might prosecute abortionists, the same conspiracy which had protected them in the nineteenth century operated right through into the twentieth. Among the women she served, the old wife as abortionist was often popular. 'The people down the street was ever so nice—wished me luck. Hoped I'd get off.'[8]

The role of abortionist was a necessary one. Until birth control became widely available, abortion remained a primary method of birth control. The majority of women who sought abortion were married and did not wish to have any more children. The *Derby Evening Telegraph* reported on 14 January 1939 the case of one woman who had died from an abortion:

The Coroner described the case as most unsavoury and most unsatisfactory. One must feel a good deal of sympathy with the woman who had died at the age of 36, and during practically the whole of her 17 years of married life had been either pregnant or recovering from pregnancy. While one could not condone it, one could well understand the desperate feeling she must have had when she found herself again pregnant . . .

The letters in *Maternity*, compiled by the Co-operative Women's Guild in 1915, provide a graphic and moving first-hand account of the desperation of many.

The mother wonders what she has to live for; if there is another baby coming she hopes it will be dead before it is born.

For fifteen years I was in a very poor state of health owing to continual pregnancy. As soon as I was over one trouble, it was all started over again . . .

I am really not a delicate woman, but having a large family, and so fast, pulled me down very much . . .

. . . when my second baby came, I had to do my own washing and baking before the weekend. Before three weeks I had to go back to working, washing and cleaning, and so I lost my milk and began with the bottle. Twice I worked to within two or three days of my confinement. I was a particularly strong woman when I married. There is not much strength left . . .[9]

---

[8] M. Woodside, 'The Woman Abortionist', in *Abortion in Britain*, Proceedings of a Conference held by the Family Planning Association at the University of London, 22 Apr. 1966 (London: Pitman Medical Books, 1966).

[9] *Maternity: Letters from Working Women* (London: Virago, 1978).

The methods used by the women varied from instruments (typically in the twentieth century the Higginson's syringe) to herbs. Mrs C. recalled:

abortion

> They'd steep the herbs in hot water and then let them stand, for drinks. Water of rue was one of them. And they'd drink it, to see if they could disperse of it if the baby wasn't wanted. Keep on with that, every day. Rue and fennel. And they've come to me, even in my older life, and asked me what they should do, tried to get it out of me. But I would never tell them anything.[10]

And then there were drugs. By far the most dangerous of the methods used were drugs bought from the chemist. Some were prepared medicines, often marketed for 'female irregularities', as some of the more unscrupulous druggists attempted to enter the market for abortions. But others were drugs bought singly and then compounded and administered at home—such as Epsom salts, castor oil, and other aperients. Many of the drugs were highly poisonous. Diachylon, for instance, was a lead compound. Women who took it often suffered lead poisoning as a result, and sometimes died. Quinine often had similarly tragic results. Others were based on mercurial compounds.

It is not clear, however, to what extent the old wife would have employed or advised the use of the more lethal drugs. Evidence seems to suggest that the reputation of certain drugs as abortifacients spread regardless of the role of the old wife. A Sheffield pathologist, for instance, commented that 'the news is handed from woman to woman by word of mouth, like any of the other household remedies or "cures" which every woman knows'.[11]

. . . Long after many doctors had dropped their moral objections to abortion, they continued to argue that the old wife was performing a risky medical operation, with little of the expertise and technological back-up necessary. But the fact that abortion was not made legal—and therefore safely performed by doctors—accounts for the survival of the old wife in this area of health care. Her role as abortionist should not, however, obscure the continuation of her other services.

Although midwives had to be registered from 1902, the use of

---

[10] Mrs C., Suffolk.
[11] *Quarterly Medical Journal*, 10 (1901–2), 148–52.

unregistered midwives continued in country areas until the 1930s largely because, until the 1936 Midwives Act, there was no state requirement which obliged local authorities to provide midwifery services. The towns were better served, but in country areas the services of the trained midwife were not always available, and the 'woman' was therefore called in.

8

'Secret Remedies' in the Late Nineteenth and Early Twentieth Centuries

Paul Vaughan

[In the second half of the nineteenth century and the early part of the twentieth century] the sale of quack remedies—likely in themselves to be far more harmful than the activities of unqualified practitioners—was on a semi-legal footing. Under the Stamp Acts, secret remedies—those which did not carry a statement of their formulae—incurred *ad valorem* duty and had to bear an Inland Revenue stamp showing that duty had been paid. Because the Revenue authorities collected large sums annually from this course they were, understandably enough, loth to accept a change in the regulations. About this the [medical] profession was justly indignant.

. . . [But] it was not until the early years of the present century that the British Medical Association came squarely to grips with the problem of secret remedies. At the Annual Representative Meeting of 1906, the Medico-Political Committee submitted a Report calling, once more, for the formulae of all patent medicines to be printed on the accompanying labels; the labels should be made to constitute a legal warranty of sale, and false description of the drug, on the label, should be made an offence.

In the same year, the *British Medical Journal* . . . began to publish a series of short articles on the composition and cost of certain patent medicines: two or three remedies would be dealt with in each issue. Week after week, the analyses were printed. In 1909, they were collected and published in book form as *Secret Remedies—What They Cost and What They Contain*. A second volume, *More Secret Remedies*, appeared in 1912.

By this time the trade in quack medicines had reached formidable proportions. The great newspaper empires of the twentieth century were in the process of construction, and a vital part of their foundations was the revenue from advertisements. There were few restrictions on what the advertiser could claim, which was generally less important to the newspaper proprietor than what he could pay for his space. The Proprietary Articles Section of the London Chamber of Commerce, in a privately circulated pamphlet protesting at 'The Agitation against Patent and Proprietary Medicines and Foods', complacently stated that between them their members spent about two million pounds a year on advertising. Some manufacturers used hoardings, others used signs in the fields bordering railway lines, but a great deal of this impressive sum was going to the newspapers, which formed the staple advertising medium. This was inducement enough to make the newspapers of the day (with only two exceptions) refuse to accept advertisements for either of the British Medical Association's books of *Secret Remedies*. Copies of both books, sent to the press for review, were studiously ignored.

The trade was an industry in its own right, embracing the activities of great companies with million-pound capitals as well as paddle-and-bucket concerns that arrived and disappeared almost overnight. It was said that in 1908 the amount of money spent by the public on secret remedies was the then enormous total of £2,500,000—enough, as the British Medical Association pointed out, to maintain 40,000 hospital beds. Every year the proprietary manufacturers now made a munificent contribution to the national budget in the form of Stamp Duty. In fact, revenue from Stamp Duty was a significant measure of how the trade had prospered. Whereas in 1860 the money from this source had been £43,366, by 1890 it had reached more than five times that amount, and in 1908 it stood at £334,142.

Some of the manufacturers had contrived to suggest that the stamp on the packet was some kind of official warrant of efficacy, with the result that, in due course, the stamp was printed with the statement, 'This stamp implies no Government guarantee'. Even so, the stamp was still ingeniously used as an advertisement of sorts, by means of artfully phrased copy; the impression of a guarantee was strengthened if the proprietor had his name, or his autograph, printed on the stamp—and this could be done if he were prepared to pay the cost of the die.

To the investigating doctors public credulity seemed limitless. A vast industry had been built up on the basis of ignorant diagnosis, usually through the post, by quacks claiming fictitious qualifications; it was an industry based on self-medication with remedies of hopeless inadequacy for diseases of every imaginable kind. Some of the diseases which the quacks claimed to cure were unknown in any medical textbook, diseases such as 'shopper's or sightseer's headache', 'brain fag', 'tobacco heart', 'catarrh of the bowels'. Among themselves the manufacturers trafficked in lists of people suffering from diseases likely to make them respond to advertisements through the post. Anyone about to market a 'cure' for cancer, for example, could buy from one of many agencies a nominal roll compiled from the records of other merchants. (It was said that lists of consumptives were dearer than others, because this class was considered likely to yield a better response.) Thanks to such workmanlike measures as this, business continued at a steady rate. Cancer sufferers smeared themselves with mineral caustics or blue dye, consumptives swallowed mixtures of glucose, tannin, peppermint, and garlic, diabetics drank neat alcohol laced with resin and bicarbonate of soda—all clinging to hopes of a cure raised in them by the makers' promises. It was an industry founded on a vast, cruel confidence trick. And the dupes were the sick people of the nation.

Secret Remedies made it clear that while the vast majority of these preparations were worthless as medicines, many were also actively dangerous. All of them were potentially so inasmuch as they might cause the sufferer to delay seeking proper medical advice. But some contained ingredients which were a positive danger to life. A brand of Soothing Syrup, 'for children teething', contained .08 grains of morphine in each bottle until legal action was taken, as a result of which the morphine was omitted. The treatment of cancerous growths with such things as zinc chloride (a powerful caustic) and birchwood tar was known to have caused unspeakable agonies to those taken in by the claim 'cancer treated without the knife'.

Among other evils which trailed after the trade in secret remedies was alcoholism. Invalids who had been induced to take a regular dose of tonic wines were innocently swallowing, daily, the equivalent in alcohol of half a tumbler of neat whisky. Many became chronic alcoholics—and fair game for the vendors of the many 'cures' for drunkenness. There was an immense sale for drugs and pills to produce abortion, to take some of which was tantamount to suicide. These abortifacients, with their alleged effects thinly disguised, were openly advertised in the press. One Sunday paper in 1912 carried nineteen separate advertisements for products described as 'a boon to ladies', 'for removal of female irregularities and suppressions', 'extra strong', 'never known to fail', etc.

In 1889, there had occurred the notorious case of the Chrimes brothers, who were the makers of a range of abortifacients, with such typical names as 'Lady Montrose's Miracle Female Tabules'. The newpapers which accepted advertisements for these products charged five times the usual rate ('a somewhat significant increase' observed the prosecution when the Chrimes brothers were tried), and altogether the brothers spent over £2,000 in advertising, achieving a brisk trade. To stimulate business still more, they sent a letter to between 8,000 and 10,000 of their clients, purporting to come from 'Charles J. Mitchell, Public Official', and threatening them with criminal proceedings for having committed 'the fearful crime of abortion'. Retribution could be averted, the letter went on, on payment of two guineas, 'being costs already incurred by me', and on the wrongdoers' swearing a 'solemn promise on oath before God' never to commit their crime again. Within the next few days, the police, who had been informed by an alert husband, intercepted 1,785 letters, addressed to 'Mitchell', of which 413 contained money. When the jury brought in their verdict of Guilty, they added a rider, that 'such a vile plot, even with all the ingenuity displayed in it, could only have been possible by the acceptance of such immoral advertisements by a section of the Press—religious and secular— well knowing their nature'.

The results of another case, heard in Edinburgh in 1906, were, if possible, even more damning. A proprietary manufacturing company sought in the courts to restrain the activities of an enterprising chemist, who was selling pills of his own manufacture under the company's brand name. Today, this would seem a straightforward case of infringement of patent rights. But the Lord Justice, pronouncing his decision, had this to say:

The evidence in this case discloses the history of a gigantic and too successful fraud. The two complainers who ask for an interdict against others, do so to protect a business which they have brought to enormous proportions by a course of lying which has been persisted in for years. The complainers cannot succeed in obtaining assistance from the law for a business based on unblushing falsehood for the purpose of defrauding the public into a totally false belief as to the origin and material of the goods they sell.

The preparation in question was a household name. What did the public think of this judgment, delivered after a thorough inquiry into the merits of the medicine? They had no chance to form an opinion. Scarcely a single newspaper mentioned the case.

The British Medical Association knew that to beat this nightmare enemy its best weapon was science and its best strategy objective inquiry. The idea behind the books of *Secret Remedies* was straightforward and deadly simple: it was that one of the main reasons why these remedies were sold in such numbers was that nobody but the makers knew what was in them. 'The surest enemy of quackery', ran the Introduction to *More Secret Remedies*, 'is increased publicity.' The tone of both books is restrained and coldly factual: if a note of sarcasm is heard it is when the claims made for some catchpenny 'cure' reach a pitch of boastful effrontery that grates upon even the hardened susceptibilities of the authors. Between their level-headedness and the bombast of the secret remedy manufacturers there is a contrast which contributes more than anything to the irresistible effect of the two books. The *British Medical Journal* remarked that *Secret Remedies* 'gives the reader the impression of hearing quacks in a market place bawling against each other'. The names of long-forgotten nostrums, some of them remedies that were once household names, ring through the books' pages, names with a Barnumesque flamboyance dreadfully misapplied: claims of uniqueness, of relief rapidly effected when all else has failed, of magically curative properties, are repeated *ad nauseam* and in language which absurdly combines pompousness with ignorance. 'A food that makes brain in five hours and blood in four . . . Chew one up with every meal, and in five minutes after you take the first concentrated tablet of this precious food it will commence to unfold its virtues . . .' 'A New Discovery for the removal of diseases, being an Electric Fluid of Intense Power in rapidly attenuating, dissolving, and removing obstructions in any part of the system . . . a subtle extract from the vegetable kingdom, the hidden fire or life of plants and flowers, the "Quint-essence of

Life!" Call it, if you please, "Bottled Fire!" "Bottled Health!" "Bottled Life!" . . .' 'I invite other ladies to participate in a discovery which reduced me 4 st. 8 lb. and got rid of my ugly double chin . . . My remedy is a woman's cure for women only. Nobody but a woman could have discovered it'—but the 'discovery' consisted mainly of pulverized seaweed. 'A Key to Health!!!', proclaimed another advertisement, 'for the treatment of many Diseases incident to the human frame', including piles, venereal diseases, gout, influenza, 'bad legs', and 'tumours': the formula—aloes, powdered ginger, and soap.

A favourite method of drumming up trade was to send to the sufferers a printed form on which a number of questions would be posed: the answers, it was claimed, would enable the authoritative person at head office to diagnose the precise nature of the complaint and arrange suitable treatment. The treatment would, of course, be founded on the remedy the questioner was selling. The doctors at the British Medical Association amused themselves by returning the forms with details of fictitious cases. Both questions and answers were then ruthlessly printed in *Secret Remedies*. Sometimes, having asked for the form the doctors would neglect to return it; frequently, when this happened, a letter would come from the manufacturers expressing solicitous surprise at the delay and offering to supply treatment at reduced rates. 'There is only one conclusion we can arrive at,' ran one such letter, 'namely, that financial circumstances make the cost of a treatment prohibitive to you. Should this be the case we would like to say, that this Association being at all times willing to extend a helping hand to everybody, is prepared to treat your patient for a fee of only 21s. per course.'

Secret Remedies and its sequel became famous. Without mercy, they revealed to the public how little care and accuracy went into the composition of these medicines. They revealed the reckless variation in the ingredients used, from batch to batch. They revealed the cost of making each remedy and contrasted it silently with the price the public was charged. Above all, they revealed the complete ineffectiveness of a large number of treatments whose manufacturers made claims for them of breath-taking scope.

As a result of these exposures, only one action was brought against the Association. The action failed.

However, the patent medicine manufacturers saw to it that the doctors had an uphill struggle to draw public notice to their findings. Not only was there a practically unanimous newspaper boycott on advertisements for *Secret Remedies* and *More Secret Remedies*, but many of the makers bought copies of both books by the thousand and hastily burnt them before—as they hoped—the secrets came out. But, fortunately, they were not spry enough to prevent considerable damage being done.

Despite the difficulty of obtaining a hearing, the British Medical Association succeeded in arousing public interest and indignation, and the attention of Parliament was at last drawn to the problem. In 1912 the Government announced that a Select Committee would be appointed to investigate patent medicines and foods.

This news aroused furious opposition from the proprietary manufacturers. The Proprietary Articles Section of the London Chamber of Commerce launched a vigorous attack on the doctors, complaining that if the manufacturers were obliged to disclose their formulae, this would invite unscrupulous imitators to pirate their products, and in any event would mean nothing to the public. The doctors' motive was quite clear, they said: all they wanted was to 'extend their monopoly'. As for the alleged harm done by secret remedies, if a preparation were harmful, the public would not buy it. 'Merit alone will permit continued advertising. If a medicine does not fulfil what is claimed for it, it soon kills itself, and the advertising ceases.'

The manufacturers had the benefit of spirited support from the press, who were generally as lavish in giving space to the trade's argument as they had been niggardly in publicizing the British Medical Association's case. The *Newspaper Owner* of 4 May 1912 carried an article entitled 'Newspaper Owners and Proprietary Articles—A Huge Revenue Threatened', which left its readers in no doubt where they should stand:

The broad question for the newspapers will shortly be which shall we support? The people who have advertised, are advertising and will keep on doing so, or the people who don't advertise, and don't believe in it, and who if they did have not the money to spend on it?

The answer of the Press should be short and sharp—deeds not words . . .

The *Daily Dispatch* took up the cue on 7 May, making sure that its readers did not shrug off the question as nothing to do with them. 'It is a question which directly and intimately affects millions of people', they insisted. 'The British public have an invincible faith—founded, be it said, on experience—in the efficacy of patent medicines.'

John Bull had already proved itself a useful ally of the medicine makers by publishing a glowing account of the splendid work done by 'The National College of Health, Limited, Eye, Ear, Throat, and Skin Institute, and Infirmary for Bad Legs'. 'The Tremol Treatment', purveyed by this establishment, had been duly examined in *More Secret Remedies*: Tremol Ointment No. 1, recommended for various kinds of leg ulcer, had been found to consist of 70 per cent prepared chalk, and 29 per cent soft paraffin, with traces of an unidentifiable but worthless yellowish-brown colouring matter. *John Bull* was then under the editorship of the egregious Horatio Bottomley, and it joined in the attack on the British Medical Association with obvious relish. The Home Secretary was 'acting under pressure of that trade union of doctors, the British Medical Association'. 'It is an open secret', the editorial went on, 'that the object of the medical fraternity is to eliminate competition and to force the public into their consulting-rooms and surgeries to be doctored at their own prices, and on their own conditions.'

The only effect, the writer declared, of the doctors' demand for publication of formulae would be 'to cripple huge businesses built up at tremendous cost and enable rivals to steal the product of other people's capital, enterprise, and ingenuity'.

John Bull made much of the triumphant proclamation by the manufacturers, that only two deaths had been 'known to occur' as a result of the sale of fifty million secret remedies a year, a lie that was well and truly nailed by the British Medical Association before the Select Committee. But, said *John Bull*:

the doctors have no such record. Almost every week the papers are eloquent of their bungling and their ignorance. Everybody grown to manhood is familiar with some case or other where patients have been wrongly diagnosed and wrongly treated by doctors, at all but ruinous expense, for week after week and month after month, to be eventually cured by a patent medicine or a 'quack' . . .

By way of peroration, there was an appeal to the Englishman's sense of civic justice and individual liberty:

In these days, the formulae of patent medicines are compounded by chemists at least as well qualified as those who dispense the undisclosed formulae of medical practitioners, and any legislative action which would harass, obstruct, or prohibit their sale would not only be a grave injustice to them, but a wholly unwarrantable interference with the right of the public to doctor itself as it pleases.

Undeterred by the opinions of the press, the Select Committee gathered its evidence. Two years later the Committee published its report, including 765 pages of verbatim minutes of the evidence heard: they had held thirty-three public sittings, heard forty-two witnesses, and asked 14,213 questions. By the time they had finished, they were no doubt a disillusioned body. There was, certainly, little left of the medicine-vendors' claims. The Committee summed up the position in these words:

For all practical purposes British Law is powerless to prevent any person from procuring any drug or making any mixture, whether potent or without any therapeutic activity whatever (so long as it does not contain a scheduled poison), advertising it in any decent terms as a cure for any disease or ailment, recommending it by bogus testimonials and the invented opinions and facsimile signatures of fictitious physicians and selling it under any name he chooses with payment of a small stamp duty for any price he can persuade a credulous public to pay.

The Committee recommended that there should be a register of licensed makers, with a list of their products, and that the registration should be renewed every year on payment of a fee. But they would not go so far as to demand that the composition of the medicines should be publicly displayed—that, in fact, secret remedies should give up their secrets. They believed, they said, that a strong case had been made out by the manufacturers against divulging their formulae: a trade secret was a trade secret, and Parliament had no right to jeopardize the prosperity of an established firm by making it possible for anyone to plagiarize their product. The most that the Committee would recommend was that the formulae of secret remedies should be placed, in confidence, in the hands of an official Government custodian.

They were not quite the thoroughgoing, root-and-branch

recommendations that the Association had hoped for. Nevertheless the British Medical Association welcomed them. But even these recommendations were not adopted. The Committee's two years of patient investigation were virtually ignored, and the Association's campaign was frustrated. For a reason for this apparent failure, one need look no farther than the first page of the Committee's Report, where the date of publication is printed: it was 4 August 1914.

Success in the struggle against secret remedies was a long time in coming. Something was achieved by such legislation as the Venereal Disease Act of 1917, which under the pressure of war prohibited the sale and advertisement of remedies for venereal disease. Lttle by little, other substances were added to the number of scheduled poisons, and the import, manufacture, and sale of opium, cocaine, and their derivatives were drastically restricted during the 1920s.

During the twenty-five years following the publication of the Report of the Select Committee, three bills came before Parliament which would have done something more to control the sale of secret remedies. All three failed to pass into law. One, which was given its second reading on the day of the 1936 Grand National, was counted out of the House, the minds of those few members present being elsewhere. Meanwhile the trade continued to flourish, and by 1937 the annual turnover in proprietaries had soared to twenty million pounds. The British Medical Association pointed out in 1933 that:

the progress of science has provided the quack with new sources for exploitation . . . Remedies claiming to possess radio-active properties are offered to the public through advertisements and literature describing their marvellous curative powers in elaborate but meaningless quasi-scientific jargon. If these remedies have the potency claimed for them there is serious danger in allowing them to be sold to the public for self-treatment, while if they have no such potency the claims are fraudulent.

In 1936 the Government stated that it had no intention of bringing in any legislation, at least in the foreseeable future, to put into effect the recommendations of the long-forgotten Committee of 1912. The Association was bleakly informed that further progress could only be made 'by public education through voluntary organizations', and was recommended to 'watch for opportunities of securing legislative control step by step'.

It was a disappointing statement. But public education and piecemeal legislation were ultimately responsible for solving the problem. The next real advance came in 1939, when the Cancer Act was passed. In this Act, the British Medical Association contrived to have a clause inserted which forbade anyone but a registered medical practitioner from treating, or offering to treat, cancer, by advertisement or any other means. At last, in 1941, the Pharmacy and Medicines Act placed similar controls over the treatment of a long list of serious diseases—Bright's disease, cataract, diabetes, epilepsy or fits, glaucoma, locomotor ataxy, paralysis, or tuberculosis. The list is almost identical with the one included in the Report of the Select Committee in 1914. The Act also makes it obligatory that the composition of all proprietary medicines should be shown on their labels.

9

Orthodox and Osteopathic Medicine in the Inter-War Years

Gerald Larkin

The responses of alternative medicine to the successes of orthodox medicine in Britain have been profoundly influenced throughout this century by a history of exclusion from public health services. This contribution examines the events and policies of the inter-war years, which resulted in alternative practitioners playing no direct part in the last forty years of the National Health Service. Osteopathy's attempt to gain recognition in this period will be used as a case-study to shed light on the closely linked growth of medical dominance and the marginalizing of competitors.

Before examining how the histories of medicine and osteopathy interlock, it is necessary to note that both occupations have developed strategies to secure professional control, despite their many evident differences. Each has been concerned to protect and enhance its identity through time, which in turn implied the elaboration of policies to control market value and image. This is not to suggest that therapeutic differences are simply market based, but rather to emphasize their part in a wider political pursuit of group interest. Foremost in this enterprise is a perceived need to win privileges of occupational self-government from the State, usually through types of statutory state registration. Occupations which retain purely voluntary terms of association often remain particularly vulnerable to competition. Health care practitioners like all professional monopolists thus seek to protect themselves against 'unfair' challenges. They protect their investment in training and their modes of practice by acquiring state-backed powers of enforcement. This form of sponsorship is integral to full professional development, and is usually claimed in terms of public rather than partisan interest. It has become increasingly important in this century, particularly as state recognition implied eligibility for employment in the growing public health sector.

Orthodox medicine achieved state registration with substantial powers of self-government in 1858. It was not challenged to share its premier position until osteopathy's attempt in the 1930s. Other health care occupations had reached forms of state registration, such as midwives (1902), nurses (1919), and dentists (1921). They remain, however, in various ways subject to medical control and in effect were licensed as secondary practitioners. By contrast the osteopaths, at this point only a few hundred in number, through a succession of bills, sought a legal status comparable to that of the medical profession. Furthermore, their challenge was linked to the advocacy of therapeutic concepts and practices quite at odds with contemporary medical wisdom. When finally pressed home in the House of Lords, it led to a public review of much significance for the future of osteopathy and other heterodox practices in this country. In outlining these events three phases will be distinguished: (1) osteopathy's advent in England and the first medical responses; (2) the activating of a Ministry of Health and medical profession alliance in opposition; and (3) the ensuing parliamentary inquiry and aftermath.

THE EARLY YEARS

Osteopathy first developed in America, under the inspiration of A. T. Still (1828–1917). Still learnt medicine through an apprenticeship to his father, and practised in the mid-West for some twenty years up to 1874. At this point he later claimed to have had the visionary insights that began to revolutionize his practice. These centred on two principal themes—that the healthy body contained all the remedies necessary to maintain itself, and that 'osteopathic lesions' could interfere with this internal balance. These lesions were taken to be morbid altera-tions in tissue, whether osseous, muscular, visceral, ligamentous, or some combination of all these types. They were principally associated with impairments to the body's structure, particularly the condition of the spinal vertebrae. Still further claimed to have discovered a system of manipulation which reduced harmful lesions.[1] These insights, however valid, at least offered an

---

[1] G. L. Albrecht and J. A. Levy, 'The Professionalization of Osteopathy', in

alternative to many of the drastic surgical and drug remedies of the day. Still successfully propagated his ideas, and founded a school in 1892 in Kirksville, Missouri. A small group of graduates from Kirksville took up practice in England, and by 1911 had founded the British Osteopathic Association. Still's ideas spread beyond this group to other practitioners, although membership of the Association was linked to Kirksville training.[2] The Incorporated Association was founded in 1926 for 'untrained' osteopaths, and despite status differences both organizations began to press for governmental recognition.

Before examining their tactics some of the contemporary organizational features of medicine should be noted. The medical division of labour had more fluid boundaries within it than is the case today. Many of the 'frontiers' with emergent and ambitious allied professions were still in a state of flux. As indicated, nurses and dentists had reached forms of state registration, but in many other cases the distinctions between 'medical' and as then termed 'auxiliary' responsibilities were subject to dispute. Many groups, such as chiropodists, physiotherapists, and radiographers, pressed their claims and were actively seeking status advance through medical recognition. Medical patronage was thought to be a step to fuller recognition, and in this sense these groups were notably different from osteopathy. They went on to join the British Medical Association's Board of Registration of Medical Auxiliaries in the mid-1930s. Osteopaths on the other hand did not seek medical patronage as a mode of advance, and thus were not subject to inclusive subordination. They saw themselves as having equal rights to practise in a full sense, embracing diagnosis and treatment based upon different principles of injury and healing.

The osteopaths' treatments brought them into direct competition with the specialisms of orthopaedic and physical medicine within the orthodox camp, which were in vigorous and marginal phases of development respectively. Orthopaedics had been revolutionized by anaesthetic and surgical improvements allied to X-ray aided diagnosis from 1895 onwards. The ensuing

J. Roth (ed.), *Research in the Sociology of Health Care*, ii (London: JAI Press Inc., 1982), 162–205.

[2] H. A. Baer, 'The Drive for Professionalization in British Osteopathy', *Social Science and Medicine*, 19:3 (1984), 717–25.

casualty requirements of the First World War also pushed the speciality into a major expansion. Through the 1920s trained orthopaedic surgeons spread throughout the country as osteopathy's claims also escalated. Physical medicine on the other hand was more of a collection of treatments linked to the chronically ill, rather than an emergent and expanding specialism. The various heat, electrical, and manipulative methods employed were thought to be archaic by a large number of doctors. Physical treatments also carried the taint of being associated with non-medically trained bone-setters, and charlatans who exploited the hopelessly crippled and incurably ill. The few interested doctors working in this area were looked down upon by many of their medical colleagues, even before the advent of osteopathy. As James Mennell, a prominent physical medicine specialist of the inter-war years, later reminisced, his early career choice was thought degrading by his fellow medical workers.[3] The marginal medical status of the specialism, however, was balanced in the 1920s by the growing popularity of physical treatments and the related opportunities that this presented for successful practice.

A concern with the 'osteopathic invasion' is evident in the rhetoric of medical journals during the late 1920s. It began to intensify from 1925, when twenty-one Members of Parliament backed state registration for osteopaths in a circular letter in Parliament. At a special meeting Dr Kelman Macdonald, a conventionally trained medical graduate of Edinburgh University who had become one of Still's pupils, argued that the public, in seeking the services of properly trained osteopaths, instead were threatened by a host of impostors. In particular he instanced a recent General Medical Council ruling that medically trained anaesthetists could not work with osteopaths. The General Medical Council was empowered to discipline any doctor engaged in 'covering'—that is, assisting an unqualified person to act as a registered medical practitioner. Macdonald thus concluded that state registration for trained osteopaths would both forbid unqualified practice as defined by the British Osteopathic Association, and establish a basis for proper collaboration with the General Medical Council.[4]

Medical responses were swift and very negative. In 1925 Sir

---

[3] J. B. Mennell, 'The Use and Abuse of Physical Treatment', *Lancet* (1924), 160.
[4] *British Medical Journal* (1925), 716.

Hubert Waring, a prominent surgeon, devoted his presidential address of the Medical Society of London to the threat that osteopathy posed to the public. Waring pointed to an alleged ambiguity in osteopathic claims. On the one hand they denied any wish to disestablish medicine but rather wanted to work alongside it, in a manner comparable to dentists. However, they also claimed a complete philosophy of healing and range of treatments for many ills. Waring called for a strengthening of the Medical Acts underpinning the dominant position of the medical profession in the health care division of labour so 'that it would not be possible for the community to be treated by them or any other unqualified charlatan or quack'.[5] His position was supported by the *British Medical Journal*, which argued that osteopaths were encroaching on medicine because they in turn were under threat from chiropractors, an even more 'bogus' group. Under these pressures, it was claimed, osteopaths were introducing bacteriology and surgery into their training to effect a 'back entrance to medical practice'. The expression of these strong feelings took the form of derision:

It may remove some misapprehension if an explanation is given of the manifest indifference with which osteopathy is received in this country on the part of medical men. It may perhaps be inferred that we consider there is nothing in it. Such is by no means the case. We are aware that osteopaths profess to make use of approved hygienic measures in their treatment, and that they attach importance, with a view to treatment, to deformities of the spine, such as lateral curvature, with which the regular practitioner is quite familiar. When, however, osteopaths refer innumerable diseases to small derangements in the form of the backbone—irregularities which we are unable to detect at post-mortem examination, with the body open before us—we regard their theories as far-fetched and fanciful, and, when applied to grave diseases such as typhoid fever and diptheria, as decidedly dangerous. When we are asked to believe that a cold in the head, a crop of pimples on the face, an attack of vomiting and diarrhoea after a gorge, an attack of gout or measles— that these and a host of other diseases too numerous to mention are, one and all, due to small spinal irregularities which may be readily corrected by manipulation of the back, we experience a difficulty; it leaves us, so to speak, cold. It may be objected that no such difficulty has been felt in America, where osteopathy has had an enthusiastic reception. It should

[5] *British Medical Journal* (1925), 679.

be remembered, however, that America is the land of freedom—freedom
for faddists among others.[6]

THE MEDICAL–MINISTRY ALLIANCE

In response to these denunciations, osteopaths in turn
claimed that much of contemporary medical practice was misconceived. However, beneath the surface of debates over
effectiveness were other issues. Osteopathy by this time had
developed more successfully and extensively in the United States,
with its notably different social and political system. The British
system of government by contrast was centralist rather than
federal in structure. Professional licensing was monitored and
controlled at a national level, rather than devolved as a state or,
in the British case, a local authority responsibility. The older
medical corporations had a long tradition of close association
with this process through the Crown and central government.
This enabled them to convert their accretion of legal privileges
into active and practical monopolies of employment. Heterodox
practitioners, they argued, had to be excluded from participation
in any public or state-administered service, lest the progressive
impact of the Medical Acts be eroded. This viewpoint found
strong support amongst the medically trained administrators of
the Ministry of Health, created after the First World War. To these
Ministry officials the preservation of improved standards in
medical education and practice was intimately linked with
denying state recognition to any less orthodox group, as Dr
Charles Newman's note as Chief Medical Officer on the Medical
Herbalists Bill of 1923 indicates:

training

safety

*legal
standing*

The object is obviously to secure legal recognition for herbalists, and the
next step would be to claim for registered herbalists all the rights of
qualified medical practitioners. No doubt the argument of the promoters
would be that if people wish to be treated by herbalists, it is better that
they would be treated by herbalists who have had some kind of training
than by those who have had none. I do not know how herbalists are
trained, and it is at least doubtful whether a trained herbalist is any less
dangerous than an untrained one, but if any official recognition is to be
given to herbalism it cannot be denied to any other type of unqualified
medical practice.[7]

---

[6] Ibid. 706. [7] Public Record Office, Ministry of Health, 58.106.

The close co-operation between ministry and medical profession became further evident in a co-ordinated response to the
first Osteopaths' Registration Bill in 1931. Mr Arthur Greenwood,
the Minister of Health, was on the Management Committee of the
British Osteopathic Association's clinic. This, *inter alia*, may have
led to a raising of osteopathic ambition and the observation by
Newman that in this instance there was 'no insuperable obstacle
to the Bill's ordinary progress through Parliament'. Newman
then wrote to Sir Donald Macallister, President of the General
Medical Council, and raised the spectre of 'confusion in the
public mind and prejudice to the credit and integrity of medicine'.
Macallister in reply set out a number of objections which added
to the strands of existing Ministry opposition to the Bill. These
were that (1) it gave a particular status to a theory of medicine,
contrary to Section 23 of the Medical Act of 1858; (2) osteopaths
were to sign birth and death certificates without regular medical
training; (3) the Bill was unnecessary as doctors could offer
osteopathic treatment if they wished; and (4) no satisfactory legal
definitions could be devised to distinguish medicine and osteopathy as practised by two different and separately recognized
classes of practitioner. Macallister further argued that the more
reputable osteopaths were American trained, and that the British
schools were of a low standard. The British Osteopathic Association also wished to enforce a four-year training period via the Bill
which was vulnerable to the charge of inferior provision to that of
medical education. Greenwood, despite his links with the
Association, made arrangements for the blocking of the Bill, and
a further attempt to enhance the position of osteopaths through
parliamentary means in 1933.[8]

Government blocking of these Commons' bills increasingly
served to unite the osteopathic factions and to persuade them to
seek sponsorship in the less easily managed House of Lords. In
1934 Viscount Elibank introduced a Registration Bill, backed up
by a joint manifesto from both the British and Incorporated
Association of Osteopaths. This attacked the hostile, obstructive,
and jealous attitudes of doctors to their 'sixty years of a new
independent system of drugless medicine and bloodless surgery'.
They complained of a 'stigma of outlawry', which brought some

[8] Public Record Office, Ministry of Health, 58.107.

modification to the Ministry position. Briefing notes for the Minister of Health suggest a change from outright rejection to proposing a form of subordinate inclusion. This was to be based on a distinction between osteopathic theories and allied manipulative techniques. Such techniques might be very useful to medicine, it was argued, if their exponents worked under medical direction, as did other auxiliaries. They could, for example, manipulate patients under general anaesthetics provided a registered medical practitioner controlled the case. Authority and acceptability were thus closely linked.[9]

The British and Incorporated Associations of Osteopaths had no desire to acquire an auxiliary status in medicine. Even with equal status they eschewed absorption. The reduced status of homoeopathy within medicine had served as a warning in their eyes that the medical fraternity was neither pluralistic nor tolerant. Whatever the precise terms of the 1858 Medical Registration Act, it had in effect created an allopathic closed shop given to excesses of its own dogmas and assumptions. As Lord Elibank put it in debate, 'the ordinary medical man relies in the treatment of disease upon the giving of drugs or the surgical knife, whereas the osteopath relies upon the curative action of the body's own resources'. This, he claimed, was a fundamentally different view of the origins of disease, and an innovatory one obstructed by the medical profession. In response Lord Moynihan and other medical peers derided the Bill as 'an endeavour to destroy the Hippocratic unity of medicine'. Perhaps unwisely they also termed osteopathy as worthy only of 'the derision of all competent and experienced minds'. A number of peers professed to have benefited from manipulative therapies followed hunting, polo, and cricket injuries. They took exception to what Lord Ampthill termed the strictures of 'the most jealous trade union in the world'. The Bill was read a second time, and referred to a Select Committee of the House of Lords with leave to hear counsel for both sides.[10]

THE INQUIRY AND AFTERMATH

The Select Committee held twelve sessions during 1935, and was composed of both supporters and medical opponents drawn from

---

[9] Ibid. 205.   [10] *Lancet* (1934), 1399.

the House of Lords. Aristocratic sponsorship had so far assisted the osteopaths to press their case, but their counsel still found it wise to open the discussion with a number of concessions to medical objections. These included amendments to the Bill to exclude osteopaths from the practice of major surgery, from obstetrics, and the signing of birth and death certificates. They also included medical representation on the proposed Osteopathic Council. Opening counsel further denied all charges of hostility to conventional medicine, and assertions that osteopaths claimed to cure all diseases. Their case, he emphasized, did not rest upon any superiority or desire to displace medicine, but simply on the legitimacy of their own claim to recognition. They were not anti-medical or 'anti-scientific', even in their belief that osteopathic lesions predisposed people to bacteriological infection. No single system, whether medical or osteopathic, deserved exclusive state recognition and registration, which should thus be extended to all reputable practitioners. This apparent mildness did not reduce or deflect medical hostility. The British Medical Association in a special memorandum set out its own case as one of science against dogma, of open-minded empiricism against a bizarre philosophy regarding the origins of disease. Osteopathy was said to dispute

the basis of modern medical and surgical practice. In its view, at least the original view, physiology and pathology as evolved by scientific research and as taught in our universities and medical schools are built upon a completely false foundation. Apart from the presence of an osteopathic lesion, bacteria are not the causative organisms in disease and bio-chemical changes are of little or no significance. It is important to realise the implications of this attitude. If osteopathic theory is sound the work of the pioneers of modern medicine—Pasteur, Lister, Koch, Manson, Ross, Mackenzie, Crile and Banting—had resulted in a completely erroneous conception of the pathology, prevention and treatment of disease . . . It involves a complete and absolute denial of the modern structure of medicine.[11]

Eight hundred medical and biological scientists signed a supportive statement submitted to the Select Committee. Osteopathic lesions, they claimed, could not exist because their presence could not escape conventional scientific scrutiny. This

[11] 'Theory, Technique and Practice of Osteopathy', *British Medical Journal*, supplement (1935), 1575.

supported the main thrust of the British Medical Association counsel's arguments against the Bill—namely, that either against all available evidence and reputable opinion its supporters believed that non-existent lesions caused all diseases or, if they modified this position, they wished to practise substandard medicine. The other principal strand of argument was that in some instances, purged of fanciful theories, 'manipulators' might do useful work under medical instruction and servicing. Much was made of the extravagance of Dr Still's visionary insights. This emphasis upon the arguably less credible dimensions to osteopathy's history led the *Lancet* to counsel against the dangers of spoiling an 'otherwise excellent case'. Osteopaths, the *Lancet* conceded, 'had largely if not overtly receded from the doctrine enunciated by their founder'. Much of the medicine practised by Still's medical contemporaries would also not survive careful scrutiny. This warning, however, was meant to refine the case for rejection, for 'diluted dogma' was now being mixed with a 'smattering of most of the subjects taught to doctors'.[12]

In the Select Committee the osteopaths emphasized their approval of many medical insights and treatments. In response to leading questions they avoided any assertion that their belief in spinal integrity and manipulation could supplant well-proven medical cures. For example, they stated that they did not manipulate for pernicious anaemia and accepted the value of liver treatment. At this stage three American doctors—Minot, Murphy, and Whipple—had won a Nobel prize, following their discovery in 1934 of the curative effects of raw liver. This treatment must have been empirical, for the precise effective factor, Vitamin B_{12}, was not isolated until 1948. Osteopathic claims to empirical success with other conditions were, however, dismissed as unscientific by medical counsel. The osteopaths in return challenged this view of science. Scientific pathology, they argued, would detect osteopathic lesions in its future development. The financial competition between the two sides broke through medical debates only once, when Dr Macdonald stated that the successful osteopaths 'made a good living, more successful than the average general practitioner, often more than many medical consultants'. It was two other factors, however,

---

[12] *Lancet* (1935), 95.

which particularly damaged the cause for state registration. One was Dr Macdonald's admission that the British School of Osteopathy, assigned a central role in the Bill, 'was not up to the level we would like'. The other stemmed from accusations that its principal, Dr M. Littlejohn, had used bogus degree titles and dubious methods of managing the School. Littlejohn's response to these charges was weak, and certainly did not appear to rebuff the assault on his integrity. At this point the osteopaths' case began to flounder, and a basis for honourable retreat was sought in the evidence of Sir Arthur Robinson for the Ministry of Health.

Robinson held that state registration implied not only occupational registration and powers of self-regulation, but also state authorization for the petitioner's mode of practice. This contradicted the previous Ministry position, that the 1858 Medical Act did not judge theories of medicine and thus no further legislation was needed for other schools of thought. He went on to argue, however, that a proper scientific inquiry, if favourable in conclusion, could lead to the authorization of a separate type of medical practice. Pending the outcome of such an inquiry it would be very confusing, he claimed, to license two types of practitioner. In the interim, osteopaths should form their own voluntary register. They in turn chose to interpret Robinson's evidence as indicating both Ministry support for a proper evaluation of osteopathy and for a type of state-backed voluntary registration. Having survived their encounter with the medical Goliath, the supporters of the Bill withdrew their increasingly beleaguered witnesses, claiming an honourable 'draw'.

In fact, the Select Committee's conclusions when reported were adverse on a number of grounds.[13] Osteopathy, it claimed, evaded any definition of sufficient legal clarity to support the state recognition and registration of another type of medical practitioner. It was clearly not only 'a craft or art limited to the treatment of maladies or defects of the bones, joints, ligaments etc. by manipulation'. In this sphere the Committee had 'no doubt osteopaths perform valuable services', but it was also a total system of treatment. As such it was not considered sufficiently developed to warrant state support. Its principal school was exposed 'as being of negligible importance, inefficient for its

[13] *British Medical Journal*, 2 (1935), 66.

purpose and above all in thoroughly dishonest hands'. This issue of state registration, the Committee concluded, had to be deferred until osteopathy clarified its unique identity and linked this to a sound system of education of intending practitioners. This led the British Osteopathic Association in 1938 to approach the Ministry of Health again for government financial support for an osteopathic hospital and research unit. This time any claims to being a total system of healing were played down, and its membership was portrayed as one composed of specialists on the links between physical structure and health. No scientific inquiry was forthcoming, and these adjustments to occupational imagery were to no avail. The Chief Medical Officer advised the Minister against any support, to avoid rekindling ambitions for state registration. Following the outbreak of the Second World War in 1939 osteopaths were rejected as participants in the Emergency Medical Service. Doctors were encouraged to use conventionally trained physiotherapists to cater for the expected major expansion of rehabilitation requirements.[14]

Throughout the 1930s the osteopathic alliance had pressed its case with at least two core tactical weaknesses. One was an ambivalence as to whether osteopathy was a 'pure' and thus different system of healing, or one which could be 'mixed' with and overlap that of conventional medicine. The other was an uncertainty as to whether osteopathy was a 'universal' or 'limited' system in its scope of practice. The alliance not only failed to break the medical–Ministry link which was the principal axis of professional power during this period. Its efforts also consolidated medical authority with the consequence that heterodox practitioners in general were more easily excluded from the ensuing planning process for the National Health Service. Osteopathy, therefore, avoided a supplementary status in the medical hierarchy of occupations, but at the cost of an enduring marginality. In the 1930s its pursuit of aristocratic patronage to address this problem may well have rested upon a confusion between symbolic and real authority in the modern British State. The medical profession's protection of its more secure legal status was derived not so much from its treatments or clients, but its close relationship with the Ministry of Health.

[14] Public Record Office, Ministry of Health, 58.286.

10

Unorthodox Medicine after the Establishment of the National Health Service

Brian Inglis

The Second World War witnessed a transformation in medical treatment of a kind unparalleled in history, and unlikely to be repeated. For twenty years after Ehrlich's 'magic bullet', Salvarsan, had been introduced no successor could be found; and in *Man and Medicine*, published in 1931, Henry Sigerist felt compelled to admit that although there had been massive advances in medical knowledge, they had done little to improve medical treatment. A few months later, however, the chemist, Gerhard Domagk, working for I. G. Farben discovered that streptoccocal infections in laboratory animals could be controlled by a dyestuff, 'prontosil red'; and shortly before the War the first of the 'sulpha drugs', M and B, came on the market. For the first time doctors could actually treat and cure meningitis, pneumonia, and other disorders, as distinct from helplessly observing their progress from the bedside. Penicillin, brought into production during the War, proved even more effective and safer than the sulpha drugs; streptomycin followed, speeding up the fall in the mortality rate from TB; and in the late 1940s the arrival of the 'broad spectrum' antibiotics—chloramphenicol, aureomycin, and terramycin—meant that Erhlich's concept became obsolescent. They were not so much bullets as grape-shot, lethal to a wide range of pathogenic bacteria.

Unorthodox forms of medical treatment consequently began to seem irrelevant, particularly in Britain, after the National Health Service had been set up in 1948. Shaw had not been alone in his belief that it was crazy for doctors to be paid by people who were ill instead of being paid to keep people well; socialists had long argued that medical treatment should be free—paid for, that is, out of taxation, or from some all-embracing national insurance scheme. It would take time, the Labour Government explained, for the backlog of ill-health to be cleared. Children who had grown up in slums might be suffering from calcium deficiency, say, or decayed teeth; for a while the profession would have to concentrate on the eradication of sickness. But in due course the National Health Service would become, as its name indicated, a national *health* service, with prevention of disease as its primary function.

THE NATIONAL HEALTH SERVICE

At last the dream of the French revolutionaries appeared to be on the verge of fulfilment. Disease, they had believed, was largely the reflection of a sick society. 'Living in the midst of ease, surrounded by the pleasures of life,' the Girondin Lanthénas had written of the aristos in 1792, 'their irascible pride, their bitter spleen, their abuses and the excess to which their contempt of all principles leads them, make them a prey to infirmities of every kind'; whereas the virtuous poor only needed to be better nourished, better housed, and provided with better facilities for enjoying fresh air and exercise, to enjoy good health. The proposition had become integral to left-wing thought. Nor could it readily be dismissed as a socialist pipe dream: common sense suggested that as living standards rose the incidence of diseases associated with poverty, overcrowding, and undernourishment must decline, leaving the medical profession more time to concentrate on finding ways to prevent the disorders of affluence. In his own self-interest, surely, every doctor would want to show patients on his list how to keep well. The healthier they became the less work he would be called upon to do.

Although the medical profession regarded the proposed Health Service as a threat, and fiercely resisted it, their fears centred around the possibility that the State would convert doctors into civil servants, and exercise more control over them by restricting their right to prescribe the drugs they believed most suitable, regardless of cost. The then Minister for Health, Aneurin Bevan, went out of his way to remove their apprehensions. But in doing so, the herbalists realized when the Bill was going through Parliament, he would reinforce the profession's monopoly.

Herbalists had been hard hit during the nineteenth century by the discovery of ways in which to extract alkaloids from plants—quinine from cinchona, cocaine from the coca shrub, and several others—providing drugs which were much more effective, even if more dangerous, than herbal remedies. In the 1860s some British practitioners had made an effort to put their craft on a more specific basis by setting up the National Institute of Medical Herbalists, aiming to end the practice by which they could sell the doses they themselves prescribed, and introducing examinations. But this had caused a split, many herbalists refusing to accept the need for so drastic a change; and although the movement survived, it was on a greatly reduced scale. By the late 1940s, about the only advantage the remaining herbalists still enjoyed was that their remedies cost less than the medicines bought over the chemists' counters, and often very much less than those obtained on a doctor's prescription.

Under the National Health Service, medicines prescribed by a doctor would cost the patient nothing; and the herbalists, alarmed, asked a Member of Parliament to put their case for inclusion before the Minister. Bevan's reply was that they must set their house in order before their case could even be considered. This did not merely mean that they would have to settle their differences, and set up a single organization with a training scheme and qualifications of a kind which would meet with the Ministry's approval. It carried the further implication that if their reorganization was deemed satisfactory, they might be admitted to the National Health Service, but only on the same basis as other medical auxiliaries. They would then, like physiotherapists, come largely under the direction of the medical profession, accepting only such patients as doctors chose to send them.

Naturally this was not what the herbalists wanted. Their remedies were not designed to complement the drugs which the pharmaceutical industry was now pouring out, but to render them unnecessary. Few doctors would accept this; very few would even consider prescribing herbs. So the herbalists elected not to try to enter the National Health Service; and a hard time they were to have of it for the next few years. Yet they won little public sympathy, as the general impression was that they were expendable. Doubtless there would continue to be a small market for some of their wares—old-fashioned ladies wanting old-fashioned remedies, and gullible folk looking for an elixir (and for some quack to provide it). But surely such superstitions would gradually die out?

Nature cure practitioners—naturopaths, as they now styled themselves—were in a slightly less vulnerable position, as it was their services rather than their remedies that they had to sell; and this also applied to healers, radiesthetists, and hypnotists. But these groups had no prospect of qualifying for admission to the National Health Service. The only other medically unqualified practitioners who had to make up their minds whether to apply to join the health service, or risk deprivation outside it, were the osteopaths and chiropractors.

In the United States, they had less to worry about. In most states of the Union osteopaths had become to all intents doctors, with the same rights and privileges as members of the medical profession, and trained in many orthodox techniques . . . Chiropractic, too, though still unrecognized in a few states, was beginning to catch up. And as in many parts of the country chiropractors still provided the only medical services in the districts where they practised, when they were proceeded against for practising medicine without the requisite qualifications or for illegally dispensing drugs, sympathetic juries often refused to convict.

In Britain, osteopaths (there were still very few chiropractors) were more vulnerable. Unlike the United States, the great majority of their patients came to them to be treated for backache and associated symptoms like sciatica and rheumatism. During the War the belief had grown that the majority of cases of backache were caused by a 'slipped disc'—by one of the shock absorbers between the vertebrae protruding and impinging upon a nerve; and this had meant that osteopaths had lost many potential patients to surgeons. And 1949 saw the introduction of cortisone, which for a time looked as though it might be the answer to orthodoxy's prayers. Not merely did cortisone enable patients who had long been crippled by spinal trouble to leave their beds, walk, and even run: it broke fresh ground by being the first of the new drugs to be effective against a degenerative disease, as distinct from an infection.

Might it not be the precursor of many others, as M and B had been of the antibiotics? If so medicine would be even more strikingly transformed, as the incidence of most of the infectious diseases had already been greatly reduced even before the wonder drugs appeared, whereas rheumatism, cancer, heart attacks, and other disorders arising out of premature ageing or faulty metabolism were, if anything, on the increase.

PSYCHOSOMATIC MEDICINE

There was, however, a vitalist spectre at the feast. Medical scientists had continued to assert that organic disease could only arise from some physical or chemical cause: germ, virus, or toxin. They had paid no attention to [claims] that . . . doctors ought not to content themselves with diagnosing what was physically the matter with the patient: they ought also to look for underlying or precipitating psychological causes, asking themselves what kind of a person he was, why he fell ill at that particular time, and if he had any reason for falling ill, because the answer might provide useful diagnostic clues . . .

[This] was . . . partly because the great majority of doctors had been indoctrinated with mechanistic assumptions, partly because of the rapid development of specialist disciplines. Consultant dermatologists, say, or rheumatologists, did not as a rule relish psychological let alone psychoanalytical, speculation about the causes of acne or arthritis. When they wrote textbooks they often warned students against diagnosing symptoms as psychosomatic unless and until every other possible physical or chemical cause had been eliminated. A few eminent members of the profession actually dismissed psychosomatic medicine as a passing fad. It was unworthy, Sir George Pickering asserted in 1950, even of consideration by medical science.

How mistaken this view had been was soon to be demonstrated by a report in the *British Medical Journal* of an experiment carried out in a London hospital. A boy had been admitted suffering from ichthyosis, most of his body being covered with a malodorous horny layer, as if it were a cluster of warts. None of the treatments tried was any use; skin grafts taken from parts of his body which were unaffected were soon as bad as the skin they had replaced. One possibility remained untried: hypnotism. An experiment carried out not long before had demonstrated the effectiveness of auto-suggestion even without hypnotism, in getting rid of warts; children suffering from them had been divided into two groups, one group receiving the then standard treatment, and the other participating in 'magic'—using pictures of the warts, drawing circles round them, and daily reducing the warts' size on paper; and the magic had worked better than the standard medical treatment. It was decided that suggestion reinforced by hypnosis should be tried on the 'rhino boy', as by this time he was being described. Out of caution—and also to ensure that if the scales fell from his body, it really was the suggestion which was responsible—the treatment was carried out in stages. He was hypnotized, and told that a certain area of his skin would clear up; and when it did, leaving skin that was almost normal in texture, the process was repeated until recovery was complete.

As very few doctors had any experience of hypnotizing patients, the way should have been open for hypnotists to take advantage of the publicity. But hypnotism had never succeeded in divesting itself of the Svengali image. Although there were probably at least as many hypnotherapists, as they called themselves, as there were herbalists, they had no effective organization. The group which came forward to take advantage of the evidence which psychosomatic researchers were providing was, unexpectedly, the Churches' Council of Healing, a body backed by all denominations in Britain except the Catholics, who in those pre-ecumenical times would not formally collaborate in such ventures.

The Council's genesis could be traced back to the end of the nineteenth century, when members of the Protestant Churches who had retained a belief in the Church's healing mission became alarmed not so much by the growing materialism of the medical profession as by the way in which Christian Science was attracting recruits: recruits, too, from the well-to-do middle classes on whose allegiance the Episcopalian Church could normally have counted. The Emmanuel Movement founded in the early 1900s in Boston, and the Guild of Health, its London counterpart, were designed to revive the mission.

They accordingly sought the profession's co-operation. The British Medical Association politely set up a Committee; but its Report, though making soothing references to the valuable role of the clergy in maintaining patients' morale, insisted that all forms of healing which were designated as spiritual or psychic were attributable to suggestion, and that suggestion was effective 'only in cases of what are generally termed "functional disorders" '. It was a clear intimation that the profession did not intend to relax its rule that doctors must not allow any unqualified practitioner to *treat* patients, even if he were in holy orders; and the Guild of Health did not choose to pursue the issue further.

There were always a few churchmen who believed that the mission should be revived, among them William Temple, who became Archbishop of Canterbury during the Second World War. Although he did not live to see it, a new organization, the Churches' Council of Healing, was set up after the War along the lines he had planned; and in the early 1950s his successor and the Archbishop of York together named the members of a Commission to investigate the subject, the aim being to assist the clergy in the exercise of healing, 'and to encourage increasing understanding and co-operation between them and the medical profession'.

It was not the Archbishops' intention, clearly, to provoke any confrontation with the profession; and one of the Commission's first acts was to ask the British Medical Association to co-operate. The British Medical Association's response was again to set up its own investigating Committee; and its Report, published in 1955, differed only in emphasis from the one published before the First World War. It warily admitted the possibility that spiritual ministrations might help in treating patients 'suffering from psychogenic disorders, including psychosomatic states, in which physical symptoms result from emotional disturbances', and it conceded that 'various forms of neurosis, alcoholism and other functional disorders' ('functional' by this time being by implication a psychiatric condition) could actually be cured by religious conversion. But like its predecessor, the Committee rejected claims of cures of organic disorders—'We have seen no evidence that there is any special type of illness cured solely by spiritual healing which cannot be cured by medical methods which do not involve such claims'; and it patronizingly suggested that the clergy or their lay helpers should confine their efforts to providing patients with 'reassurance' and 'peace of mind'.

As nearly half the members of the Archbishops' Commission were also members either of the medical profession or of its affiliates, its Report—published in 1958—could hardly be expected to reject the British Medical Association Committee's findings. It contented itself with a mild protest that the Church's healing ministry 'cannot be completely described in terms of psychological medicine, nor can its ministry be regarded merely as an important environmental factor'; and it insisted that there was much more to healing than the British Medical Association had allowed. But it was not prepared to defy orthodoxy by re-affirming positively that organic illness *could* be cured by 'supernormal' means. . . .

Irritated though many of the clerical members of the Commission must have been by the British Medical Association's polite scepticism they were more worried by a new development on the other flank; the emergence of spirit, or spiritual, healing, as an alternative to what the clergy had usually described as faith healing.

The Churches had tended to think of faith as the essential ingredient, in the sense that it opened up the recipient to the divine grace which was bestowed upon him. Spiritualists believed in the divine grace, but they did not feel it was necessary for the recipient to have faith in it. They had begun to set up churches in the later years of the nineteenth century, but until after the Second World War the main emphasis had been on communicating with the spirits. A few individuals, though, had become healers; and among those who had given evidence to the Archbishops' Commission, supported by an impressive array of testimonials, was Harry Edwards, by that time the best-known healer in Britain, who claimed that his powers were mediated by spirit guides.

In the 1930s Edwards had been a rationalist, contemplating a career in politics; but he had been invited to go to a spiritualist seance, and heard from the mediums there that he had healing gifts. Experimenting, he found that he could indeed cure people of disorders for whom orthodox treatment had been ineffective; and healing became his full-time occupation. So far from being hostile to orthodoxy Edwards had spirit 'guides' who were orthodoxy's heroes, Pasteur and Lister; and he studied anatomy and physiology, so that he could not be accused of putting patients at risk while showing them that joints which had long been locked by rheumatoid arthritis could become flexible once more. He also introduced a course for members and prospective members of the National Federation of Spiritual Healers, designed to make them better acquainted with the history, theories, and practices involved. But the course events had taken made it obvious that he and the Federation could expect no recognition from the medical profession, and little sympathy from the hierarchy of the Established Church.

Spiritualism, though, could be presented as a religion (which for some spiritual healers it was); and this gave a chance for members of the Federation to carry on their work even in hospitals, however hostile the doctors might be. With management committees' consent, they could visit any patient who called for their services. As this privilege could easily have been withdrawn if the healers made it too obvious they were treating patients, as distinct from ministering to their spiritual requirements, Edwards warned them against making exhibitions of themselves in any way—for example, by going into trances. The *British Medical Journal* was not appeased. Spiritual healers, an editorial complained in 1960, had 'slipped through the guard of two hundred and thirty-five hospital management committees' by this deception, in defiance of the General Medical Council's directive that any medical practitioner who 'by his presence, advice and co-operation' knowingly assisted anybody not registered as a medical practitioner to practise medicine, was liable to erasure. Ridiculing Edwards's claims for the validity of his cures, the editorial concluded with a call to Members of Parliament to ask the Minister of Health whether it was his policy 'to admit to Britain's State hospitals healers who claim to cure disease by supernormal means': a view supported by a number of correspondents, one of whom protested that hospital committees showed 'so little confidence in their medical and surgical staffs that they have seen fit to return to the cave, by encouraging the belief in the control of man's environment by magical means', and another who claimed that all that medical science had achieved 'in the face of desperate odds' by insisting on 'the scientific method of observation and mensuration' was now in jeopardy. 'Should we allow ourselves to slip back to the hocus-pocus of medieval concepts?'

In its editorial, the *British Medical Journal* argued that though healing might appear to be successful, the 'cures' could be accounted for by mistakes in diagnosis, spontaneous coincidental remissions, and the effects of suggestion: 'hence modern statistical devices to eliminate bias in clinical trials'. All right, then, Edwards replied: let there be trials of healing with such devices. But this, too, was unacceptable. Even when the healers offered to allow themselves to be tested without entering the hospital, by using 'absent healing'—comparable to, and often including, prayer—the project was turned down. The Cambridge psychologist R. H. Thouless, who had been a member of the Archbishops' Commission, tried to set up an experiment in which hospital patients would be divided into two matched groups, in pairs: absent healing being given to one of each pair and not the other, with neither patients nor hospital staff to know which was which until the conclusion of the experiment. But although the formal attitude of the profession was that healing did not work except by suggestion, and that consequently absent healing could not work at all, the General Medical Council's rule against co-operation with unqualified practitioners was invoked, and the experiment blocked.

An alternative was to follow up cases where Edwards had claimed success, to find whether any of his cures were inexplicable in orthodox terms; and an attempt at this was made by a London doctor, Louis Rose, who came to the conclusion that in the cases of cancer which had been claimed as cures, none could positively be attributed to Edwards's healing. But to reach this verdict, Rose had to accept some ludicrous propositions: for example, that in a case where cancerous tissue had been found at a biopsy, and the man had subsequently been pronounced free from cancer, the cure might have been the result of the fortunate chance that all the cancerous tissue had been removed for the biopsy. In other cases, too, where there was no dispute about the cure, it could be attributed to the delayed results of earlier orthodox treatment. The only cures which the profession were prepared to accept, Edwards complained, were of patients who had never been treated by a doctor, but in such cases, as there would have been no medical history, 'you would dispute the healing because there could not have been a proper diagnosis. It's a case of heads I win, tails you lose.'

Edwards was, in fact, wasting his time trying to convince medical scientists of his ability to heal by supernatural means. Even the possibility of paranormal healing (the implied distinction being that in Edwards's case, the force was divine and consequently not, or not necessarily, material; whereas 'paranormal' left the door open for the eventual discovery of some force analogous to radiations, or magnetism) was rejected; usually without serious consideration, and sometimes with even greater violence than spiritual healing of the traditional kind, as if there were a deep fear that to contemplate a paranormal explanation would be to cast doubt on the mechanist principles of medicine . . .

PART III

ALTERNATIVE MEDICINE IN MODERN BRITAIN

11

Self-Help Groups and Health Care in Contemporary Britain

Jill Vincent

Self-help groups based on health issues have been growing in number and becoming more visible in recent years in Britain. Currently, this form of support is particularly encouraged by government policies which stress the value of community care within 'welfare pluralism' in which informal (family, friends, and neighbours), voluntary (not for profit), and private (for profit) care increasingly find a role alongside state provision. Consequently self-help group activity for health care (and social problems) is receiving much interest and some indirect support from state agencies even though some—though not all—groups appear to embody ideas which are opposed to traditional medical care.

This paper discusses, in the context of health care in contemporary Britain, first, what is meant by self-help and how far self-help groups in reality conform to the popular image. Next, the similarities between explanations offered for the recent upsurge in interest in self-help groups and in alternative medicine are drawn out. Finally, the characteristics and activities of self-help groups and alternative medicine are discussed and their paradoxical positions in respect of mainstream orthodoxies are set out.

WHAT IS MEANT BY SELF-HELP?

The term self-help is used here because it is common currency. However, this implies an individualistic—'self'—approach to care, while what is at issue is groups which are organized around a commitment to mutual aid, co-operation, and reciprocity. The tensions and contradictions that are embedded in the term are illustrated by its use over time, but all the approaches share a faith in grass-roots activity.

Samuel Smiles wrote about self-help at the height of nineteenth-century Victorian faith in individual effort. He extolled the virtues of liberal, bourgeois individualism, arguing that energy, purpose, application and hard work, cheerfulness, prudence, virtuousness, and learning would bring reward. Smiles said, 'Heaven helps those who help themselves . . . help from without is often enfeebling in its effects, but help from within invariably invigorates.'[1] Peter Kropotkin, an anarchist and atheist writing at the turn of the century took a different position. He stressed the necessity of co-operation in human endeavours, seeing mutual aid as a natural human force which binds people together.[2] Modern social anarchist or libertarian ideas have developed those of Kropotkin, and look towards the development of self-reliant and responsible individuals who will create a community characterized by mutuality and freedom. To this end, large, hierarchical, centralized, and élitist institutions must be superseded by small, participative, egalitarian organizations. In this approach, responsible individuals remain free by co-operating in settings which they all control. Landry *et al.* discuss radical, libertarian projects in publishing, in community politics, and in the voluntary sector over the last ten years: they also look at those factors which in their view help to account for the collapse and failure of many of these projects.[3]

Recent developments within a feminist frame of reference have also been important in the exploration of the meaning of the concept of self-help. Not least of these has been the attempt by some feminists to develop a form of organization opposed to male-dominated, hierarchical, bureaucratic forms. The alternative adopted by women's groups is small, leaderless groups that engage in collective, participative work characterized by mutuality and reciprocal support. This is reflected in the health field where the power of medical and scientific knowledge to define and control the human condition has now been recognized. Discussion here has centred on the appropriateness of allowing such power to rest in the hands of a small, largely male, medical élite,

[1] S. Smiles, *Self-Help: With Illustrations of Character, Conduct and Perseverance* (London: John Murray, centenary edn., 1958).

[2] P. Kropotkin, *Mutual Aid* (Harmondsworth: Allen Lane, 1972).

[3] C. Landry, D. Morley, R. Southwood, and P. Wright, *What a Way to Run a Railroad: An Analysis of Radical Failure* (London: Comedia Publishing Group, 1985).

and developed into a critique of medicine as a whole. Self-help groups, clinics, and advice centres have been established, and publications such as *Our Bodies Ourselves* give an opportunity for women to speak to women.[4]

The ambiguities and contradictions within the term self-help remain. The simplest and broadest definition of self-help groups is that of Richardson and Goodman who view them as 'groups of people who have a common problem and have joined together to do something about it'.[5] This has the advantage that it avoids prescription and allows for a range of possible outcomes. An alternative approach is to set out the key components of a self-help or mutual aid philosophy on which the 'prescriptive ideal' rests. The key components for groups in the health field are that members share a health problem, with only sufferers or carers being admitted; that there is no distinction, in principle, between givers and receivers of health care, so that reciprocity, either direct or serial, is the primary mode of exchange; and that decisions about the form of the group and its activities are the preserve of all members, with a commitment to participative democracy informing organizational arrangements.

It is these assumed characteristics which have brought self-help activity in health and other fields such a good press and a warm welcome from across the political spectrum. Groups are believed to be small, localized, and caring, encouraging face-to-face meetings and mutual support. They are seen variously as a means of providing evidence of individual responsibility and rolling back the frontier of the State; rejecting or at least questioning the power of experts and professionals; instigating a learning process in which local, grass-roots power and creativity is recognized and used; and forming part of a potential social revolution. However, more sober reflection suggests that self-help groups in the real world may vary in the extent to which they embody these model or 'ideal typical' characteristics, and that they may not be extensive enough or strong enough to carry such weighty political implications. Hence the model can be used as a benchmark against which to measure the gap between reality and rhetoric.

---

[4] A. Phillips and J. Rakusen, *Our Bodies Ourselves* (Harmondsworth: Penguin, 2nd edn., 1989).
[5] A. Richardson and M. Goodman, *Self-Help and Social Care: Mutual Aid Organisations in Practice* (London: Policy Studies Institute, 1983).

SELF-HELP GROUPS IN REALITY

Some indication must be given of the extent of self-help activity. It is not a phenomenon that is peculiar to Britain, and, as Branckaerts and Richardson point out, increasing attention has been given to the formulation of policies on self-help at international as well as national levels.[6] The outcome has been a range of initiatives and conferences but little in the way of a coherent policy. Branckaerts and Richardson argue that 'while there may be little broad pressure *for* self-help, there is unlikely to be strong pressure *against* it'. They conclude that self-help is—and probably will remain—'a fringe activity, concerning a small proportion of the population'.

Evidence about the extent of self-help activity specifically in Britain is limited, although a range of initiatives demonstrate the increased legitimacy and attention afforded to such groups. For example, in 1979 a research project was established which built on several years of investigation and preparatory work carried out within the Wessex Regional Library and Information Service. The project started by looking at the needs of health staff for information on voluntary organizations (including self-help groups), and grew into a major resource centre providing information to health care professionals, patients, and relatives. The Help for Health Information Service now holds data on over one thousand national and two thousand local (Wessex) voluntary organizations and self-help groups and receives over four thousand enquiries each year.[7]

Similar growth specifically in the area of self-help is shown by the Self-Help Team in Nottingham which works as a clearing-house for information and as a support for new and established groups for health and social problems. Their first directory of local (Nottingham) groups was published in 1982 and contained sixty-eight entries. The seventh edition of the directory, published in 1987, contains two hundred groups, many of which were helped

[6] J. Branckaerts and A. Richardson, 'Politics and Policies in Self-Help: Notes on the International Scene', in S. Humble and J. Unell (eds.), *Self-Help in Health and Social Welfare* (London: Routledge, 1989), 29–44.

[7] R. Gann, *Information for Care: The First Five Years of the Help for Health Information Service* (Southampton: Wessex Regional Library and Information Service, 1984).

in their early stages by the Team. Some of the groups are local branches of national bodies but most are local groups for local needs.

Two recent initiatives which were set up in 1986 indicate that the rate of growth of the number of self-help groups is increasing and that they have gained official sanction. First, the National Self-Help Support Centre was established with a small staff, and based at the National Council for Voluntary Organizations. The Centre publishes its bulletin, *Mutual Aid and Self-Help*, quarterly. Secondly, a three-year scheme managed by the Self-Help Alliance (a temporary consortium of national voluntary organizations) was set up. The scheme consisted of eighteen self-help support projects based in local development agencies in various parts of England and was funded by the Department of Health and Social Security as part of its 'Helping the Community to Care' initiative. It was evaluated by a research team from the Tavistock Institute of Human Relations which is publishing a series of papers based on its research.[8]

Morgan, Calnan, and Manning comment upon the difficulty of obtaining precise figures on the total numbers and membership of self-help groups because of the fluctuations in membership as groups become established or decline and the problems of determining whether particular groups come within the category of a self-help group.[9] They point out that a directory published in 1977 lists 233 groups concerned with health and health-related conditions. However, Webb found 2,080 self-help groups in and around London in 1981.[10] Such a discrepancy may be explained by the definitions employed, the range of problems encompassed, the size of membership, and the level of formality (or informality) of the group. In any event it demonstrates the problem of establishing quantitative accounts of non-statutory activities.

[8] See E. Miller and B. Webb, *The Nature of Effective Self Help Support in Different Contexts: Self Help in Rural Areas: Is It Different?*, COVAS Occasional Paper No. 2 (London: Tavistock Institute of Human Relations, Sept. 1988), and F. Abraham and E. Sommerlad, *Self Help Support and Black People: Start Up Strategies in Four Self Help Alliance Projects*, COVAS Occasional Paper No. 4 (London: Tavistock Institute of Human Relations, Nov. 1988).

[9] M. Morgan, M. Calnan and N. Manning, *Sociological Approaches to Health and Medicine* (London: Croom Helm, 1985).

[10] P. Webb, 'Ready, Willing but Able?—The Self Help Group', *Journal of the Royal Society of Health*, 103:1 (1983), 35–41.

Research by the author in a semi-rural borough in Leicestershire (population: 132,900) in 1986 found thirty-five self-help groups in the field of health care, seven of which were no longer active.[11] This research casts light on the range of conditions around which groups had been formed, and also on the patchy and fragile nature of such provision. Thus groups were available for a diversity of health problems, including alcohol and tranquillizer addiction, anorexia, epilepsy, migraine, cystic fibrosis, multiple sclerosis, and diabetes. Group membership differed widely, from two groups in which three or four people met on a regular basis to a group with 264 'members', and four others with more than one hundred. The surge in self-help activity in Charnwood, as elsewhere, was shown by the twenty-one groups which had been established since 1978. Membership of the groups represented only a fraction of their potential; for instance, while one in two hundred persons has chronic or active epilepsy the associated group had only twelve members; and while about 4 per cent of school-age children have asthma the group had eighteen members. Self-help groups tend to be fragile in that they have high birth and death rates. The Charnwood research showed that the high birth rate had produced twenty-two groups since 1978, and the high death rate had reduced this by one-third (seven groups were no longer active). Thus self-help groups are fragile and their provision is patchy. None is necessarily available in a particular locality for a particular problem, and not all those who are potential members will join a group.

A review of the available evidence on the characteristics of self-help groups in health care suggests that group members usually share a common health problem or are friends and helpers of the afflicted; are usually women, reflecting their caring role in our society; and are mainly drawn from the middle class.[12] There is no systematic route for recruitment although members are most likely to hear about such groups through 'word of mouth' and the media. Unell's research shows that health and welfare

[11] J. Vincent, *Constraints on the Stability and Longevity of Self-Help Groups in the Field of Health Care* (Centre for Research in Social Policy, Loughborough University, 1986).

[12] See Richardson and Goodman, *Self-Help and Social Care*, and Vincent, *Constraints on the Stability and Longevity of Self-Help Groups*.

professionals who work in the community and are in a good position to make referrals seem generally sympathetic, but express reservations about the effectiveness of self-help—occasionally tinged with anxiety about threats to their professional authority.[13] They often appear to lack knowledge of available groups and to be selective about which ones they recommend. These research findings about the nature of the membership and of recruitment reinforce the point made earlier about the 'patchiness' of self-help.

There are two strands of evidence about helping and reciprocity in such groups in the health context, and these hold in Britain and in West Germany.[14] On the one hand, many members are aware of the advantages of self-help. They recognize the particular benefits derived from meeting with others who share the same health problems and exchanging experiences and information and, as their condition or their ability to cope improves, they are keen to help others in their turn. On the other hand, within many self-help groups with a health focus there are members who have received, but not given, help. There may be a core of members who do all or most of the work and thus can be seen as giving a service to the rest—indeed, in some groups, service-giving by the few is the predominant activity.

Few self-help groups in the health arena manage to establish an organizational structure in which participation can be fostered and maintained. In general this is not recognized as a problem and confronted by members; the committee form of organization is widely adopted without consideration of its appropriateness. Participation in the sense of active involvement and responsibility for group tasks is therefore limited, and the opportunity for members to learn and become confident in their own abilities is restricted. Thus excessive demands are sometimes made on the active members, and this, along with the difficulties of attracting members, makes self-help groups fragile—many are formed, but

---

[13] J. Unell, *Supporting Self-Help in Health Care and Social Welfare* (London: Bedford Square Press, 1986).
[14] See J. Matzat, 'Self-Help Groups in West Germany: Developments of the Last Decade', *Acta Psychiatrica Scandinavica*, suppl. 337, 76 (1987), 42–51; Richardson and Goodman, *Self-Help and Social Care*; and Vincent, *Constraints on the Stability and Longevity of Self-Help Groups*.

many collapse under the weight of work placed on a few or even one active person. It is only fair to say that an early account of the achievement and potential of self-help groups by Robinson and Henry was extremely enthusiastic about their place in health care.[15] The authors contacted eighty-four groups and national organizations, mostly in and around London. Not all were studied in depth. They concluded that, in self-help-helping, the problem is integrated with the member's life in such a way that self-help becomes a way of life, and self-help groups transform people. The later research and analyses, which cast some doubt on the ability of groups to conform to the 'ideal-type' model of self-help, should be seen in this context.

It becomes evident, then, that self-help groups involved with health issues embody a number of tensions and contradictions: between mutuality and individualism; between reciprocal caring and either giving or receiving services; and between active involvement and participation and passive membership. The difficulties encountered in deciding what is to count as self-help derive from these tensions and contradictions. Self-help groups in this field can be seen in reality to form a continuum. At one pole are self-help groups which conform to the 'ideal type' or model in which all are therapists, offering reciprocal care and support; along the continuum come groups in which only some members take the therapeutic role and/or responsibility for the tasks of the group; then come groups which offer services in a traditional way, that is, given by the few to those defined as deserving (in this case, only to their members); finally, at the opposite pole, are groups which may retain a core of self-help but whose main activity is providing services in the mould of a traditional voluntary organization. There may be a tendency for self-help groups in health care to change over time towards the more formal, service-giving end of the continuum, not least because of pressure towards conformity from orthodox and dominant modes of medical belief and organization.

The challenge that self-help groups in health care can make to dominant medical practices lies not in their number, but in the broader characteristics that those towards the self-help pole of

[15] D. Robinson and S. Henry, *Self-Help and Health: Mutual Aid for Modern Problems* (London: Martin Robertson, 1977).

the continuum share with lay health initiatives, patient participation and alternative systems of medical care. The relevant characteristics are as follows: they involve their members as responsible persons, active in the definition of their problems and their solution or management; this active participation takes place in a setting which encourages mutuality and a recognition of the shared and thus social nature of the source of problems as well as their solution; and the individualization of disease and the power of professionals are called into question. It is these characteristics which are highlighted in explanations of the welcome accorded to self-help group activity in health and other fields.

WHY THE RISE OF SELF-HELP GROUPS NOW?

Explanations of the recent upsurge of interest in self-help groups in health and other fields and the expansion of their number must take account of the context of state welfare. Current government policies embrace a pluralist approach to welfare in which informal, voluntary, and private provision are to assume enhanced roles at the same time as financial limits are placed on state provision. However, while these broad changes can be expected to accelerate the expansion of self-help activity, the phenomenon was already established in advance of them.

Morgan *et al.* set out two kinds of explanation which have been put forward to account for the earlier surge.[16] The first is that self-help groups form part of a more general protest against the dominant values and institutions of our society. They place groups organized by the women's movement and some established by the gay liberation movement and by disabled people in this category. The second explanation is that groups arise to meet needs that are not catered for by the existing institutions. One type of need arises from the inadequacies of existing medical services. These are seen to neglect those suffering from conditions like alcoholism or obesity which have never come fully within the medical sphere, and to fail to support those with chronic illness (after the acute phase). A second type of need regarded as explaining the rise of self-help groups is the feeling of isolation,

---

[16] Morgan *et al.*, *Sociological Approaches*.

loss of identity, and rootlessness associated with the process of industrialization and the growth of bureaucracy.

A further set of explanations set out by Wilson rests on what are seen as the failures of the welfare state.[17] These include the failure to make any substantial inroads into poverty and economic inequalities; to challenge the power of professionals and lack of information available to clients; to mitigate the dehumanizing effect of services delivered through centralized bureaucratic bodies; and to involve communities and individuals in planning and decision-making about services and their own health care. In addition, it is pointed out that the illness spectrum of industrialized societies has moved towards chronic diseases, with the result that better ways had to be found of coping with chronic conditions. However, as Morgan *et al.* point out, it is also necessary to explain why the response took the form of setting up a self-help group rather than some other course of action.[18] They look to parallel changes for explanation—namely, the increasing emphasis on individual responsibility for health, the growing consumer movement, and the increasing recognition of the limits to medical knowledge and expertise. More recent policy changes, with their individualistic emphasis, can be expected to quicken the pace of the development of self-help groups in health and other fields. They may also deepen the tension between individualism and mutuality that is inherent in self-help.

Many of the developments that led to the emergence of self-help are echoed in the explanations for the resurgence of interest in alternative medicine. These include a range of causes which rest on similar dissatisfactions with the organization and delivery of medical care. Thus Salmon argues with regard to the United States that whilst vast accomplishments in disease eradication are acknowledged, a number of problems remain: the high costs which follow from the production for profit of pharmaceuticals, hospital equipment and construction, and—though this is less evident in Britain at present—the delivery of services; the power held in the hands of the medical profession; and the racist and sexist assumptions (that white males set the norm or standard

---

[17] J. Wilson, 'Supporting Self-Help Groups: An Action Research Study of the Work of Nottingham Self-Help Groups Project between 1982 and 1983', unpublished M.Phil. thesis, Loughborough University, 1987.

[18] Morgan *et al.*, *Sociological Approaches*.

against which others are measured) which underlie medical practice.[19]

However, criticism of the predominant mode of medical practice is taken further by some commentators. In these accounts both the paradigm of scientific medicine—including its basic assumptions about health and disease—and its practical approach to the patient are subjected to critical appraisal. For instance, scientific medicine is seen by Berliner as 'a specific mode of healing characterised by: (1) the assumption that all disease is materially generated by specific etiological agents such as bacteria, viruses, parasites, genetic malformations, or internal chemical imbalances; (2) a passive patient role; and (3) the use of invasive manipulation to restore/maintain the human organism at a statistically derived equilibrium point (health)'.[20] In Berliner's view popular discontent with, and awareness of, the limitations of this model stem from factors which include changes in the disease structure of modern societies so that chronic degenerative diseases like cancer, heart disease, and stroke have become the major problems; shifts in demographic patterns as more people live on into old age, creating a larger 'at risk' sector of the population; the fragmentation and specialization of medical care beyond the primary care given by general practitioners; the medical focus on disease as opposed to preventative medicine, and, associated with this, medical training which ignores or underemphasizes epidemiology, nutrition, psychology, and environmental and occupational health; the negative implications of the passivity of the patient role in hospital and other medical contexts; the costly, high-technological approach of modern medicine, which is of questionable efficiency and has counter-productive, iatrogenic effects; the 'machine' model of the person that splits mind from body and the person from his or her social, environmental, and occupational contexts; and, finally, the struggle against death, irrespective of the resultant quality of life.

The consideration of these deficiencies of scientific medicine

---

[19] J. W. Salmon, 'Introduction' and 'Defining Health and Reorganising Medicine', in id. (ed.), *Alternative Medicines: Popular and Policy Perspectives* (London: Tavistock, 1985), 1–29, and 252–80.

[20] H. S. Berliner, 'Scientific Medicine Since Flexner', in Salmon (ed.), *Alternative Medicines*, 30–56.

brings into focus the similarities between the problems which explain the upsurge of interest in self-help groups and alternative medicine. This is not to say that all participants in self-help groups recognize or grasp their full significance—or reject orthodox forms of health care. None the less, small groups can and often do offer a critique and an alternative to orthodox provision in the health arena. This leads to a consideration of the relevance of self-help to alternative medicine.

SELF-HELP GROUPS AND ALTERNATIVE MEDICINE

Both self-help groups and alternative systems of healing may challenge the traditional doctor–patient relationship and offer the alternative of equality in the medical encounter. In their most radical form, self-help groups present a challenge to traditional paternalism and professional power. They do this through the recognition and celebration of the knowledge and experience that members bring to the group and are invited to share with others. It is argued that this increases members' confidence, and may encourage them to perceive and acknowledge their potential power, and that this affects their lives as a whole. Further, group meetings take place between equals who can develop an understanding such that emotional and psychic needs are attended to and broader, social interpretations of health and disease are developed. The sufferer or carer thus becomes an active participant in the care or control of his or her own problems.

These principles are also significant in the field of alternative medicine. More specifically, Taylor explains the resurgence of alternative medicine as resting on the nature of the relationship between the practitioner and the client which alternative systems of healing offer.[21] She argues that 'the fragile and complex relationship between healer and healed is collapsing, placed under enormous pressure at a time when the bases of authority relationships in many other social institutions have changed, when health has become a popular obsession and when the institution of medicine has become more central than ever before

[21] R. C. R. Taylor, 'Alternative Medicine and the Medical Encounter in Britain and the United States', in Salmon (ed.), *Alternative Medicines*, 191–228.

in people's lives'. In so doing, Taylor draws attention to the intensive, personal attention and treatment tailored to the person's particular temperament, history, and peculiarities in homoeopathy, and to the active participation demanded of the patient in natural therapy, involving diet, exercise, and way of life. Further, Taylor looks at the relationships in self-help groups, in which shared experience is the central component, and at the support these groups bring for a wide range of afflictions. This highlights the parallels between self-help activity in health care and alternative systems of healing, both of which may cut across the orthodox doctor–patient relationship—and foster a greater degree of equality between those involved in the encounter. They also share an approach which draws on the healing potential of participants.

The radical version of self-help exemplifies a form of organization which is small scale, face to face, and non-hierarchical. It encourages the responsible, active participation of members in defining their problem, its causes, and its cure, management, or control. All members are drawn into democratic participation in the life of the group.

Similar aims are subscribed to, and approaches taken, within alternative medicine. Salmon suggests that the following features are common to such practice: a holistic approach which asserts in principle the notion of the fundamental and integral unity of the body, the mind, and the spirit; concepts of health and illness that go beyond the materialism of scientific medicine; a more human connection between practitioner and patient in the healing encounter; and a notion of 'energy' linked with the presupposition of an innate healing potential within the person.[22]

Self-help groups take a form which gives expression to these beliefs and provide a forum in which people can actively engage their whole selves. A therapist or healer who is committed to this approach can guide and support the members of the group in a way which draws on and increases their individual and collective strengths. Professionals who take the role of expert, who dominate the group, and who attempt to use it for purposes defined in their terms, undermine the self-help qualities of the group. An enabling and empowering approach enhances the

[22] Salmon, 'Defining Health and Reorganising Medicine', in id. (ed.), *Alternative Medicines*.

potential of members and their mutual bonds. An example of this approach is given in the words of a healer, 'we're living in an ocean of energy, as physicists now agree. It's possible to tap that energy, and move it through your body and into another person. I don't believe anyone heals anyone else, but what I'm doing is creating a context for people to initiate their own healing process.'[23]

The members of self-help groups bring to the groups the knowledge and understanding they have won through their experience of the health problem. Engagement with the lives of others encourages understanding which goes beyond the parti- cular individual to recognition of the social and environmental factors in disease and disability. Further, members share ways of coping, information about statutory and voluntary forms of support and about alternative approaches, and practical advice and aid—and the group acts as a channel to more formal sources of information. Newsletters from national levels of organization draw on an even wider field for information and advice. Knowledge gained in the context of a self-help group is assimilated and evaluated through the filter of group discussion; it is not therefore reified and separated from the self, but is made personal and useful.

In the same way alternative medicine may stress channels and modes of knowledge and understanding that differ from those of conventional medicine. Thus Stanway argues that the solely intellectual approach to science generally and medicine in particular is not providing the answers.[24] On this view, aware- ness at a 'higher, supersensible dimension', beyond the limits of ordinary, routine perceptions, has been used in healing for centuries. Stanway draws attention to the achievements of yogis as an example of this ability. He adds that all human beings share the potential to develop this dimension of their psychic abilities. Fulder emphasizes the diversity of approaches that are found outside mainstream conventional medicine.[25] However, he sees

[23] Denise Linn, quoted in A. Purvis, 'Healer at One with the Light', *Weekend Guardian* (14 Jan. 1989).

[24] A. Stanway, *Alternative Medicine: A Guide to Natural Therapies* (Harmonds- worth: Penguin, 2nd edn., 1986).

[25] S. J. Fulder, *The Handbook of Complementary Medicine* (Oxford: Oxford University Press, 2nd edn., 1988).

the common bond which unites them as an attempt to recruit the self-healing capacities of the body. This emphasis on self-healing draws the patient into the healing process. All alternative therapies are partly instructional and some, such as the Alexander or relaxation therapies, are almost entirely so. Virtually all encourage patients to discover why they are sick and to work for their own cure in partnership with the therapist. Thus alternative approaches celebrate and draw on the potential within the human body and the human being as a person to enable healing to take place.

The self-help group form of organization can be seen as opposed to bureaucratic forms and hierarchical authority structures. Groups are thus similar in form to the consciousness-raising groups of the women's movement, which intentionally oppose the typical authority structures of patriarchal society.[26] The appeal of this form of support for women is twofold. First, as Dalley points out, women are usually the carers in our society.[27] It is women who take on the caring roles in the home and in the wider community and their paid employment reflects and reinforces this idea of 'women's work'. Consequently, groups whose focus is a health problem have a strong appeal to women. Secondly, the self-help form of organization mirrors the way women ordinarily interact. Some members are aware of the radical potential that self-help groups embody, but this is not true of all members, and it is not a necessary condition of group functioning.

Black self-help offers another example of self-help which has developed out of disadvantage—in this case the discrimination that separates black people from white ones. Some indication of its extent is given by the National Federation of Self-Help Organizations (NFSHO) whose thousand member groups operate in a variety of fields, far wider than just health, and including community, youth, education and training, housing, business and co-operatives, and the arts. The NFSHO characterizes black self-help as 'The Black Community, through its initiatives, its ideas, and organisations, attacking jointly multiple stresses

---

[26] An account of the 'dreams and dilemmas' of the movement for women's liberation is given by S. Rowbotham, *Dreams and Dilemmas* (London: Virago Press, 1983).

[27] G. Dalley, *Ideologies of Caring* (London: Macmillan, 1988).

affecting that community'.[28] On this view, black self-help is likely to be consciously oppositional. It is worth noting here that Abraham and Sommerlad's paper for the Tavistock Institute which looks at support for ethnic minority self-help has been strongly criticized.[29] Huby argues that it tacitly accepts that any difficulties encountered were a product of ethnic minority culture and not the culture of self-help funding and policy-making institutions.[30] Consequently, it is claimed that it reinforces the traditional exclusion of black and ethnic minority groups from the well-established and powerful core of the voluntary sector and that black self-help has opposition thrust upon it.

Any discussion of self-help as opposition must consider the idea of a self-help movement. Despite the rise in the number of self-help groups and the use of the term in popular writing, Wilson argues that the idea of such a movement in Britain cannot be upheld.[31] She says that there is no evidence of either national or local federations of self-help organizations and groups, and no co-ordinated movement is emerging from self-help groups themselves. And despite the radical model of self-help activity, she finds no evidence that more than a few groups are consciously demanding change in society or demonstrating commitment to an ideology of self-help which challenges dominant medical practices.

A similar conclusion may be drawn for alternative or complementary medicine. On the one hand, Stanway argues for the name 'alternative' medicine because of the fundamental difference between the philosophies underlying this form of medicine and conventional Western medicine.[32] This formulation emphasizes the opposition between the approaches. On the other hand, Fulder adopts the term 'complementary', preferring to see the therapies referred to as partners with scientific medicine— even though they are different in nature from it.[33] From this perspective, such therapies are not alienated or embattled, but

---

[28] National Federation of Self-Help Organizations, *Self-Help News*, NFSHO Newsletter, 13 (June 1988).

[29] Abraham and Sommerlad, *Self Help Support and Black People*.

[30] G. Huby, 'Work with Black People', *Mutual Aid and Self-Help*, Bulletin of the National Self-Help Support Centre, 10 (Winter 1988), 1–2.

[31] Wilson, 'Supporting Self-Help Groups'.

[32] Stanway, *Alternative Medicine*.

[33] Fulder, *Handbook of Complementary Medicine*.

are more and more accepted by lay people and medical professionals. Thus both self-help groups and alternative—or complementary—medicine can be taken up and used without an oppositional intent or outcome for participants.

The broader question of the political implications of self-help and of alternative medicine can be raised here. It has been shown that self-help can develop into provision of services in a traditional mould and that the groups can be hijacked by interested professionals for their own aims. Hence self-help may be seen by the State as a way of increasing cheap voluntary and self-care and as legitimating cuts in statutory provision. Similarly, alternative medicine can influence orthodox approaches and add to their basis of knowledge and understanding. Or it may be marginalized, available only to the few who can afford to pay, leaving traditional entrenched interests untouched.

CONCLUSION

The strength of self-help groups in health care and alternative medicine in Britain lies in their empowering of their members and the challenge they may pose to medical orthodoxy. They can call into question the medical model of health and illness as well as the practice of medicine in a situation in which the number of self-help groups and use of alternative medicine is growing. However, self-help groups are a patchy and fragile mode of support, and are readily incorporated into professional power structures in the health field, while alternative medicine may exist in a complementary, comfortable, and unchallenging relationship alongside orthodox practices, in a way that contravenes its fundamental philosophies and potential for opposition. None the less, both approaches now have a wide, popular appeal which may help to make them a more central influence on medical institutions and traditions, especially if they are already open to change.

12

Pentecostalists as a Medical Minority

Gillian Allen and Roy Wallis

The socially constructed world is an ordering of experience. A meaningful order, or *nomos* in Peter Berger's[1] terminology, is imposed upon the discrete experiences and meanings of individuals. This ordering activity is a collective enterprise. Meanings are shared and thus acquire an 'objective' character. Common interpretations of experience come to be seen as 'objective knowledge' by the members of a society. This paper is concerned with the 'objective knowledge' about the causation and cure of illness ... shared by members of a small congregation of a Pentecostal Church, the Assemblies of God, in a Scottish city.

THE ASSEMBLIES OF GOD AS A RELIGIOUS SECT

The Assemblies' basic doctrines are generally similar to the teachings of other evangelical movements. The Bible is accepted as the literally true and inspired Word of God, 'the Infallible and All-Sufficient Rule for Faith and Practice';[2] all other sources of knowledge are suspect. The doctrine of the Second Coming of Christ is formally adhered to, but it is not now a central feature of Pentecostal preaching. The essential evangelical doctrine of individual guilt for sin, and the need to obtain redemption through Christ's substitutionary atoning death, are continually emphasized. Salvation can be won when the individual's sense of guilt for sin leads him to 'accept Jesus Christ as his personal saviour' who bears his sins, and was crucified for them. It is the subjective experience of 'asking Jesus to come into your heart', and the subsequent gratitude for the relief of guilt and the promise of eternal life which charges the Assemblies' meetings with emotion. It is the experience of salvation and of a

[1] P. Berger, *The Social Reality of Religion* (London: Faber and Faber, 1967).
[2] *Assemblies of God Yearbook 1968–1969*.

developing personal relationship with God that is the crucial aspect of their religion for Assembly members. Doctrine is not so important.

Pentecostalists are distinctive in their belief in the 'baptism of the Holy Spirit' as a reality for present-day believers as much as for the early disciples on the day of Pentecost. Baptism in the Holy Spirit is manifested by an emotional reaction and the receipt of 'spiritual gifts' which include the gifts of speaking in 'divers kinds of tongues', 'the working of miracles', and 'healing' (1 Cor. 12).

The Assemblies of God is the largest Pentecostal sect in the United Kingdom,[3] with an officially estimated 20,000 members in England and Wales and 500 members in Scotland in 1950. In the Scottish city considered here, Pentecostalists form a tiny minority of the population. The Assembly of God has about twenty adults and thirteen children attending regularly (0.02 per cent of the city's population), with approximately another twenty occasional attenders. Including the Elim Foursquare and Apostolic Churches, Pentecostalism in this city claims less than 0.1 per cent of the population.

Membership in the Assembly is by proof of a conversion experience, baptism in water, and knowledge of the Assembly's twelve Fundamental Truths,[4] and entails obligations to attend regularly, contribute financially, live righteously, and try to be baptized in the Holy Spirit. Members who do not live up to these obligations can be expelled at the discretion of the pastor and elders, or of the whole meeting in serious cases. In fact this rarely happens, and social control is mainly informal.

Separation from the world is very limited. Physical or linguistic isolation is not practicable for a conversionist sect.[5] Endogamy is encouraged, but the in-group includes all 'born-again believers'. Insulation is mainly from popular leisure-time activities which are displaced by church-going; most Assembly members attend three to five times a week. Services are lively and quite entertaining in themselves, however, with singing, clapping, and banging tambourines to modern hymn tunes. Self-expression is

[3] J. Highet, 'Scottish Religious Adherence', *British Journal of Sociology*, 4 (1953), 142–59.   [4] In *Assemblies of God Yearbook 1968–1969*.

[5] For the notion of conversionist sect, see B. R. Wilson, 'An Analysis of Sect Development', *American Sociological Review*, 24: 1 (1959), 3–15.

encouraged, the more emotional the better, as long as it is within the narrowly prescribed range of themes, and couched in stereotyped religious phraseology, except, of course, when 'the Spirit descends' and spiritual expression breaks the bounds of language.

The Assembly is a community. 'We're like a family.' Members refer to each other as 'brother' or 'sister', visit each other socially and help each other, particularly in sickness. Control can therefore be exercised over a wide area of the member's life, and his or her commitment must be fairly intense to endure it.

THE ASSEMBLY OF GOD AS A MEDICAL MINORITY

Theories of illness causation

What theories of illness causation are employed by members of the Assembly of God? In general, the prevailing naturalistic explanations of disease are accepted. In answering questions about actual illnesses they have had, causes were given as physical (germs, viruses, cold, and damp), or psychological (strain, worry, shock). Their ideas about disease causation were not always strictly scientific, and could perhaps best be described as metaphysical in some cases, due to their limited knowledge of scientific medicine rather than to any belief in opposing theories.

However, some of the Assembly members also explained their illnesses in spiritual terms. For eight out of the twenty-nine illnesses mentioned (27 per cent), the question 'Do you think that it was just bad luck that you got it?' was answered negatively, because it was seen as God's will. Disease, in these cases, was explained in both scientific and theistic terms, each operating at a different level. While the immediate physical mechanism was explained scientifically, God was believed to exercise ultimate control over these physical events.

More details of the supernatural theories of disease causation held by the Pentecostalists were obtained in answer to questions about the causes of disease in general, rather than their own specific illnesses. The questions were: 'You've probably heard people arguing over why God allows people to suffer, even saved Christians; what do you think about it?'; 'Do you think God still sends sickness as a punishment for sin, like he did in the Old Testament?'; and 'Is disease ever caused by the Devil?' The theories of disease causation revealed in their answers can be classified under *demonic, theistic,* and *metaphysical* headings.

Demonic theories Sixteen out of the twenty Assembly members thought that disease could be caused by the Devil; only one heretic asserted 'Disease is caused by germs!' Assembly members accept a strict dualism between God and the Devil: 'A non-Christian life is a life with the Devil—there's no half-way house.' Since God is the source of goodness, it follows that 'all badness ultimately comes from the Devil—the source of evil', so it must usually be the Devil who sends illness because, as one person expressed it, 'I can't see why the Lord would, unless someone was backsliding and the Lord wanted to draw them closer to him.'

The Deacon of the Assembly categorized the ways the Devil can cause disease into 'direct' and 'indirect'. He can cause disease directly as he did to Job: 'So went Satan forth from the presence of the Lord, and smote Job with sore boils from the sole of his foot unto his crown' (Job 2: 7). Or he can cause disease indirectly through sin, ignorance, and apathy. One member of the Assembly, a health visitor, emphasized the role of the Devil in perpetuating ignorance: 'He blinds people to knowledge, particularly the rules of hygiene', and one old lady found that the Devil tempted her to adopt the sick role too readily: 'If you bucked up you could be better but the Devil says don't bother, just be ill.'

Whether or not the Devil causes disease is essentially an academic question for Assembly members. None of them mentioned the Devil as a causative agent in *actual* illnesses they had had, and some pointed out that 'you can't distinguish between diseases caused by the Devil, or allowed by God'.

'Possession by evil spirits', on the other hand, is actively used to explain not only mental illness but also some cases of dumbness, blindness, and epilepsy. Demon possession is considered to be transferable by touch; and is exorcizable by prayer, by appealing to the Spirit of God to overcome the evil spirits.

Theistic theories Half the members of this congregation of the Assembly of God believed that God sometimes sends sickness as a punishment for sins. Illness might be a punishment for specific sins which provoked God's wrath, for example sexual misconduct:

'There was an unmarried couple who had a baby—it had spina bifida. This was a punishment for sin.' Or it might be a punishment for more general spiritual faults: 'If you get ill it makes you sit up and see what you're doing wrong—you're being disobedient somewhere.' It might sometimes be designed to lead the sinner back to righteousness: 'God has to chastise us, but it's for our own good. It's done in love'; 'Sometimes people say it was through illness that they got converted.'

Disobedience to God was thought by some to result naturally in punishment, which might take the form of sickness: 'Just as a child, if it's disobedient, it has to be punished.' This belief that God can send illness as a punishment for sin is commonly held among fundamentalist Protestant groups.

The other half of the Assembly felt that God never sends illness as a punishment. They either believed, stressing God's role in the *healing* of sickness, that he does not deliberately send illness at all, or they believed that God sometimes sends illness, but not as a punishment. He might, for example, send illness to bring us closer to him: 'The only way the Lord can get people to listen sometimes is to lay them on their back.' This view of illness causation is again in agreement with fundamentalist Christianity.

Metaphysical theories A view of the relationship between sin and sickness emerged which was not mediated by God's direct intervention. It can therefore be categorized as metaphysical rather than theistic. There were two broad versions of this theory. Illness was seen as sometimes the result of sinful actions. Mental and physical illness was explained by this variant as the result of natural mechanisms, but the explanation was couched in moralistic terms: 'Leading a loose, wicked life leads to illness as a natural result.' Disease might also result from the sin of a whole society: 'For example, Biafra. Man's sin leads to wars which lead to starving children.'[6]

An even less direct connection between sin and sickness can be observed in a variant of this theory in which sickness is seen as a

---

[6] These theories have a quasi-karmic character. For a non-Christian parallel, see R. Wallis, 'The Aetherius Society: A Case Study in the Formation of a Mystagogic Congregation', *Sociological Review*, 22:1 (1974), 27–44, reprinted in id. (ed.), *Sectarianism: Analyses of Religious and Non-Religious Sects* (London: Peter Owen, 1975).

concomitant of the sinful state of man, a result, therefore, of original sin. 'If there'd been no Fall, there'd be no sin and no sickness. Sickness is part of our heritage owing to the Fall.' One person accounted for the world-wide distribution of disease in these terms: 'We've brought it on ourselves through original sin and it's multiplied over the years, and through migration illness has been spread over the world.'

The two levels, natural and supernatural, of the theories of disease causation held by Assembly members fall within the competence of the medical and clerical professions respectively. The naturalistic theories, understood in scientific or quasi-scientific terms by Assembly members, do not conflict with those held by the medical profession. The supernatural theories do not differ markedly from those held by the Church of Scotland, particularly on its fundamentalist wing. Pentecostalists accept a similar conciliation of natural and supernatural causes as does the Established Church, though the supernatural is accredited with more power by Pentecostalists, for example in their belief in demons. . . .

Theories of treatment

The Assemblies of God do not explicitly accept or reject scientific theories of treatment. But they subscribe officially to a belief in divine healing. The eighth Fundamental Truth states that: 'We believe that the gifts of the Holy Spirit . . . have been set by God in the Church.' These include the 'gifts of healing' and the 'discerning of spirits' (1 Cor. 12: 9–10). Divine healing can thus be a gift of the Holy Spirit, given to some people who have a special power to transmit the healing forces of the Holy Spirit. Similarly, the power to exorcize demons is believed to be God-given.

There is a second source of divine healing, mentioned in the tenth Fundamental Truth: 'We believe that deliverance from sickness, by Divine Healing, is provided for in the Atonement.' In the same way that Christ is believed to have been sacrificed vicariously for man's sins, by taking it on himself and relieving man of it, he is also thought, by Pentecostalists, to be able to take the sickness of believers. They quote Matthew 8: 17: 'Himself [Christ] took our infirmities and bore our sicknesses.' Divine healing can, in theory, be obtained by anyone in the same way as salvation from sin, by faith in Christ. The procedure is laid down in James 5: 14–16:

Is any sick among you? Let him call for the elders of the church; and let them pray over him, anointing him with oil in the name of the Lord: And the prayer of faith shall save the sick, and the Lord shall raise him up; and if he have committed sins, they shall be forgiven him.

Confess your faults one to another, and pray one for another, that ye may be healed. The effectual fervent prayer of a righteous man availeth much.

The divine healing of James 5 rests on a holistic conception of health. The healing of sickness is a part of the healing or salvation of the whole man.

Neither the New Testament nor the Assembly of God Fundamental Truths distinguish between miraculous and non-miraculous healing. Members of the Assembly in fact use the term 'divine healing' in both senses, although it is most commonly used to mean healing by miraculous supernatural intervention in natural processes. In three-quarters of the twenty-six cases of divine healing reported by Assembly members, the healing had occurred without medical treatment, or after the treatment had been perceived to be unsuccessful. Half of the recoveries were instantaneous or occurred within a few days. These healings were interpreted as miraculous.

But 'divine healing' was also applied in some cases where medical treatment and prayer had been used concurrently. This non-miraculous healing was considered divine in so far as God is believed to control all natural processes. One member explained: 'The Lord can heal you in any way, through tablets for example . . . It all comes from the Lord if we are healed.'

While in this latter, non-miraculous sense 'divine healing' is perfectly compatible with dominant scientific notions of causation and treatment, miraculous 'divine healing' is not. The idea of supernatural healing is contrary to the basic assumptions of scientific medicine. The fact of remarkable physical cures following spiritual ministrations is not denied by the British Medical Association, but in their report on divine healing such cures are explained in psychological terms.[7]

[7] British Medical Association, *Divine Healing and Co-operation between Doctors and Clergy*, Report of the BMA Committee (London, 1955).

Utilization behaviour

In its beliefs about illness, the Assembly of God constitutes a medical cognitive minority. How far is the illness behaviour of members influenced by these beliefs?

Healing procedures Prayer for healing in the Assembly of God occurs at the end of normal services, when those who need healing, or help and advice, are asked 'to come out to the front'. There the pastor and elders perform the laying on of hands and sprinkling with holy oil, and pray simultaneously: 'Oh Lord, heal this woman! Yes, Lord! we know you can heal her.' The occasional case of demon possession is dealt with in a similar way, when the pastor or evangelist addresses the demon along these lines: 'Get out, foul demon! In the name of Jesus, leave her!' The pastor may visit and pray for the sick person at home or in hospital if he discovers someone is ill. Alternatively, prayer for the sick may occur at a distance, if the patient cannot attend church, for example; or via a material medium, such as a handkerchief, which is prayed over in church and taken to the patient in hospital.

Utilization The use of divine healing in relation to orthodox medical services was investigated for both 'serious' and 'minor' illnesses. Data were collected for the most recent 'minor' illness like flu or a cold, and for a serious illness recalled by the respondent in answer to the question: 'Have you ever had a serious illness or accident?' It is likely that the selection of serious illnesses was biased towards those for which prayer had been used. Seventeen minor illnesses and twelve serious illnesses were reported.

The two help-seeking actions investigated were consulting the doctor, and being prayed for by the pastor in church or at home. Respondents were asked 'What happened from the time you first felt ill?'; 'Did you see the doctor about it?'; and 'Did you go out in church to get prayed for?' No Assembly members were private patients, so ... 'National Health Service' will be used as synonymous with 'going to the doctor' and 'use of orthodox medical services'. 'Prayer' will refer to prayer by the pastor either in church or at home, not to private prayer, though in practice they are generally used together. Utilization of paramedical practitioners such as chemists, other unorthodox practitioners, and self-medication were not specifically investigated.

Factors influencing choice of pattern of utilization among Assembly members in the Scottish city were found to include the type of disorder, its seriousness and suddenness of onset, and its imputed cause. Greater variability in illness behaviour occurred for minor illnesses.[8] Six typical help-seeking careers could be distinguished:

1. Divine healing as an *alternative* to the National Health Service.
2. Divine healing as a *first resort* followed by use of National Health Service.
3. Divine healing as a *supplement* to the National Health Service.
4. Divine healing as a *last resort*.
5. National Health Service only.
6. Neither.

1. *Alternative*. Divine healing is used as an alternative to the National Health Service mainly in minor illnesses. Seven of the seventeen minor illnesses reported were dealt with by prayer alone, whereas none of the serious illnesses were. Use of prayer as an alternative to the doctor was closely related to the perception of illness as spiritually caused. Prayer-only users when compared to doctor-only users more often attributed their illnesses to supernatural causes.

Some Assembly members see prayer for divine healing as a rule which ought to be followed 'in obedience to the Word of God'. Their faith in God as 'the Great Physician' is confirmed by their own experiences of divine healing. Sixteen of the twenty Pentecostalists interviewed claimed to have been divinely healed at some time in their lives, and past successes were given as reasons for current use of prayer. 'The Lord had healed my stomach a while back, so I assumed he could heal my sinusitis. But he didn't.'

Prayer may be expedient in some cases, when for instance, 'as far as I know doctors have no cure', or when 'The Lord could heal

---

[8] As David Mechanic's finding would lead one to expect; D. Mechanic, 'The Concept of Illness Behaviour', *Journal of Chronic Diseases*, 15 (1962), 189–94.

you much better than the doctor—you'd get a complete healing, whereas the doctor can't do much for you. They can't do much for varicose veins.' Divine healing may be used by some in an almost magical way, to avoid the pain and inconvenience involved in medical treatment. One woman chose prayer instead of the doctor because 'I was afraid he might tell me to rest and I can't afford to.' In minor illnesses, prayer is frequently used in conjunction with self-medication.

2. *First resort.* Prayer for divine healing may be followed by a visit to the doctor if results are not forthcoming. This happened in two of the twelve serious illnesses reported. Although many feel that 'God should be the first resort', they recommend that 'after being prayed for two or three times and it doesn't work, go to the doctor'. . . .

Whether God or the doctor is the first source of help depends partly on the type of illness; for faults in the mechanics of the body, such as broken bones, it is 'common sense to go to the doctor'; while some thought that for psychiatric illness or illness which would involve surgery, prayer should come first 'because the body is the Lord's'. Prayer may be used both to assist in making the decision whether to seek professional medical help, and as a form of treatment in its own right.

3. *Supplement.* Prayer is used as a supplement to medical treatment particularly in serious illnesses. In seven of the twelve serious illnesses reported, prayer for divine healing was used in conjunction with medical treatment, whereas this occurred in only one of the seventeen minor illnesses. Typically, in serious illnesses of sudden onset, relatives or neighbours fetch the doctor immediately, and send for the pastor once the doctor has established the treatment regime.

Fetching the doctor is a procedure followed almost automatically in an emergency. About half the Assembly felt that even in less urgent cases they would use the medical services in the same way as anyone else, but pray as well. They rejected the way prayer was used almost magically by some Pentecostalists to achieve healing without any effort. They thought that 'God's willing to do his part, but we've got to do ours'. There was some criticism of those who refused medical treatment.

It was a common opinion that: 'There's nothing wrong with going to the doctor. God has given people the ability to be doctors and he's put medicine in the world.' Nevertheless, the doctor was generally regarded merely as an instrument of God, human and fallible, in whose knowledge and skills one could not place much faith. But because doctors are regarded as the instruments of God, the use of prayer plus doctor utilizes God's healing power most effectively. The Assembly's pianist expressed it as follows: 'God's methods are sometimes through men. Prayer makes the doctor's treatment successful.' Prayer, then, is often for 'divine healing' in the broader sense, including miraculous and non-miraculous healing.

The use of prayer and doctor together is seen as the most effective means of returning to complete health, physically, mentally, and spiritually. The doctor may be used for physical treatment, but some Assembly members believe that a complete return to health involves a spiritual healing as well. In this way, their beliefs in the spiritual causation of disease, and the close relation of divine physical healing with spiritual salvation, influence their utilization behaviour.

4. *Last resort.* Divine healing was occasionally used as a last resort after the medical services had failed to cure the disorder. Only two of the twelve serious illnesses and one of the seventeen minor illnesses fell in this category. One woman with flu, for example, sent for the doctor first because she 'took it for granted that he would clear it up'. When the side-effects of the drug he prescribed made her worse, she sent for the pastor to pray for her. A small minority of the Assembly (three out of twenty) thought that divine healing should *only* be used as a last resort.

5. *National Health Service only.* Prayer for divine healing was not used in three of the twelve serious illnesses and eight of the seventeen minor illnesses. Use of the health services only was closely related to the imputation of a purely physical cause. In none of these cases was a spiritual cause assigned to the disease. Lack of opportunity for going out for prayer limited its usefulness: 'You can always send for the doctor, but you can't always get to a meeting.' Prayer for the sick is a minor part of the pastor's role, so Assembly workers were often reluctant to bother him.

6. *Neither.* In four of the minor illnesses, neither the doctor nor the pastor was consulted because the complaints were 'too trivial'. Self-medication was used in these cases. 'A cold isn't a disease. Jesus Christ only healed diseases. When you can take a

tablet yourself, I don't think it's out of place.' Similarly: 'I wouldn't class a cold as a sickness, so I wouldn't go to the doctor. I'd try all the treatments I could myself without bothering the doctor.'

The peculiarly Pentecostal beliefs about illness held in the Assembly of God are used by members in deciding on courses of help-seeking action. Belief in divine healing, as a theory of treatment, provides an alternative system to the health services, which may be employed in relation to the health services in the variety of ways described above. Theories of causation were found to be influential especially in minor illnesses, where belief in a spiritual cause was closely related to the use of prayer as an alternative to the doctor. In more serious illnesses, perception of a spiritual component in causation and cure resulted in the joint use of doctor and prayer.

13

Alternative Therapists in Britain

Stephen Fulder

WHO ARE THE THERAPISTS?

The public image of a complementary practitioner has been at a nadir for over a century. However, there has been a considerable change in recent years. The public is now more ready to see therapists as true professionals. The therapists themselves, especially if young and recently qualified, are more confident, more forthcoming, and more politically and socially active in the furtherance of their profession. Their older colleagues are less concerned with their public status and keep a low profile, tending to devote themselves completely to their practice. Complementary practitioners are usually male, and in early middle age. A survey of United Kingdom osteopaths put their average age at 37 years and showed that they had been in practice for an average of thirteen years.[1]

Characteristics of therapists would seem to be similar to those of any other set of health care professionals although they come from diverse backgrounds, certainly more diverse than the average professional, who tends to come from a middle-class home. No less than 80 per cent of Australian therapists have had previous occupations of one kind or another.[2] One can understand why, for the profession of complementary practitioner is marginal, holding an uncertain status. Entrants are usually motivated more by the calling itself than by any of the ancillary

---

[1] A. K. Burton, *A Work Study of the Osteopathic Association of Great Britain: Part I: The Structure of Practices; Part II: The Characteristics of Patients* (Osteopathic Association of Great Britain, 1977).

[2] R. Boven, G. Lupton, J. Najman, S. Payne, M. Sheehan and J. Western, *A Study of Alternative Health Care Practitioners*, Appendix 7 of the Committee of Inquiry, Parliamentary Paper No. 102, 1977. This is the second Report by the University of Queensland team, based on interviews with 594 practitioners throughout Australia.

social benefits that may result. Entrance to medical school, by contrast, usually occurs immediately after completion of secondary education, at an age when social and parental pressures are still determining factors on careers, and status is an important goal.

NUMBERS OF THERAPISTS PRACTISING IN THE
UNITED KINGDOM

In 1981 the Threshold Survey made a serious attempt to estimate the total number of therapists in the United Kingdom. Questionnaires and follow-up forms were sent to all the organizations representing or training complementary practitioners. Every organization was contacted or eliminated as defunct or irrelevant. Steps were taken to eliminate therapists appearing on more than one register and distinguish practising United Kingdom members from retired, honorary, foreign, or associate membership. The figures are given in columns 1 and 2 of Table 13.1 and refer only to practising United Kingdom therapists. However, this is only half the story, because many therapists choose not to join professional bodies. Furthermore they may be full-time therapists or part-time untrained therapists who treat an occasional person in their spare time. Their numbers were obtained by combining rough estimates from the various organizations, and are given in column 3. They are basically informed guesses.

In 1981, there were over 11,000 therapists belonging to professional bodies practising in the United Kingdom, including all possible therapies. This was no less than 41 per cent of the number of general practitioners in the United Kingdom. If healers are eliminated as an inappropriate comparison with medical practitioners, and the creative therapies (art, music, and drama) as outside the definition of complementary medicine, there were 4,069 full-time professional therapists, which was 15 per cent of the number of general practitioners. This was a minimum: if one takes into account the estimated numbers of therapists who do not belong to professional bodies, it increased to 33 per cent of the number of general practitioners. There are no data on the number of practitioners in practice in 1987. However, allowing for an increase of 10 per cent a year ... it is possible that

No. of practitioners

TABLE 13.1. *Complementary practitioners in the United Kingdom (1981)*

Therapy	Medically qualified[a]	In professional association	Not in professional association	Total
Acupuncture	160	548	250	958
Alexander technique	5	170	50	225
Chiropractic	1	156	200	357
Hakims, Chinese doctors	0	40	40	80
Healing	20	6,300	13,000	19,320
Herbalism	10	228	200	438
Homoeopathy	425	41	230	696
Hypnotherapy	1,000	507	170	1,677
Massage/ manipulation[b]	350	1,000	1,500	2,850
Miscellaneous physical therapies[c]	0	300	800	1,100
Music, art, drama therapy[d]	0	815	90	905
Naturopathy	5	204	200	409
Osteopathy	212	777	150	1,139
Radionics	21	98	100	219
TOTAL	2,209	11,184	16,980	30,373

[a] Implies doctors. However, as organizations mostly failed to distinguish between doctors and other health professionals, it is possible that in some cases paramedical and auxiliary medical professionals will also have been included in column 1. Otherwise they would be included in column 2 or 3.

[b] Excludes beauty therapists.

[c] Includes reflexology, rolfing, metamorphic therapy, polarity therapy, and applied kinesiology. As there are no proper professional bodies with registers in these therapies, and they are taught to the public, the number given in column 2 is an estimate of the number of instructors plus full-time practitioners. The number in column 3 is an estimate of the part-time and occasional practitioners. All estimates are derived from the organizations themselves.

[d] These therapies are included as they are arguably alternatives to conventional rehabilitation and are based more on anthroposophical than medical principles.

Certain other therapies such as colour, aroma, and sound therapies are not specifically included, but practitioners have been incorporated into the estimates in column 3 of naturopathy, homoeopathy, and herbalism. Data derived from the Threshold Survey (see n. 4).

there are approximately 6,000 therapists in professional bodies, corresponding to 20 per cent of the number of general practitioners.

The 1981 Threshold Survey found that over 2,000 doctors, or 8 per cent of the number of general practitioners belonged to complementary medical professional bodies. This figure seems to be underestimated, however, as a recent study reported in the *British Medical Journal* indicated that no less than 45 per cent of general practitioners in one area of the United Kingdom practised some kind of complementary medicine.[3] These general practitioners, however many there are, play a highly important part in the spread of complementary medical services.

There is a very large number of healers in the United Kingdom; organizations in the field agree upon a figure of around 20,000. However, this figure includes healing circles in churches and healing by prayer groups. Healing has a much stronger tradition in the United Kingdom than in other Western countries. The largest complementary profession is osteopathy, which has always been regarded as the most senior, respected, and powerful of the therapies. However, acupuncture is rapidly catching up and is now in second place, despite its relatively recent appearance in the United Kingdom.

Numbers of therapists have been increasing rapidly. The annual trends in numbers of practising United Kingdom therapists were calculated from membership organizations for 1978–81 and show that acupuncture is indeed the fastest growing therapy, doubling its number of professional practitioners between 1978 and 1981.[4] Homoeopathy has also increased considerably, as a result of the establishment of a body of lay homoeopaths. No therapy has declined. . . .

THE COST OF COMPLEMENTARY MEDICINE

In 1981, the Threshold Survey found that most first consultations fell within the range of £6–£15 and almost all subsequent consultations within £6–£10. These fees are less than those of a

[3] R. Wharton and G. Lewith, 'Complementary Medicine and the General Practitioner', *British Medical Journal*, 292 (1986), 1498–1500.
[4] S. J. Fulder and R. Monro, *The Status of Complementary Medicine in the United Kingdom* (London: Threshold Foundation, 1982).

medical specialist and roughly twice the total cost per consultation of providing general practitioner services, excluding drugs. They are likely to be 30 per cent greater in 1987.[5]

If we assume that the average fee is £10 for each visit to a complementary practitioner, and 15.4 million consultations are given annually,[6] then £154 million are spent annually on consulting complementary practitioners. The additional cost of vitamins, supplements, herbs, X-rays, and mechanical aids could reasonably bring the figure to £250 million per year. This is equivalent to only 1.2 per cent of the total health services bill, despite serving some two million people annually.

cost of

Europeans as a whole spent over £1,200 million on complementary medicine in 1986, 60 per cent of which was for consultations and physical therapies and the rest for remedies and supplements.[7] The amount is forecast to rise by about 10 per cent a year in the next few years.

HOW MANY PATIENTS DO THERAPISTS SEE?

The demand for therapists is an indication of the popularity of the practices, the popularity of the practitioners, and the room for future expansion. The Threshold Survey's statistics are given in Table 13.2, together with those from the University of Queensland alternative practitioner study,[8] as a comparison.

In the United Kingdom, a surprising number of practitioners, 16 per cent, saw hardly any patients. This reflects the proportion of part-time and occasional therapists who obtain their livelihood by other means. The Australian figures tend to ignore part-time practitioners, since the research team restricted their study of practitioners to professional organizations. In the United Kingdom, more than half the total consultations are accounted for by less than a quarter of the practitioners. Chiropractors and osteopaths see the greatest number of patients. This is both because treatment takes less time than other therapies and

[5] P. Davies, *Report on Trends in Complementary Medicine* (London: Institute of Complementary Medicine, 1984).

[6] S. J. Fulder and R. Monro, 'Complementary Medicine in the United Kingdom; Patients, Practitioners and Consultations', *Lancet*, 2 (1985), 542–5.

[7] Frost and Sullivan Ltd., *Alternative Medical Practices in Europe*, Report No. E874, Sullivan House, Grosvenor Gardens, London SW1, 1987.

[8] Boven, *et al.*, *A Study of Alternative Health Care Practitioners*.

TABLE 13.2. *Numbers of patients seen by complementary practitioners per week in the United Kingdom[a] and Australia[b]*

Number of patients seen	United Kingdom practitioners (%)	Number of patients seen	Australian practitioners (%)
< 5	16	< 20	22
6–20	24	21–60	38
21–50	31	61–100	16
51–100	19	101–200	14
101–200	10	< 201	1
> 201	0		

[a] From the Threshold Survey.
[b] From the Queensland survey of complementary practitioners.

because the therapists themselves tend to be more organized. Acupuncture and naturopathy follow, then hypnotherapy, and finally, healing. Many healers see very few clients. The average number of weekly consultations overall was forty-three in 1981,[9] and, according to a more recent Report, is now about fifty.[10] This is between one-third and one-half of that of general medical practitioners, who see twenty-one patients per day.

THE CONSULTATION

At a first consultation with a complementary practitioner, the patient will usually be required to give a full personal history. The individualistic nature of complementary medicine, in which the practitioner takes time to decode the origin of the disease from the cipher of character and constitution, makes this necessary. First consultations in traditional acupuncture and homoeopathy can take up to two hours. The Threshold Survey found that most first consultations take between thirty and sixty minutes and average time for all consultations is thirty-six minutes. This is *six times* that of a general practitioner. We need look no further for one of the reasons for the popularity of complementary medicine. Modern medicine, outside the hospital, does not require lengthy

[9] Fulder and Monro, *The Status of Complementary Medicine in the United Kingdom.*
[10] Davies, *Report on Trends in Complementary Medicine.*

personal contact with the physician. Although general practitioners rightly claim that they are too overworked to give sufficient time to patients, if they were given thirty-six minutes per patient per visit it is doubtful if many of them would know what to do with it.

Because a complementary practitioner sees one-third to one-half of the number of patients as a general practitioner, but for six times as long, he would have, on average, two to three times as much total patient contact as a general practitioner. Even allowing for the house calls of the latter, we can conclude that complementary practitioners are as busy as general practitioners and that demand is considerably outstripping supply.

COURSES OF TREATMENT

The once-only visit to a complementary practitioner is a rarity. The practitioner is involved in a programme to steer the patient to his state of maximal health. Often the patient will be suffering from chronic or deeply rooted conditions which require lengthy management. The practitioner in virtually all the therapies is concerned with the fundamental causes of a patient's condition and thus his patients should expect continuing, rather than extempore, all-at-once, treatment.

The statistics reflect this. The Threshold Survey found that the numbers of visits in a linked series (during less than a year) were highly variable, especially in the case of acupuncture. Acute cases generally needed three to four visits, chronic cases ten to twelve. Some healers, hypnotherapists, and radionicists gave up to and over thirty treatments in a course: the average was 9.7.[11] . . .

CLINICS, HEALTH CENTRES, AND HOSPITALS

Many professional therapists practise from private houses, with simple treatment rooms that would remind one of a family doctor with a small practice, minus receptionist. In fact, it would be quite difficult to tell therapists apart, were it not for their equipment. Osteopaths have a padded raised table and medical-looking diagnostic instruments; chiropractors usually have a much more complex hinged, spring-loaded table, and sometimes

[11] Fulder and Monro, 'Complementary Medicine in the United Kingdom'.

equipment

an X-ray room; herbalists their tinctures and bottles, naturopaths their charts; radionicists their instruments; homoeopaths their bottles of little pills; and acupuncturists, packets of sterilized needles and perhaps electro-acupuncture apparatus.

There is a growing trend for therapists as well as general practitioners to share their treatment facilities rather than work in isolation. Two or more therapists of the same or different discipline may work together in a shared clinic at which they are likely to be able to employ a secretary and provide a more efficient service to the public. Half of all therapists now work in a group practice of this kind.[12] It is worth remembering that complementary therapists do not have any general administrative infrastructure to channel patients to them and their code of ethics does not permit advertising. So they are, like general practitioners, dependent on patients' recommendation through the local grapevine to provide new clients. When therapists pool resources their influence increases. For example, an acupuncture clinic at Farmoor near Oxford was established for a number of years, building up sufficient clientele to be able to support no less than nine acupuncturists. The existence of this centre was instrumental in the growth of an awareness of acupuncture itself throughout Oxfordshire. There are now fifteen full-time acupuncturists serving the city of Oxford and its immediate surroundings.

A growing number of therapists feel that practice in clinics is only a prelude to a much more powerful establishment: the natural or holistic health care centre. Such a centre (which under a new ruling cannot be called a 'health centre' to avoid confusion with National Health Service health centres) employs the services of several therapists practising different disciplines. There are often classes in yoga, relaxation, diet, or other self-care methods. It is an attractive arrangement to both therapist and patient as it can deal with a wider range of problems more effectively. For example, acupuncturists and osteopaths both treat a large number of back-pain cases. However, while the osteopath can provide relief and the opportunity for repair of the physical frame, the acupuncturist can deal with underlying metabolic or energetic disturbances. A mixed treatment of this kind is better than the sum of its parts. For the patient, this kind of centre is a boon. It drastically reduces the laborious search for the right

---

[12] Ibid.

therapist, which understandably discourages so many potential patients. The patient can instead put himself in the hands of a group of natural therapists whose skills complement each other, enabling them to guide the patient to the most appropriate therapy for his condition. The Nature Cure Clinic in London is perhaps one of the best-known examples of this kind of polyclinic, but there are now hundreds throughout the country.

A centre that is solely a group practice of professionals is still to some extent a sickness centre. A health centre that is true to its name should play a preventive, health-promoting role in the community, and there are a growing number that do this. Like the United States Holistic Health Centres, these places become a focus where lectures, workshops, and classes are held, self-help groups meet, and techniques for developing human health and well-being, such as yoga or T'ai-chi, might be taught. Examples include the Wellbeing Centre in Cornwall and the Bristol Natural Health Centre. Some centres, in fact, are dominated by instructional and educational activities, to which may be added the more consciously social goal of the spread of natural health measures and complementary medicine among the public.

While the number of these centres is fast increasing, there is little to offer in the way of natural therapy hospitals or residential clinics. This is a sad state of affairs, for many people with chronic conditions, such as high blood pressure, could be substantially cured by intensive residential natural treatment combined with a drastic alteration in their life-style. There are very few naturopathic hospitals, and none of them is bigger than one hundred beds.

The best-known and most successful is the Tyringham Clinic near Newport Pagnell in Buckinghamshire. Set up as a charity in the mid-1960s, this manor house is booked up virtually all the year round by both in- and out-patients. On admission a patient is seen by a multi-disciplined consultant and therapies are assigned according to individual need. A large number of therapies is available and careful attention is given to a patient's diet. The Kingston Clinic in Edinburgh is noted for its purificatory procedures and emphasis on nature-cure. Other clinics include Shrubland Hall in Ipswich, Enton Hall in Godalming, and Grayshott Hall in Hindhead. There are, of course, health resorts too, the best-known being Champneys at Tring. However, these are less naturopathic hospitals than health farms or health resorts at which relatively healthy people can clean out the residues of their indulgences in an amenable but expensive environment.

THE TRAINING OF COMPLEMENTARY PRACTITIONERS

There are basically two ways to learn the healing arts. At one extreme is the apprenticeship. A student learns his skills through a gradual process of osmosis from long periods of working with accomplished therapists. This experiential training is more suitable for the intuitional healing arts which involve special sensitivities, for example healing, radionics, Alexander technique, or reflexology. At the other extreme is the highly formal and standardized training.

At one time complementary therapies were virtually always taught by apprenticeship. The knowledge was passed down as a semi-secret art from therapists to disciples, whose only entrance requirements were enthusiasm and endurance. Under these circumstances, there was every opportunity to be very good or very bad. Small colleges were set up, but they too were of greatly differing qualities, depending on the competence and ability of their founders. The colleges taught different interpretations of each therapy, fragmenting the knowledge and preserving the fragments with professional rivalries. Attempts to set up standards were fruitless. Therapists therefore arrived into the mid-twentieth century as a mixture of the highly competent and incompetent, highly trained or untrained.

Modern medicine started its colleges in a somewhat similar vein. However, its education is now at the other extreme: precisely delineated teaching sequences, producing similarly trained practitioners, all of reasonable competence. The lack of standardized training in the complementary therapies has given, and still gives, the medical profession ammunition with which to criticize the therapies. The therapists reply: 'Why should the medical school be an appropriate model for other healing arts?'

Today, complementary therapists are rapidly becoming more professional. Their new attitude is producing an intense preoccupation with education and training; the therapists are attempting to found new, and upgrade existing, teaching establishments and the Government and organized medicine is

using education as a test of complementary medicine's acceptability. This is a mixed blessing. While the need for acceptance by
professional peers is undoubtedly improving education, it also
produces a subtle shift in the way a therapist is judged by society
at large. Instead of being judged by results, as in the pre-
professional era, a therapist will be judged on qualifications. This
does not matter too much in conventional medicine, where
doctors share a single canon. It might, however, matter in
complementary medicine, which does not have a single, crystal-
lized body of knowledge.

If, as is the case with complementary medicine, there is no
single standard body of knowledge, there can be no single
standard training. The fluid world of the complementary therapies
requires great flexibility in matters of training and assessment.
Otherwise the very strengths of these systems—their adaptive
and unconventional healing strategies—will be crushed.
Admittedly, there is no substitute for therapists who are selected
as to ability, who are carefully and intensively trained, and who
have built up a resource of experience, sensitivity, and understanding. Even spiritual healing can be, and is, taught so that
healers learn to amplify their energy and channel it into the
required therapeutic form. There are entry standards into the
profession just as with other therapies. However, training should
always expand ability, not distort or reduce it.

THE CURRENT STATE OF THERAPISTS' EDUCATION

The author's first contact with a complementary therapy college
was as a young patient seeking osteopathic treatment. The college
used a large and rather gloomy Victorian house. The secretary
who made the appointments also seemed to run the entire
establishment, from a partitioned office on the ground floor.
Nearby were classrooms with ancient books in glass-fronted
bookcases, old wooden desks, and a skeleton or two dangling in
the corners. Apart from the secretary, the place had a rather
quiet, sleepy air, with an occasional student in a crisp white
jacket calling patients for treatment. The course there was a full-
time, four-year course, which students might enter straight after
school, with certain minimum O and A level entrance requirements. The students were mostly in their late teens or early

twenties. They gave a pleasing impression of devotion and dedication to their therapy.

It turned out that this first impression was rather typical of the full-time colleges, although they are more modern now. Anthroposophy, chiropractic, herbalism, naturopathy, and osteopathy are all available as full-time courses of at least three years' duration. Acupuncture and homoeopathy are taught in part-time courses of equivalent duration. All the therapies, with the exception of anthroposophy, can also be studied in a briefer, part-time, and often more superficial manner. This includes correspondence courses.

Standards are set by the practitioners' associations in each therapy. Usually, students must pass an examination and undergo a certain prescribed amount of clinical training before being awarded a Diploma or Licentiate, such as DO (Doctor of Osteopathy) or Lic. Ac. (Licentiate of Acupuncture). The diploma entitles the student to practise; however, sometimes the student is required to practise under the supervision of a senior therapist for a set period before being included on a register.

Just as there is no legal hindrance in the United Kingdom to an individual setting himself up in practice, so there is none to prevent him teaching others to do so, and setting the standards to boot. There has been a continuous splintering process in all the therapies as therapists succumb to the temptation of founding their own colleges. Naturally this has resulted in a proliferation of courses and colleges whose standards vary from the excellent to the abysmal. In no case would the teaching come up to the academic level of universities, but in no case is this an ambition of the colleges. Rather, the best of teaching standards, for example at the Anglo-European College of Chiropractic, the British School of Osteopathy, the European College of Osteopathy, or the revised National Institute of Medical Herbalists full-time course, are equivalent to polytechnic or technical college standards.

. . . It should be pointed out that some subjects do not require extensive courses—a four-year, full-time course in reflexology, for example, would be a ridiculous idea. On the other hand, where full-time courses of several years' duration exist in a subject it is an indication that that subject needs it, and colleges offering only minimal training in the same subjects should be looked at with suspicion.

Two other kinds of teaching are also available. The first is the short course, which is given to laymen to acquaint themselves with the rudiments of a therapy for first-aid or self-care purposes, or given to other therapists to broaden their knowledge of different therapies in the mosaic of overlapping complementary systems. These courses are a unique and important facet of complementary medicine. The second kind is postgraduate teaching, which in some cases is very extensive indeed. Acupuncturists, in particular, seem never to stop learning more of the deep mysteries of Chinese medicine. Other therapists also continue to develop their skills, part of the tradition of apprenticeships in complementary medicine.

There is a great deal of argument dividing therapists from each other concerning the minimum length and depth of training courses. The colleges which provide full-time, four-year courses are somewhat righteous about this. Others counter that as much can be taught part-time. There is also a perpetual debate about the wisdom of the scientific–medical model within teaching. For example, some naturopaths are keen to adopt the American-style multidisciplinary 'Doctor of Naturopathy' (ND), training, which generates practitioners who are almost indistinguishable from holistic doctors. The more traditional naturopaths see the way the NDs hand out vitamin pills as a mirror of the symptomatic treatment offered by conventional medicine. They want to preserve the emphasis on diet and hygienic methods which allow proper self-healing, and to teach a purer course.

One consequence of being on the medical fringe is a lack of government support for complementary medical education. This means that practitioners must establish colleges themselves and teach in them. There is rarely a possibility of attracting full-time professional lecturers. Therefore, teaching is usually part-time and carried out by practising therapists. On the one hand, this compromises standards. On the other hand, it has had the result of keeping teaching closely connected to practice, preventing the development of excessive esotericism at the expense of the patient. Some local authorities will give discretionary grants to students at the major chiropractic, naturopathic, and osteopathic colleges. However, they are the lucky few, and most students must pay their way, in contrast to conventional medical education, which is free. This is certainly unfair, although in the long term it may not make much difference and may even help the budding professions by selecting the more motivated as entrants.

Unhindered by the need for accreditation, each college has set about designing education for its own therapy in an original and individualistic way. At one extreme this has produced some novel and exciting courses tailor-made to the unique situation of an 'alternative' therapy inside a modern, scientific-based, cultural milieu. For example, one might pick out the two main traditional acupuncture colleges and the new College of Herbal Medicine. At the other extreme it has generated some chaotic establishments where the students are subjected to burdensome amateur teaching by egotistic practitioners whose schools are set up mostly for financial gain. . . .

training)

THE TRAINED, THE UNTRAINED, AND THE QUACK

There is no statutory register of complementary practitioners who have reached an agreed standard of competence, as there is with physicians, nor are there laws in the United Kingdom which restrict members of the public from practising any therapy they choose. This creates an environment in which quackery, the practice of medicine for profit by the untrained and incompetent, can flourish. In actual fact real quackery is relatively rare. The Threshold Survey found only four untrained practitioners out of 137, and these claimed to have been in practice for some time and to have been taught by apprenticeship . . .

Although quackery is not a great problem, the superficially trained therapists who belong to impressive-sounding organizations cause more serious disturbance, both to the therapy they practise and often to patients. For example, there is one hypnotherapy organization in the United Kingdom which trains practitioners in a brief correspondence course, after which it gives them recorded tapes and a franchise on an area of the United Kingdom. The practitioners advertise hypnotism as a cure for smoking or overeating, and the public pay dearly for what can only be described as utterly inadequate treatment. In a slightly different case, a student can also receive a diploma in a number of complementary therapies, including, for example, psycho-therapy, solely through correspondence courses. The school makes it clear that their courses are introductory, yet they do nothing to stop someone hanging their elegant Latin diploma on the wall and starting a practice.

There is little that can be done about this except to make sure that the public is well informed. Patients can certainly sue incompetent therapists, but they never do. In the absence of legal registration of therapists, it is, in the last analysis, a case of *caveat emptor.*

Another kind of poorly trained therapist who sometimes plays at professionalism, is a member of the public who has taken a bit of self-help instruction and has been tempted to take on patients. The author has witnessed one typical episode of therapeutic theatre in which a middle-aged lady chased someone around the house with bottles of Bach-flower-remedies, to which she had been recently converted. Since complementary medicine gives so much more responsibility to the patient than conventional medicine, there is the inevitable risk that the patient grabs more responsibility that he or she ought to. This probably does little harm, and may even be helpful in raising more interest in self-care, providing it is kept to a domestic scale.

THE ORGANIZATION OF COMPLEMENTARY MEDICINE

Professional associations of therapists have usually borrowed a structure from medical associations. They have an elected council, a management committee, a code of ethics, a register to which only suitably qualified practitioners will be admitted, and sometimes a research section. Some are charities, others companies limited by guarantee. For example, the strongest acupuncture organization started off as the Association and Directory of Acupuncture Ltd., and became the British Association of Acupuncture by permission of the Board of Trade in 1977. Its Executive Council sets standards and appoints examiners. Acupuncturists can only be admitted to the Association and included on its published register if they have passed the examination of the British College of Acupuncture, which the Association has set up to train its practitioners. If acupuncturists have been trained elsewhere, they have to satisfy the examiners as to their qualifications.

. . . There are some sixty professional bodies in the United Kingdom, with members ranging from half a dozen to several thousand. Virtually all the professional associations have codes of practice which are mostly voluntary, although some organizations state that they would be prepared to use the only sanction available, dismissal from the register, when a member was in breach of the code. The larger and more established bodies are stricter in relation to membership and will normally only draw their membership from specific approved colleges. Very few associations hold examinations for membership, but it is quite common for budding practitioners to be required to practise for a certain period, say a year, before being admitted to the association and inscribed on its register. It is, of course, the stringency of entry requirements that select the major from the minor organizations.

Complementary medicine is beset by divisiveness. Many parallel organizations, often having little to choose between them as far as standards are concerned, have been at loggerheads for years, although the situation is changing rapidly. For example, the osteopaths are the most established therapists in the United Kingdom, yet have eight professional bodies. The largest organization, the General Council and Register of Osteopaths (GCRO), has recently joined forces with an earlier rival, the Society of Osteopaths, on the basis of their equivalent standards.

They are now in the midst of a seemingly endless dialogue with the British Naturopathic and Osteopathic Association (BNOA), previously shunned because of its more naturopathic and less medical orientation. This may result in a merger, but at present ... there is much uncertainty. The British Osteopathic Association and the Osteopathic Medical Association, which both represent the medically qualified osteopaths, are not only set off against each other, but also against the remainder of the osteopathic organizations because they are not sufficiently medical. Meanwhile the College of Osteopathy, the British and European Osteopathic Association, and the Natural Therapeutic and Osteopathic Society and Register are not accepted by the former organizations because of a disagreement on standards. Therefore these organizations have formed the Association of Osteopathic Practitioners as an umbrella body. It bickers continually in public with the General Council and Register of Osteopaths, and leaves the British Naturopathic and Osteopathic Association somewhat uncomfortably suspended in between them. Members of each register appear on other registers in a confusing way. One or two outsiders have been omitted as they are completely unacceptable to any of the above organizations.

The rivalry between those therapeutic organizations whose members are medically qualified and lay therapist organizations is perhaps more understandable, although none the less unfortunate. The societies of medical osteopaths, acupuncturists, and hypnotists still strongly hold the position that they alone should dominate the therapy and that lay practitioners be banned. However, the secretary of the Faculty of Homoeopathy recently made a courageous recommendation to its medically qualified members to co-operate with lay practitioners for the benefit of the therapy as a whole.

Disagreements have, of course, been highly damaging to the political development of the therapies . . . For example, when Joyce Butler MP put forward a motion in Parliament in 1976 for the statutory registration of osteopaths, it was undermined by the failure of certain osteopathic groups to support it. However, it should have been clear by that time that lay therapists did not need to continue to behave so defensively as attitudes were changing. The Threshold Survey noted that 42 per cent of therapists polled utilized more than one therapy. This included all the naturopaths and masseurs, and about 33 per cent of the acupuncturists, although few chiropractors or osteopaths. Organizations are still disputing over therapeutic boundaries which are rapidly disappearing.

14

The Paradox of Incorporation: Acupuncture and the Medical Profession in Modern Britain

Mike Saks

Acupuncture, which can be broadly defined as involving the insertion of needles into the body for therapeutic purposes, has a long history in Britain which goes back to the seventeenth century.[1] The strongest flurry of medical interest in this early history was in the first half of the nineteenth century when a number of doctors employed the technique pragmatically for a narrow range of conditions, including rheumatic complaints. While non-medically qualified practitioners continued to use the method as a panacea for a period after the mid-nineteenth century, the limited medical involvement with acupuncture went into sharp decline at this time, as a clear climate of rejection was established.[2] Interest was resurrected in this subject, though, in the second part of the twentieth century, not least under the impetus of the 'ping-pong' diplomacy between China and the West in the early 1970s that reopened communications with the society in which acupuncture had its origins many centuries ago. This contribution outlines and analyses the reception of acupuncture by the medical profession in Britain from its new beginnings in this country in the 1960s and 1970s through to the start of the 1990s.

The response of the medical profession to acupuncture in the 1960s and the first half of the 1970s is viewed as largely perpetuating the long-standing climate of rejection faced by both the method and its small number of medically and non-medically

---

[1] Lu Gwei-Djen and J. Needham, *Celestial Lancets: A History and Rationale of Acupuncture and Moxa* (Cambridge: Cambridge University Press, 1980).

[2] M. Saks, 'Professions and the Public Interest: The Response of the Medical Profession to Acupuncture in Nineteenth and Twentieth Century Britain', unpublished Ph.D. thesis, Department of Sociology, London School of Economics, University of London, 1985.

qualified exponents in the preceding period. However, it is argued that, following the mid-1970s, acupuncture has been progressively incorporated into the orthodox medical repertoire, even though it has not yet fully become part of mainstream medicine and the profession maintains a none-too-positive attitude towards lay practitioners of this technique. Accordingly, the paper examines how these apparently contradictory trends might best be explained. After careful consideration of the evidence—in an area of study in which assertion is often substituted for analysis[3]—it is claimed that the initial blanket rejection of acupuncture by the medical profession in the period leading up to, and including, the first half of the 1970s is most compatible with an explanation based on the operation of professional self-interests. The paper then explores why there should have been an increasing shift towards the incorporation of the procedure into the practice of medicine—and in particular whether an explanation focused on the notion of professional self-interests still remains appropriate in accounting for this paradoxical development.

THE RESPONSE OF THE MEDICAL PROFESSION TO ACUPUNCTURE IN MODERN BRITAIN

The paper begins, though, by documenting the initial upturn of interest in acupuncture amongst medical practitioners in Britain after the mid-twentieth century, following a rather bleak period for the technique over the preceding decades. At this time, enthusiasts in the medical profession like the pioneer Louis Moss and Felix Mann, who founded the Medical Acupuncture Society in the early 1960s, propagated the use of acupuncture for a broad band of conditions—from asthma and bronchitis to depression and sciatica—in a manner linked to its traditional Chinese roots.[4] Even in the 1960s, however, there were no more than a handful of medical practitioners of the method in this country. This is not surprising given the lack of support that it received within the

[3] M. Saks, 'Removing the Blinkers? A Critique of Recent Contributions to the Sociology of Professions', *Sociological Review*, 31:1 (1983), 1–21.

[4] See F. Mann, *Acupuncture: The Ancient Chinese Art of Healing* (London: Heinemann, 1962), and L. Moss, *Acupuncture and You* (London: Paul Alek Books, 1964).

medical profession; acupuncture was not taught in medical schools, medical research into the subject was not officially funded, and the technique was barely mentioned in the leading medical journals of the day.

A small, but growing, number of acupuncturists outside the profession, though, had also begun using the procedure in its wide-ranging classical form, aimed at balancing out the polar forces of Yin and Yang in the body through the insertion of needles at strategic points along a series of channels known as meridians. These practitioners, who were mainly trained in such institutions as the newly founded College of Traditional Chinese Acupuncture and the British College of Acupuncture, faced even greater hostility from the medical profession than their orthodox counterparts. Acupuncture in the period up to the beginning of the 1970s, therefore, generally attracted the scorn of the medical profession, which considered it as being beyond the pale, both inside and outside its professional boundaries.[5]

Following the renewal of diplomatic relations with China in 1971, this response to acupuncture from the British medical profession rapidly became tinged with incredulity. Almost all of the attention given to this subject focused on the much publicized and dramatic use of 'acupuncture anaesthesia' in China which led several doctors—including Medical Research Council representatives—to visit the People's Republic in the early 1970s to witness its application in major surgical procedures.[6] Items began to appear on acupuncture in the mainstream medical journals in comparative profusion at this time with a particular focus on its employment in surgical analgesia and cases of severe pain.[7] At first medical practitioners and researchers either expressed complete disbelief or put forward rather dismissive psychological theories to account for its operation based on factors like hypnotism, cultural stoicism, and the placebo effect,[8]

[5] For an interesting reflection on this period see C. Ewart, *The Healing Needles: The Story of Acupuncture and Its Pioneer Practitioner, Dr Louis Moss* (London: Elm Tree Books, 1972).

[6] See, for example, I. Capperauld, E. Cooper, and D. Saltoun, 'Acupuncture Anaesthesia in China', *Lancet* (25 Jan. 1972), 1136.

[7] A. J. Webster, 'Scientific Controversy and Socio-Cognitive Metonomy: The Case of Acupuncture', in R. Wallis (ed.), *On the Margins of Science*, Sociological Review Monograph No. 27 (University of Keele, Keele, 1979), 121–38.

[8] See, for instance, P. Wall, 'An Eye on the Needle', *New Scientist* (20 July 1972), 129–31; M. Ramsay, 'Anaesthesia by Acupuncture', Correspondence,

but gradually a range of legitimating neurophysiological explanations began to emerge—spanning from the 'gate control' theory
to the 'busy cortex' hypothesis.[9] Acupuncture in Britain at this
stage, though, was still little practised by doctors and a very long
way from receiving any substantial backing from the medical
establishment, either in terms of education or research.

At the same time, relationships were strained between the
medical profession and non-medically qualified acupuncture
practitioners who had an especially strong adherence to the
traditional theories of the technique that were seen in
orthodox professional circles as 'intuitive nonsense'.[10] The
antagonism was particularly marked between medical acupuncturists, who had begun to limit the scope of their practice,
and lay acupuncturists—with the former having major reservations about the ability of the latter to practise the method safely
and to achieve positive results.[11] Such reactions were reflective of
an era in which the General Medical Council continued to
prohibit the co-operation of doctors with unorthodox practitioners on ethical grounds. An understanding of this context
helps to explain why only a small minority of general practitioners
in the early 1970s approved of their patients receiving acupuncture treatment from lay therapists.[12]

Since the mid-1970s, though, there have been several changes
that have suggested a move towards the medical incorporation of
acupuncture. Significant growth has occurred, for instance, in the
use of acupuncture by doctors and such auxiliary personnel as
physiotherapists operating under their supervision, which has
been paralleled by the rapid expansion of short training courses
in this subject for orthodox health care practitioners.[13] Research
into the mechanism and effects of acupuncture has also been

British Medical Journal (27 Jan. 1973), 233; and R. MacIntosh, 'Tests of
Acupuncture', Correspondence, *British Medical Journal* (25 Aug. 1973), 454–5.

[9] See respectively F. Mann, D. Bowsher, J. Mumford, S. Lipton, and J. Miles,
'Treatment of Intractable Pain by Acupuncture', *Lancet* (14 July 1973), 57–60, and
G. Bull, 'Acupuncture Anaesthesia', *Lancet* (25 Aug. 1973), 417–18.

[10] 'Tests of Acupuncture', *British Medical Journal* (2 June 1973), 502.

[11] This is illustrated by F. Mann, *Acupuncture: Cure of Many Diseases* (London:
Pan Books, 1973).

[12] Consumers Association, 'Acupuncture', *Which?* (Feb. 1972), 49–51.

[13] See G. T. Lewith, 'Acupuncture and Transcutaneous Nerve Stimulation', in
id. (ed.), *Alternative Therapies: A Guide to Complementary Medicine for the Health
Professional* (London: Heinemann, 1985), 1–56.

proceeding apace, some of which has been supported through small occasional grants from official bodies like the Medical Research Council and the Department of Health and Social Security, with the results published in such major medical journals as the *British Medical Journal* and the *Lancet*.[14] Survey evidence meanwhile shows that the interest of grass-root members of the medical profession in acupuncture and other forms of alternative medicine has been rising.[15] It is revealing to note here that the membership of the reformed British Medical Acupuncture Society, which was established in 1980 to promote the use and scientific understanding of acupuncture amongst medical practitioners, has developed from an initial figure of around fifty to almost 700 doctors today—in addition to a similar number of general practitioners and hospital specialists outside the Society who are now also believed to practise the method regularly in Britain.[16]

However, it should be emphasized that despite moves by the medical profession in this country to incorporate acupuncture into its repertoire, this procedure has not yet completely emerged from the shadow of marginality in British medicine. Research into acupuncture remains grossly undersupported by medically dominated research bodies in both the public and private sector—notwithstanding the fact that the Government has recently broken the funding mould by giving a small amount of grant aid to the Research Council for Complementary Medicine.[17] Acupuncture is also still not routinely taught in medical schools at undergraduate or postgraduate level and official financial subsidies for registered health personnel taking well-regarded privately run courses on this subject are by no means guaranteed.[18] Moreover, while there is no shortage of demand

[14] See, for instance, D. Stewart, J. Thomson, and I. Oswald, 'Acupuncture Analgesia: An Experimental Investigation', *British Medical Journal* (8 Jan. 1977), 67–70, and V. Clement-Jones, P. Lowry, L. McLoughlin, G. Besser, L. Rees, and H. Wen, 'Acupuncture in Heroin Addicts: Changes in Met-Enkephalin and β-Endorphin in Blood and Cerebrospinal Fluid', *Lancet* (25 Aug. 1979), 380–2.
[15] This is indicated by, for example, R. West and B. Inglis, 'Taking the Alternative Road to Health', *The Times* (13 Mar. 1985).
[16] S. Hayhoe, 'Editorial', *Acupuncture in Medicine*, 7:1 (1990), 1.
[17] R. Thomas, 'Surprise £60,000 Grant to RCCM', *Journal of Alternative and Complementary Medicine* (Nov. 1988), 11.
[18] W. Stephens, 'Consultant Attitudes to Acupuncture in a District General Hospital', *Acupuncture in Medicine*, 6:1 (1989), 20–3.

from doctors for such courses,[19] the number of practising medical acupuncturists in contemporary Britain only represents a tiny fraction of the total complement of doctors in this country. This highlights the generally restricted medical application of acupuncture—which is further accentuated by the fact that, although some doctors now apply this technique more broadly to, amongst other things, treating addictions[20] and suppressing nausea following anaesthesia and chemotherapy,[21] the predominant focus is on the alleviation of pain. The justification for employing acupuncture in this limited role in pain clinics and other settings is to be found in fashionable orthodox medical theories about the part played by the release of endorphins and other neuroactive substances in producing analgesia.[22] These are usually seen as being superior to the traditional Oriental rationale for the method that continues to be rejected as being unscientific and irrational.[23]

It should be stressed too that, despite the thawing of hostile medical attitudes towards the restricted use of acupuncture within the profession in recent years, the negative response of the medical establishment has been maintained towards non-medically qualified practitioners of this procedure who still characteristically employ the method for conditions as far flung as allergies and angina on the basis of its classical Yin–Yang philosophy. Although some doctors have been willing to refer their patients to these practitioners following the relaxation of the restrictions by the General Medical Council on such activity,[24] non-medical acupuncturists continue to be largely

---

[19] See D. T. Reilly, 'Young Doctors' Views on Alternative Medicine', *British Medical Journal* (30 July 1983), 337–9, and R. Wharton and G. Lewith, 'Complementary Medicine and the General Practitioner', *British Medical Journal* (7 June 1986), 1498–1500.

[20] A. Macdonald, *Acupuncture: From Ancient Art to Modern Medicine* (London: Allen and Unwin, 1982).

[21] J. Dundee, 'Acupuncture/Acupressure as an Antiemetic: Studies of Its Use in Postoperative Vomiting, Cancer Chemotherapy and Sickness of Early Pregnancy', *Complementary Medical Research*, 3:1 (1988), 2–14.

[22] S. Lipton, 'Acupuncture for Pain Relief', *Acupuncture in Medicine*, 5:2 (1988), 26–8.

[23] See British Medical Association, *Report of the Board of Science and Education on Alternative Therapy* (London: British Medical Association, 1986).

[24] This can be illustrated with reference to P. A. Nicholls and J. E. Luton, 'Doctors and Complementary Medicine: A Survey of General Practitioners in the Potteries', Occasional Paper No. 2, Department of Sociology, North Staffordshire Polytechnic, 1986.

held at a distance as regards collaboration in research and practice and are frequently associated in the medical literature with causing dangerous side-effects in their patients, such as hepatitis and collapsed lungs.[25]

The attack on lay acupuncturists has been made particularly forcefully by members of the British Medical Acupuncture Society, who have not only opposed the inclusion of acupuncturists who lack medical qualifications in the National Health Service, but also strongly cautioned against patients seeking treatment from, or being referred to, such practitioners.[26] In spite of this, the numbers of non-medical acupuncturists has continued to grow, with around 800 alone in practice in the late 1980s in the four major lay acupuncture organizations—the British Acupuncture Association and Register, the Traditional Acupuncture Society, the International Register of Oriental Medicine, and the Register of Traditional Chinese Medicine— which together now form the Council for Acupuncture.[27]

EXPLAINING THE MEDICAL REJECTION OF ACUPUNCTURE

This raises the question of how the aforementioned patterns of response by the British medical profession to acupuncture are to be explained. In relation to the overwhelmingly negative reception given to this method in the period immediately preceding the mid-1970s, it is important to note at the outset that the political leverage exerted by the pharmaceutical and medical equipment companies to protect their profits does not seem to have been of major significance in shaping the line taken by the medical profession. Whilst such companies most certainly do control extensive resources—including the large sums spent on advertising their wares and sponsoring medical research—it is all

---

[25] This is witnessed by, for instance, 'Acupuncture-Related Hepatitis in the West Midlands in 1977', *British Medical Journal* (17 Dec. 1977), 1610, and 'Pneumothorax after Acupuncture', *British Medical Journal* (26 Aug. 1978), 602–3.

[26] See 'Acupuncturists', Hansard (House of Commons), 16 Dec. 1977, cols. 1174–85; 'Acupuncture and AIDS', *Lancet* (30 May 1987), 1275; and A. Grant, 'Curb Non-Medical Acupuncturists', Letters, *Journal of Alternative and Complementary Medicine* (Oct. 1987), 8.

[27] Personal communication from Maura Shifrin, Secretary to the Council for Acupuncture, 1 Sept. 1987.

too easy to overstate their influence on the profession and ignore their diverse production policies which make them potential future beneficiaries of any substantial expansion in the use of acupuncture, especially if developed in a manner compatible with orthodox medicine.[28] In the light too of the long acknowledged domination by the medical profession of both local and national health care decision-making structures,[29] there seems little doubt that the profession is the group that must assume direct responsibility for establishing the blanket climate of rejection of acupuncture before the mid-1970s in Britain. In this respect, its power seems to have been employed at two broad levels—by the medical élite, consisting mainly of leading members of the Royal Colleges and the British Medical Association, against deviant insiders, and by the medical profession as a relatively cohesive whole, against external, lay practitioners of acupuncture. The effectiveness of the deployment of this power, moreover, seems to have been enhanced by the splits between the various acupuncture organizations in existence at this time, centred on their differing approaches to practice in this area.[30]

Why then should the profession have acted in the way that it did? Its initial resistance in this period could not have been primarily due to a lack of knowledge about acupuncture, for even in the 1960s the method had a number of committed advocates and influential patrons, as well as a definite profile in the international medical literature and the mass media—which played an important part in building up a substantial public demand for acupuncture treatment even before the historic visit of President Nixon to China in the early 1970s.[31] Nor could its response be said to be related to a lack of therapeutic promise as regards either pain or certain other, more broadly defined, conditions,[32] particularly when set against the shortcomings of conventional medicine, with its inability to cope with many of the chronic and degenerative complaints of the increasing

[28] M. Saks, 'Power, Politics and Alternative Medicine', *Talking Politics*, 3:2 (Winter 1990/1), 68–72.

[29] M. Saks, 'The Politics of Health Care', in L. Robins (ed.), *Politics and Policy-Making in Britain* (London: Longman, 1987), 52–69.

[30] S. J. Fulder and R. Monro, *The Status of Complementary Medicine in the United Kingdom* (London: Threshold Foundation, 1982).

[31] B. Inglis, *Fringe Medicine* (London: Faber and Faber, 1964).

[32] See, for instance, Mann, *Acupuncture: Cure of Many Diseases*.

middle-aged and elderly population, and growing evidence of the damage caused by the routine application of orthodox procedures.[33] These comparisons also make explanations based on considerations of safety recede into relative insignificance—for while accidents have occurred in rare cases of acupuncture treatment, most trained non-medically qualified acupuncturists even in the period up to the mid-1970s could have been expected to have had a rudimentary grounding in anatomy and physiology as well as sterilization techniques. This latter point also limits the viability of accounts centred on the dangers of 'quackery' in a field in which non-medical acupuncturists in organized associations have increasingly established stringent codes regulating their behaviour in recent years.[34] Nor can cost seriously explain the resistance of the medical profession to acupuncture either before or after the mid-1970s, given its comparative cheapness in relation to the huge amounts of money currently spent on high-technology and drug-based medicine in Britain.[35]

It might be argued, however, that the holistic Oriental philosophy with which acupuncture has traditionally been associated has created problems for the profession in accepting the procedure, in so far as it clashes with the main principles of Western medicine, and generates difficulties in conducting the controlled trials of the method which have become the main orthodox touchstone in gauging therapeutic effectiveness. But although the classical view of the *modus operandi* of acupuncture does conflict in certain respects with the mechanistic, biomedical approach of British medical orthodoxy, this has not stopped the two philosophies from operating side by side in the Chinese health care system, nor blocked the development of Western medical explanations of acupuncture in the period up to the mid-1970s and beyond.[36] Similarly, difficulties with controlled trials do not appear to have been a significant obstacle to its acceptance

[33] R. C. R. Taylor, 'Alternative Medicine and the Medical Encounter in Britain and the United States', in J. W. Salmon (ed.), *Alternative Medicines: Popular and Policy Perspectives* (London: Tavistock, 1985), 191–228.

[34] See, for example, Council for Acupuncture, *A Code of Practice* (1987).

[35] See B. Griffith, S. Iliffe, and G. Rayner, *Banking on Sickness: Commercial Medicine in Britain and the USA* (London: Lawrence and Wishart, 1987).

[36] M. M. Rosenthal, 'Political Process and the Integration of Traditional and Western Medicine in the People's Republic of China', *Social Science and Medicine*, 15A (1981), 599–613.

given the intense philosophical debates about whether or not these are the most appropriate means of assessing the efficacy of modern medicine and the fact that many orthodox health care procedures (such as surgery and physiotherapy) have not yet been firmly substantiated using such an approach.[37] The traditional philosophy underpinning acupuncture, moreover, has not prevented doctors from transforming what was originally conceived as a method tailored to the needs of the individual patient into the more routinized application of 'formula acupuncture' to specified clinical conditions—which not only fitted in with the profession's self-proclaimed 'scientific' methodology, but also enabled acupuncture to be readily adopted by orthodoxy in relative abstraction from its ancient Chinese roots.[38]

But if none of the reasons so far considered for the negative reception of acupuncture by the British medical profession in the years before the mid-1970s is ultimately very convincing, the response to acupuncture at this time does appear to be largely explicable in terms of professional self-interests—inasmuch as the benefits to the profession of pursuing a strategy of rejection far outweighed the costs. This is certainly true of its aggressive stance towards lay acupuncture, for the typical subscription of non-medically qualified practitioners to traditional theories of acupuncture challenged the esoteric biomedical knowledge claims underpinning the status and power of the profession. At the same time, if they did not oppose the development of lay acupuncture, members of the medical profession in private practice stood to lose out financially from the economic competition that its practitioners provided across a range of specialisms as a result of their use of the method as a broad-ranging therapy outside the National Health Service.

Although the threat to the interests of the medical profession was not very great at this stage, as the numbers of lay acupuncturists in practice in the first half of the 1970s was still comparatively modest,[39] this was a period when the numbers of

[37] E. Hemminki, 'Problems of Clinical Trials as Evidence of Therapeutic Effectiveness', *Social Science and Medicine*, 16 (1982), 711–12.

[38] See P. H. Richardson and C. A. Vincent, 'Acupuncture for the Treatment of Pain: A Review of Evaluative Research', *Pain*, 24 (1986), 15–40.

[39] By the mid-1970s, for example, there were just over one hundred practising acupuncturists in the British Acupuncture Association—one of the leading non-

non-medical acupuncture organizations and their members were growing in parallel with other alternative therapies, against a backcloth of progressively spiralling levels of public and political support.[40] This context, together with the fact that such therapists seemed to have little desire to follow the path of groups like physiotherapists and radiographers by being incorporated into orthodoxy as subordinate professions allied to medicine,[41] goes a long way towards explaining why the response of the medical profession to lay acupuncturists was so icy at this time.

This is not to say that there were no advantages to be derived by doctors from the escalating numbers of lay acupuncturists and other alternative therapists in these years, not least because they undoubtedly eased some of the pressure on medical services from patients suffering from chronic conditions for whom orthodox medicine could do very little.[42] But it does seem, on balance, that the climate of rejection established in relation to outsiders before the mid-1970s was in the interests of the medical profession as a whole. The overall benefit of this action, though, was perhaps most apparent in the case of the small cluster of medical acupuncturists who were most threatened by lay practitioners of the technique. The sensitivity of their position is highlighted by the fact that non-medically qualified acupuncturists not only frequently had a longer training in, and deeper classical understanding of, acupuncture, but also cast doubt on their professional respectability and challenged the private fee income on which most of their practices were based.

However, as has been indicated, medical acupuncturists were themselves under siege within the profession—most conspicuously from the medical élite. The marginal position in which they found themselves also appears to be best explained in terms of professional self-interests. In this respect, such deviant practitioners can be seen as endangering the interests of those at the

medical acupuncture bodies at this time. Acupuncture Association, *Register and Year Book* (1975).

[40] B. Inglis, *Natural Medicine* (London: Fontana/Collins, 1980).

[41] G. V. Larkin, *Occupational Monopoly and Modern Medicine* (London: Tavistock, 1983).

[42] P. Strong, 'Sociological Imperialism and the Profession of Medicine: A Critical Examination of the Thesis of Medical Imperialism', *Social Science and Medicine*, 13A (1979), 199–215.

apex of the medical hierarchy, especially before the 1970s when they had a firmer commitment to the traditional, wide-ranging application of acupuncture favoured by the expanding numbers of acupuncturists operating outside the profession. This arguably reinforced the challenge to the knowledge base underlying the dominant position of the profession in general and the more highly rewarded medical élite in particular. From the viewpoint of this élite, the threat was heightened by the fact that medical acupuncturists at this juncture were mainly drawn from the less prestigious ranks of general practitioners, for whom acupuncture represented a rare window of private market opportunity. In this light, it is easy to understand why some leading consultants at this time seemed extremely reluctant to refer even last resort cases to medical acupuncturists operating in this field—not to mention to their lay counterparts.[43]

THE MOVE TOWARDS THE MEDICAL INCORPORATION OF ACUPUNCTURE

This still leaves open, though, the question of why there should have been a slow, but increasing shift towards the medical incorporation of acupuncture, despite the persisting marginality of the method, in the years following the mid-1970s in Britain. The fact that since this earlier period the shortcomings of modern medicine have become even more starkly apparent and Western convictions have grown about the efficacy of acupuncture suggests that this turn-around may have been a function of a more enlightened response from the medical profession, which undoubtedly continues to exercise a large degree of independent responsibility for determining policy in this area. However, this explanation does not entirely square with the selective nature of the trend towards incorporation. As such, the concept of professional self-interests may still provide the explanatory key to unravelling the changes in the medical reception of acupuncture in the contemporary era.

A crucial starting-point here lies in examining the continuing attack by the medical profession on lay acupuncturists in this country. This is not consistent with a more benevolent inter-

---

[43] Saks, *Professions and the Public Interest.*

pretation of events, especially given the recent tightening up of the standards of trained acupuncturists in organized associations outside the medical profession. Any remaining notion of the profession protecting the public from 'quacks' is further attenuated by the high proportion of consultations with non-medical acupuncturists and other alternative therapists that occur after unsuccessful conventional medical treatment.[44] Taken together with the persisting commitment of most lay therapists to holistic theories that conflict with the mechanistic philosophical basis of modern medicine, an explanation centred on self-interest seems more plausible to account for the hostile medical response to lay acupuncture in the latter half of the 1970s and the 1980s.

The case for explaining the continuing hostility of the British medical profession towards acupuncturists who operate outside the orthodox health care professions in these terms is greatly strengthened, moreover, by the ever-increasing public demand for not only lay acupuncturists, who form one of the largest and fastest expanding groups in the alternative health care sector, but also other non-medically qualified alternative practitioners— whose numbers are now estimated to run into tens of thousands in Britain alone.[45] Placing lay acupuncturists within this broader frame of reference emphasizes the challenge that they currently pose to the profession, a challenge which is amplified by the gradual decline of many of the previously deeply enshrined and politically damaging rifts between the dozens of associations into which alternative therapists are divided. The specific formation in 1980 of the Council for Acupuncture which brings together the major non-medical acupuncture organizations in this country has already been mentioned. The move towards greater unification in acupuncture, however, has since been paralleled at a national level by the formal launch in 1985 of the Council for Complementary and Alternative Medicine which aims to represent the interests of, and increase communication between, a more varied range of organizations of unorthodox therapists, and the establishment in 1989 of a National Consultative Council

---

[44] See, for example, Consumers Association, *Which?* (Aug. 1981), 473–7.
[45] S. J. Fulder, *The Handbook of Complementary Medicine* (Oxford: Oxford University Press, 2nd edn., 1988).

for alternative therapies intended to give an even greater sense of unity, direction, and co-ordination to this sector.[46]

All this needs to be seen in conjunction with the strong all-party political support that Members of Parliament are now providing for the alternative medicine lobby in this country, which has raised the hopes of medically unqualified exponents of acupuncture that they may eventually gain some form of official recognition on more favourable terms than groups like the professions supplementary to medicine.[47] If this were to happen the floodgates could well open, leaving the medical profession to face greater competition from lay acupuncturists and other unorthodox therapists in the increasingly contested area of private practice, as well as encroachment on its legal monopoly in the National Health Service which is still much prized despite the drift away from an overarching commitment to state involvement in health care in the Thatcher era.[48] Given this very real threat to the status, power, and income of the medical profession, its current generally negative stance towards lay practitioners in fields such as acupuncture appears to be even more compatible with professional self-interests than in the period before the mid-1970s.

This conclusion, of course, again particularly applies to the interests of the sharply rising number of medical acupuncturists in Britain over the past decade in relation to the mounting challenge from without. This challenge comes at a time when the vulnerability of medical acupuncturists to attack has been augmented by the fact that their main credentials in acupuncture are now more than ever often simply that they have attended one of a growing profusion of short courses for doctors in this subject—the adequacy of which has been questioned compared to the lengthier, and more detailed, programmes undertaken by many of the rapidly expanding band of non-medically qualified acupuncture practitioners.[49]

It is argued here that the same pressures that have resulted in

[46] Saks, 'Power, Politics and Alternative Medicine'.

[47] See, for instance, B. Griggs, 'Well on the Road to Alternative Health', *Observer* (3 Mar. 1985).

[48] J. Higgins, *The Business of Medicine: Private Health Care in Britain* (London: Macmillan, 1988).

[49] For a number of such recent attacks see 'You Give Us the Needle Dr Grant!', *Journal of Alternative and Complementary Medicine*, Letters (May 1988), 6–8.

the maintenance of the negative response to lay acupuncturists and other unorthodox practitioners in the period since the mid-1970s, also help to explain the increasingly incorporationist stance taken by the medical élite towards insiders who practise acupuncture. Admittedly, medical acupuncturists—who are now more frequently drawn from hospital specialists as well as general practitioners[50]—can be seen to threaten in a more substantial manner the position of doctors engaged in conventional practices, both directly and through the potential legitimation of the competing activities of alternative practitioners outside the profession. But these costs seem to be outweighed by the benefits from the standpoint of professional self-interests, especially in light of the terms on which the method has been incorporated into orthodox medicine.

These terms are worth exploring further. As has been seen, the medical establishment has not supported the employment of acupuncture in its traditional form, but only primarily as a limited means of dealing with pain, legitimated by orthodox neurophysiological explanations. This serves to contain the threat within the profession by restricting the medical areas under challenge. Moreover, some protection is also available to those segments of the profession operating in such exposed areas. Even anaesthetists not employing the technique in surgical procedures are relatively well insulated from attack because the practical capabilities of acupuncture in this specialism do not, in most cases, appear to be as great as conventional methods.[51] And in its more promising application to painful conditions, the medical use of acupuncture seems more likely to enhance, rather than reduce, the standing of doctors in view of the crisis of credibility that the profession faces as a result of its frequent failure to offer even basic relief for the chronic pain associated with such common complaints as back injuries, arthritis, and rheumatism.[52] At the same time, it is also significant that acupuncture has not been fully included in undergraduate medical education or mainstream medical research programmes and that the relevance of the classical theoretical underpinnings of the

---

[50] V. Camp, 'Acupuncture in the NHS', *Acupuncture in Medicine*, 3:1 (1986), 4–5.

[51] Webster, 'Scientific Controversy and Socio-Cognitive Metonomy'.

[52] Taylor, 'Alternative Medicine and the Medical Encounter'.

method has been subverted by the insistence that the knowledge required for practice can be obtained through a brief period of training in this subject firmly situated within the orthodox medical tradition. From the standpoint of professional self-interests, this both gives minimal encouragement to non-medical acupuncturists and clearly marks out the field as being ripe for medical colonization—either directly by members of the medical profession or through a process of delegation to subordinate groups within the orthodox health care division of labour—against a backcloth of growing public demand.

Professional self-interests appear therefore to lie behind not only the negative response of the medical profession to lay acupuncturists, but also the limited trend towards the medical incorporation of acupuncture in the latter half of the 1970s and 1980s in Britain—particularly in view of the increasing challenge to the profession from the range of unorthodox practitioners from without. This perhaps explains why even the recent British Medical Association Report, which was generally quite un-complimentary about alternative therapies, saw some merit in the restricted medical usage of acupuncture[53]—which stands in sharp contrast to the predominant climate of rejection of the method established by the medical profession in the era before the mid-1970s. Herein lies the paradox of the contemporary medical incorporation of acupuncture; the form of the medical response to this procedure has significantly changed, while the motive force of professional self-interest underlying this shift of position seems to have remained. Only time will tell whether or not this strategy will help to hold back the challenge to the profession from alternative therapists in general and lay acu-puncturists in particular. But the possession of such chameleon-like qualities is certainly one of the reasons why the medical profession has been so successful to date in defending its interests against competitors in the arena of alternative medicine.

[53] British Medical Association, *Report of the Board of Science and Education on Alternative Therapy.*

PART IV

ALTERNATIVE MEDICINE:
THE FUTURE

15

Alternative Medicine: Prospects and Speculations

Ruth West

Alternative medicine is witnessing a scene that a few years ago it would not have dreamed of. It has the favour of the media, the public voting for it with its feet, and the medical profession taking note of its existence. It is even gaining enough of a voice to begin asking questions about taking up its rightful place within the country's health care system. However, for those practitioners who remember the earlier years, when they were all but back street operators and the mention of their names was anathema to doctors, this new-found acceptance is regarded warily. The sight of the British Medical Association's juggernaut hurtling after them lurks in their mind's eye.

It was only in the 1960s that the practice of alternative medicine was labelled 'fringe medicine'. Meant in a kindly way by those who coined the term—it was around the time of the Edinburgh Fringe—the association with 'lunatic fringe' was perhaps a little too close for comfort. And so a more fashionable, though challenging, title was substituted—that of 'alternative medicine', after 'alternative London' and 'alternative life-styles'. Since then two other labels have been invented, both of which seek a more comfortable place alongside orthodox medicine. The World Health Organization has adopted the title 'traditional medicine'. This has worked well in developing countries, where the traditional healers and medicine men represent the indigenous non-Western medicine. But in 'developed' countries it has proved to be confusing as people have associated traditional with orthodox Western medicine and so wondered what all the fuss was about. The most recent title to be introduced is 'complementary medicine'. This has found currency with those who wish to make it clear that they are not doctor-bashers, but are wanting to achieve a partnership with orthodox medicine, each recognizing the need for the other.

WHAT IS 'ALTERNATIVE MEDICINE'?

effectiveness

If the choice of a title raised problems, then decisions as to what the title is meant to cover compounds them. There are two main options on offer. The first is to follow the World Health Organization and include all forms of health care provision that 'usually lie outside the official health sector' including formalized traditional systems of medicine such as Ayurveda, Unani, and traditional Chinese medicine; the practice of traditional healers, such as traditional birth attendants and medicine men; and the practice of biofeedback, chiropractic, naturopathy, osteopathy, homoeopathy, 'and even Christian Science'.[1]

safety

In the United Kingdom, such a categorization would mean the inclusion of about sixty therapies, which may be divided as follows. First, the physical therapies: these include naturopathy, herbal medicine, manipulative therapies (osteopathy, chiropractic, the Alexander technique, rolfing, and reflexology), Oriental therapies (shiatsu, acupressure), systems of medicine (acupuncture, homoeopathy, anthroposophical medicine), exercise/movement therapies (T'ai chi, yoga, dance) and sensory therapies (music, art, colour). Secondly, the psychological therapies: psychotherapy (analysis, hypnotherapy), humanistic psychology (*Gestalt*, transactional analysis, primal work, rebirthing, encounter . . . to name but a few), and transpersonal psychology. And lastly, paranormal therapies: healing (hand healing, exorcism, radionics, and the like) and paranormal diagnosis (palmistry, astrology, iridology).

training

A possible objection to this option is that it treats the alternatives rather like the contents of a dustbin, some of which are of value and may with luck be rescued, but the majority of which belong in the dustbin and should remain there. A second possibility is to divide the alternatives into two basic types: those that require a high degree of professional training and skill and those that are at heart variations on first aid, do-it-yourself, and self-care techniques. Osteopathy, chiropractic, medical herbalism, homoeopathy, naturopathy, and acupuncture would fit under the first category; and everything else, barring a few psychotherapies, under the second. Assuming for the moment that their

---

[1] R. H. Bannerman, J. Burton, and C. Wen-Chieh, *Traditional Medicine and Health-Care Coverage* (Geneva: World Health Organization, 1983), 292.

efficacy and safety could all be established, the first category could take its place alongside the medical profession, whilst the second category could join the ranks of the professions supplementary to medicine.

PROFESSIONAL AND PUBLIC ATTITUDES TO ALTERNATIVE MEDICINE

Judging from articles in the medical and scientific journals, attitudes within the medical profession are not changing. Their pages from time to time deride alternative medicine as 'the flight from science'; they have been known to compare chiropractic which goes beyond the 'treatment of bone and joint abnormalities' with the 'occult business of divination of the future by examination of a bird's entrails', and to put much of the survival of alternative medicine down to the 'needs of desperate patients for whom orthodox medicine has not succeeded'.[2] Small wonder that the recent action of the medical trade union, the British Medical Association . . . , raised such alarm and suspicion among alternative therapists. The Association seemed to be responding to the criticisms levelled at it by their President, Prince Charles, during his term of office;

I would suggest that the whole imposing edifice of modern medicine, for all its breath-taking success is, like the celebrated Tower of Pisa, slightly off balance . . .

Don't overestimate the 'sophisticated' approach to medicine. Please don't underestimate the importance of an awareness of what lies beneath the surface of the visible world and of those ancient unconscious forces which still shape the psychological attitudes of modern man . . . When it comes to helping people it seems to me that account has to be taken of those sometimes long-neglected complementary methods of medicine . . .

It was shortly after this second message that the British Medical Association announced that it had set up a Committee to investigate alternative therapies. The alternatives have good reason to worry about the outcome of this Committee's work.

---

[2] See, for example, 'The Flight from Science', *British Medical Journal* (5 Jan. 1980); 'Alternative Medicine Is No Alternative', *Lancet* (1 Oct. 1983), 773; 'Homoeopathy, Fact or Fiction?', *New Scientist* (22 Mar. 1984), 46.

They know all too well the sceptics' reaction to the success of their treatment. It can all be put down to a good bedside manner and/or the strength of the placebo effect: if you think something is going to work, no matter how hocus-pocus it is, then there is a 40 per cent chance it will. Of the former, Dr Tony Smith, writing in the *British Medical Journal*, has this to say: 'The patients are given time, courtesy and individual attention . . . which may relieve many of the symptoms of a chronic or terminal disease, but do nothing to arrest the disease process.'[3] Two alternative systems often cited as mere placebo are homoeopathy, in which any real effect is challenged on the grounds that it mostly uses medicines diluted to the extent that not one molecule of the original substance remains; and osteopathy, in which the effective treatment of anything except back-pain is ridiculed on the grounds that manipulating the spine could not conceivably cure such problems as headache. Moreover, scoff the sceptics, 'if patients are resorting to practices based upon the obsolescent relics of the prehistory of modern medicine', then 'this requires urgent attention'.

But this habit of linking orthodox medicine with modern, scientific ways of thinking and alternative medicine with pre-scientific thinking; of equating scientific with good, effective medicine, and anything else with irrational quackery, has been described as nothing more than an example of a doctor's trained incapacity to accept any medicine as legitimate beyond his own, so dominant has the modern medical profession become in the health care system of most societies. It belongs naturally with those who hold a monopoly position: and as Lowell Levin warns: 'there may be . . . sinister reasons for professional neglect of the lay resource in health. Bluntly stated, there may be some protecting of professional (for which, in many areas, read "financial") power preserves'.[4] While the pundits cling to their placebo theories, or argue the ethics of using or recommending the use of potentially dangerous treatments for their patients, a growing proportion of their customers, it seems, are expressing doubts and criticisms regarding the value of *orthodox* medical care. Taylor Nelson Medical is a marketing research company that has

[3] 'Alternative Medicine', *British Medical Journal* (30 July 1983), 307.
[4] L. S. Levin, 'Self-Care in Health: Potentials and Pitfalls', *World Health Forum*, 2:2 (1981), 177–84.

been monitoring changes in attitude to doctors, medicine, and health over the past ten years. In 1978, 52 per cent of the population said that they trusted the doctor to know what they needed; this fell to 39 per cent in 1980, when 22 per cent also confessed to having less faith in doctors than they used to. General practice consultations have also been declining since 1978.

THE RISE OF ALTERNATIVE MEDICINE

A survey carried out in 1980 on behalf of the Threshold Foundation found that the number of alternative medicine consultations was increasing at the rate of 10–15 per cent per year; and the estimates for the numbers of practitioners and consultations showed that alternative medicine is growing five times as rapidly as orthodox medicine.[5]

The reasons for these changes can, in the main, only be guessed at. A survey, carried out by *Which?* in 1981, revealed that two-thirds of those who had received alternative medicine treatment during the last five years said that they had been having treatment with conventional medicine, but that it was not helping or they did not like it—because of side-effects, for example.[6] The increasing hazards to health of taking modern drugs must be contributing significantly to the trend away from conventional medicine. It has been estimated that two out of every five patients taking prescribed drugs are likely to suffer from side-effects of the drug; some drugs also produce dependence; and then there are the problems created by interactions between the drugs a patient may be taking. It is also becoming evident that there is a serious mismatch between health care provisions and real needs. Modern medicine is hospital based, yet the vast majority of medical problems do not require hospital care. In any one month, a recent study has shown, out of 1,000 adults, 750 will develop a symptom of some kind; 250 of these will go to their general practitioner; ten will be referred to hospital; and only one will be admitted. The World Health Organization (Europe) is in fact now suggesting that the centralized notion of

---

[5] S. J. Fulder and R. Monro, *The Status of Complementary Medicine in the United Kingdom* (London: Threshold Foundation, 1981).

[6] Consumers Association, 'Alternative Medicine', *Which?* (Aug. 1981).

medical care, based on the large, expensive, industry-modelled, high-technology hospital, 'providing leadership, controlling other levels and generally exercising the main responsibility for the entire spectrum of patient care' is misconceived. Perhaps what is needed are 'services . . . [to be] provided using the lowest necessary level of care, as close to the community as possible. In this perspective, the starting point for health services is the people themselves and their families, with primary health care personnel providing the necessary professional care.'[7]

While the medical world awaits its reorganization, alternative medicine takes up the slack—as is witnessed by the growing transfer of allegiance from the doctor's surgery to the alternative medicine clinic and practitioner.

Reports, such as they are, on the outcome of treatment are favourable. Government Commissions of Inquiry, and Consumer Association surveys, all provide evidence in support of the alternatives: New Zealand (on chiropractic), Australia, and The Netherlands (on a range of alternatives in practice) have all reported favourably; the consumer magazine *Which?* found that nine out of every ten people surveyed said that they would use again the form of alternative they had tried and only 10 per cent felt that the treatment had been useless. The pattern seems to be that people's first use of alternative medicine is as a last resort; but then they stay and use it again, but this time as a first choice if there is a recurrence of the problem; then gradually begin to substitute it for orthodox medicine to supply their primary health care needs—their osteopath or acupuncturist, for example, taking the place of their general practitioner. One per cent of the United Kingdom population, Taylor Nelson Medical finds, now say that they use an acupuncturist; 2 per cent go to homoeopathic physicians; and, in terms of self-care, 3 per cent are practising meditation, 7 per cent use natural medicine, and 16 per cent buy health foods.

THE FUTURE

Increasingly, alternative practitioners are worrying that such progress is not enough. Although the majority feel that it would

[7] From a document submitted for discussion by the World Health Organization Regional Committee for Europe at its 33rd session in Madrid in Sept. 1983.

injure their practice to be brought into the National Health Service (because of constraints on time and freedom to practise as they see fit, unsupervised by doctors), there is a growing sense of urgency to secure some formal recognition by Act of Parliament. But just how, and for whom, is difficult to sort out.

For many reasons, it might be best to leave things as they are: everyone practising what they want, providing that they do not claim to be a doctor or to treat certain diseases. But there is a threat from orthodoxy. Already the medical acupuncturists are pressing to be the only group able to practise acupuncture, and if the trend by young doctors to learn an alternative therapy continues, then the worry is that the alternatives that appeal to the doctors will be medicalized. They will be learnt as extra techniques on weekend courses, the monopoly will thus reassert itself, and all lay practitioners will be outlawed. The emergence, in September 1983, of a new association for doctors, the British Holistic Medical Association, which includes in its statement of principles that the holistic practitioner will be 'willing to use . . . an expanded range of interventions' to include 'acupuncture, counselling, dietary advice, exercise, osteopathy and meditative techniques' has certainly added to this concern.

If one looks for encouragement to other countries to see how they are legislating for alternative health care, then the situation is fairly bleak. There are only two countries which have managed truly to integrate Western orthodox medicine with other systems; these are China and Nepal. Certain other developing countries (mainly in South Asia) have legalized alternative medicine to the extent that it is allowed to coexist with orthodox medicine. But the rest of the world, on the whole, legislates only for the practice of orthodox medicine. And this, alternative medicine's detractors would argue, is right and proper. Alternative medicine should only receive official recognition if it is able to gain its laurels in the same way as any orthodox branch of medicine—by laboratory work with *in vitro* or animal experiments, followed by a double-blind, controlled trial (to eliminate any possible placebo effect).

Alternative medicine feels caught in a cleft stick. In order to survive, it needs research to demonstrate its efficacy. But many practitioners object to animal experimentation and all are adamant that the above methods are not suited to them. Those therapies, for example, that involve touching the patient claim that technique and therapist, like the song and the singer, cannot be separated. So a blind, controlled trial of osteopathy would mean that one person simulates the manipulation in order to compare manipulation with no manipulation for a particular disorder. The fact that the osteopaths say you cannot pull the wool over people's eyes in this way, and that they have an alternative research design that they believe to be acceptable to both parties, leaves the funding bodies unconvinced. And so the research is not done. Similar problems are raised with acupuncture, in which the individual acupuncturist's taking of the patient's pulses and putting in the needles are essential parts of the treatment; and with reflexology, where the practitioner, rubbing the feet and talking to the patient, does not divide his technique from his art.

Left to orthodox research, the prospects for alternative medicine are exceedingly gloomy. Given the present state of affairs, the following is all that can be accepted as valid medicine: acupuncture analgesia (because it is now 'known' that it causes the brain to produce endorphins—natural morphine-like substances); certain medicines based on extractions from plants; certain vitamins for the treatment of specific deficiency diseases; and manipulation for back-pain, if the criterion for success is a speedier return of the sufferer to work, i.e. it is more economical as a treatment than orthodox medicine. Yet there are some (small, vaguely perceptible) signs of change. For example, a research group at Harvard Medical School has established that there is a very real physiological response that is evoked in the body by relaxation techniques that encourage the body's own self-healing forces. This helps unravel the mechanisms of meditation, for example, and it may be a means of understanding the gift of healing that some people claim to possess.

In the meantime, whatever may be surmised about the success of the alternatives, in one particular respect they are being acknowledged as having the edge on orthodox medicine—in that they recognize that most diseases afflicting Western nations today are psychological, not organic, in origin. In fact, many alternative practitioners would say that the service they are providing, rather than covering the gaps left by orthodoxy's inadequacies, is a new, or rediscovered, holistic medicine. Instead of concentrating on illness, they look at the person who is ill and ask *why* they have become susceptible to disease. 'Organic illness is what we say we cure but don't', the maverick F. G. Crookshank wrote half a century ago. 'Functional disease is what the quacks cure and we wish we could.' Instead of looking for magical cures, alternative practitioners expect patients to collaborate in their treatment by making changes in their life-style. It is, after all, nearly a quarter of a century since René Dubos concluded that the improvements that had taken place in people's health had been brought about not, as we assumed, by medicine, but by improved standards of nutrition and sanitation. Furthermore, today's diseases, says Thomas McKeown, are the 'result of behavioural and environmental changes associated with industrialisation'. For McKeown the shape of things to come depends upon public action and modification of behaviour. In the present circumstances, any sensible foetus should take the following advice. He will:

come about as near to immortality as human genes permit by electing to become the wife of a rural clergyman; well-to-do but living frugally; fertile but with few children; physically active but avoiding field sports, especially hunting; taking no drugs, alcohol or tobacco; and keeping to a diet low in salt, fat, sugar and meat, and so rich in fruit, vegetables and grains that the addition of bran would be an indulgence.[8]

Some alternative therapies have already established their usefulness within a society afflicted by 'psychosocial disease'. But whether alternative medicine will grow as a genuine alternative is difficult to say. At the moment, the amount of attention it is receiving is way out of proportion to its actual size. In the United Kingdom today, there are only 2,000 practitioners in some form of professional organization compared with 30,000 general medical practitioners. It could just be that members of the public are clinging to any bit of driftwood for help as orthodoxy sinks— or whilst waiting for the official rescue party. This would fit in with the finding that, apart from the purchase of health foods, which is a middle-class preoccupation, the use of alternative medicine is spread evenly across the population.

A perhaps more appealing interpretation is one that sees its popularity as a sign of a wider social change that is taking place. The pendulum is swinging—away from dependence on experts

---

[8] T. McKeown, 'A Basis for Health Strategies: A Classification of Disease', *British Medical Journal* (27 Aug. 1983), 287.

and specialists, towards more consumer participation and self-reliance. Alternative medicine is just one way of exercising a belief in the importance of the democratization of life as witnessed by the growth in self-help groups.

However, looking to the year 2000, there are three possible futures in which alternative medicine may have a place. In one, we continue much as we are. The economy survives; material well-being is maintained; and the health services are extended, modified, and improved to cope with an increasing population that is weighted towards old age. In a second, disaster strikes, and we are in a life-boat economy. Alternative medicine takes up a 'barefoot doctor' role in the struggle to provide any kind of health care. In the third, society is transformed. People change from being 'outer-directed', looking for the achievement of material goals, to becoming self-explorers, seeing inner growth as the way forward. Alternative medicine takes its place as a resource for self-care, leading to health, well-being, and personal development. Now this, according to the experts, is not such a far-fetched vision of the future.

16

Report on Alternative Medicine

British Medical Association

The Board of Science and Education [of the British Medical Association] set up the Working Party on Alternative Therapy in 1983 in order to examine the claims made for therapies advocated as alternatives to modern medicine. It was believed that enquiry into their nature and clinical evaluation of their methods was needed to discover whether potentially valuable methods of treatment were being overlooked. In addition, it was thought important to detect whether false claims were being made.

At a preliminary stage the terms of reference were clarified to read as follows:

To consider the feasibility and possible methods of assessing the value of alternative therapies, whether used alone or to complement other treatments and to report on the evidence received to the Board of Science and Education.

Accordingly, it is the purpose of this discussion and review to identify where the most important of the points of difference lie, the implications for those who seek treatment for their ills, and their relevance to the evaluation of the success of treatment.

ORTHODOX MEDICINE AS A SCIENTIFIC DISCIPLINE

Though some of the barriers which exist between approaches to 'orthodox medicine' and 'alternative therapy' are more a matter of terminology and understanding than substance, there is one fundamental and consistent strand to the argument which creates a division consistently separating medical orthodoxy from alternative approaches.

This is that the work and approach of the medical profession are based on scientific method, defining 'science' in the strictest sense of the word, namely the systematic observation of natural phenomena for the purpose of discovering laws governing those phenomena ... Since the beginning of the twentieth century medical science has focused on the biological aspects of disease and evolved in parallel with associated sciences, including anatomy, physiology, pharmacology, biology, chemistry, physics, and mathematics, with interlinking research findings of increasing strength, consistency, and reliability.

As an integral part of the society in which we live, scientific methodology is generally held to be an acceptable basis on which to set reliable judgements, free from overriding social values and political bias. In the specific case of scientific medicine, this term has come to be associated with the theoretical structure and medical procedures employed by Western society, emerging in Europe and the United States with the decline of nineteenth century allopathy and the subsequent acceptance of a concept of disease based on proven aetiologies. Modern medical science holds that diseases have causes—congenital, infectious, metabolic, toxic, traumatic, neoplastic, degenerative, or psychosomatic—and that they can respond to specific treatments or, if such treatment is lacking, to the palliative management of symptoms. No competing system has systematically assembled a body of knowledge expressed more fully in textbooks, in scientific papers in journals subject to review by referees, and through clinical studies. The dominance of scientific medicine is founded on its theoretical exposition, its clinical elaboration, and its technological advancement.

Inasmuch as scientific method lays such firm emphasis on observation, measurement, and reproducibility, historically it has become inevitably and increasingly separated from doctrines embracing superstition, magic, and the supernatural. It is important to realize that this separation was (and is) quite independent of therapeutic effectiveness: it seemingly represents a completely different conception of why observable phenomena have the effects they do. It is not necessarily the case that in the early days the evolving science of medicine led immediately to more effective treatment but it was the case that its evolution was in accordance with the definition of natural laws as fundamental as that of gravity. An all-embracing and internally consistent theory of medical science was the result, with direct and logical consequences for success in therapeutics.

Thus, herein lies the first and most important difficulty that orthodox medical science has with alternative approaches. So many of them do not base their rationale on any theory which is consistent with natural laws as we now understand them. It is simply not possible, to take one simple example, for orthodox scientists to accept that a medicine so dilute that it may contain not so much as one molecule of the remedy in a given dose can have any pharmacological action. In addition there is a related problem: the rationales of the various forms of alternative therapy differ widely one from another, and there is little or no consistency of concept or practice between their various approaches.

. . . About the only aspect of these therapies which is common to all is that they are not based on orthodox scientific principles: in other respects, with a few minor exceptions, they differ totally. A few examples will suffice. Disturbances in energy flows and pathways, and in the balance between Yin and Yang, are central to the beliefs of many therapies. More spiritual beliefs, however, are at the core of the methods employed by Christian Scientists and scientologists. Some therapies isolate particular (but different) parts of the body for attention: the spine (chiropractic), the iris (iridology), or the foot (reflexology). Diet is identified by many therapists, but not all, as a fundamental factor in causation and treatment.

The fact is that the steadily developing body of orthodox medical knowledge has led to large, demonstrable, and reproducible benefits for mankind, of a scale which cannot be matched by alternative approaches.

One unparalleled example of the success of modern medicine is in the field of public health, world-wide. Using observation, measurement, and deduction, Jenner introduced the practice of vaccination against smallpox, a successful procedure entirely consistent with the laws of natural and biological science. It was subject to considerable opposition at the time, towards the end of the eighteenth century. Now, towards the end of the twentieth century, we live in a world where smallpox has been totally eliminated, and this could not have occurred without the application of scientific principles. Similarly, poliomyelitis, measles, and tuberculosis are no longer the threats to human populations in developed countries that they used to be, and they are decreasing in the developing world.

In the United Kingdom we have come to assume that our tap water is no longer a source of infectious disease. The methods that Snow used in order to identify the Broad Street pump as a source of infection were entirely consistent with the more sophisticated but essentially similar methods employed by statistical and environmental scientists today. The possibility of the control of malaria lies in the realization that it was not 'bad air' (*mal-aria*) which caused the disease, but identifiable parasites transmitted by identifiable vectors in a predictable, measurable, and preventable manner.

The same principles as those relating to public health measures apply to the treatment of acute organic illness and physical trauma. For such cases, none of the information given to the Working Party supports the use of any substitute for conventional medical care. There is no doubt whatever that conditions such as acute appendicitis, stomach ulceration, or fractures of the skull and other bones should be managed by conventional medical techniques, using where appropriate all the facilities available in, for example, a National Health Service district general hospital. In the United Kingdom the medical, surgical, and support facilities available in secondary-care institutions are highly developed, with proven success in dealing with illness and trauma. We see no role for alternative therapies in treatment of this kind. The process of diagnosis is undertaken, the physiological phenomena are defined, the treatment serves a purpose rationally aligned with observable mechanisms, and outcomes are measurable in both comparable (success of one treatment versus another) and absolute (success versus failure of a given treatment) terms.

That is not to say that all such efforts have been totally effective, that all or even most diseases have been totally eliminated, or that new challenges—such as the rapid emergence of AIDS—do not face medical science. It will be to medical science that the world's people will continue to turn for continued control, with the objective of better health for all.

What ties all these approaches together is the thread of science-based theory and practice, entirely consistent throughout. Even where modern technology cannot be afforded in a developing country, the rational principles should still be applied.

To medical scientists, the methods and approaches of many alternative therapies seem closely allied to philosophies long since discredited by advancing knowledge. While scientific methodology has moved steadily along a clearly marked trail, to critical observers it is apparent that many of those who adhere steadfastly to belief in a given 'alternative' therapy have halted in their intellectual progress, as if existing knowledge was sufficient for all time.

ORTHODOX MEDICINE OR ALTERNATIVE THERAPY: A PERSPECTIVE

It has now become apparent that a multitude of factors are at work in generating the current interest now displayed in the so-called alternative therapies. These differing aspects received differing emphasis by the many groups that offered evidence, so much so that it seems wise to identify the more important of these and to attempt a perspective.

Against a growing interest of society at large in the new advances in science, biology, and medicine is the dominant role of the communication media in furthering this desirable innovation. One result identified is the awakened sense of enquiry and a need for more information; and with it a critical questioning attitude from which medicine, in all its aspects, is properly not immune.

Also identified is the acceleration of social, political, and material change in society, and side by side a growth of an underlying hostility to technology and science, and a distrust of innovation. With this is an imperfect understanding of the recent very great achievements made in modern medicine, and their significance.

The modern developments in rational therapeutics and the equally significant advances in diagnostic aids that greatly enhanced the expectations of medicine are themselves seen to have changed the erstwhile established relation between doctor and patient. Now, life-saving therapeutic intervention is a commonplace, its quite recent introduction largely forgotten or unknown, and the significance of the consequences overlooked.

Not only have the pressures and technical demands of modern medicine eroded the opportunities formerly devoted to counselling and sympathetic support, but the circumstances thus created are perceived as largely unacceptable to doctor and patient alike.

One consequence of the advances made in medicine is the changed nature of the doctor's training, with increasing emphasis on the scientific aspects of the curriculum, and a growth of specialization including general practice at the postgraduate stages. These changes are evident in the enhanced quality of primary care and are reflected in the expectations of patients.

Sadly, the provision of complementary support services to meet the new and growing demand from today's patients for communication, information, and instruction is often lacking, and almost universally less than its need. The very provision of modern diagnostic aids, for example by the pathological, haematological, and other services so essential to modern therapeutics, themselves create in their matter-of-fact and impersonal nature an intrusion between patient and doctor.

Almost as a consequence of the revolutionary developments in medicine there is voiced a demand which is hardly rational for instant cures for the currently incurable diseases of mankind. In addition, there is detected ill-founded suspicion that nothing is being done to advance these pressing problems and little perception of the long-term nature of the painstaking research involved.

In noting the need first to identify and then to redress the underlying causes of criticism, we have to recognize that a consequence of ignoring these factors is a reversion to primitive beliefs and outmoded practices, almost all without basis. Some are not without danger, others appear to be promoted for less than laudable purposes.

In identifying a number of the components of the current criticisms of orthodox medicine and of the interest in alternative therapies, we recognize in particular criticisms a need for general information about the recent advances in medicine and of its immediate prospects.

While the cultivation of sane attitudes to the preservation of good health and to the nature of common illness is clearly an obligation of society as a whole, the need to define the many areas in which orthodox medicine can provide effective treatment, and also to indicate those areas where support can be offered for conditions as yet not amenable to current therapy, is the duty of the craft of medicine in particular.

CULTS

In the following pages we will turn to some selected examples of alternative therapies, with particular importance in the United Kingdom, and discuss their relevance to orthodox scientific medicine. First, however, we wish to refer to a matter about which, during the course of our enquiries, we have encountered a great deal of concern. Our attention has been drawn by many people to the activities of what have become known as 'new religious movements', a term which is perhaps more acceptable and descriptive, if not more accurate, than 'religious cults and sects'. In Europe, this concern extended in 1984 to the passing of a resolution by the European Parliament, which focused attention on practices associated with certain religious beliefs and proposed a voluntary code of conduct for such movements.[1]

Our particular interest is in the fact that many of these 'religious' organizations make direct claims to be able to cure disease, including cancers and fractures. One of the much-publicized organizations is the Unification Church of Sun Myung Moon, whose followers are known as 'Moonies', and another is the late L. Ron Hubbard's Church of Scientology. There are now over one hundred groups operating in the United Kingdom in such a manner as to have come to the attention of FAIR (Family Action Information and Rescue), which was formed in 1976 in response to requests for help and information from distressed relatives and friends of young adults who had come under the influence of such groups.

Features which are common to most of these cults, apart from a markedly idiosyncratic view of health and the treatment of disease, include a leader with a powerful and authoritarian personality, the use of influential inducements (especially) to young people to join, and attempts to separate new members

[1] 'The Cottrell Report: A Practical Response to the International Cult Problem', paper presented to the Aktion Für Geistige Unde Psychische Freiheit (AGPF) Conference, Bonn, West Germany, on 20 Sept. 1984 by David Wilshire MA, Head of the Private Office of Richard Cottrell, Member of the European Parliament.

from families and previous friends. Most such sects are said to have an inner circle which derives benefits in terms of power, sex, and money, and responds with bitter resentment to any criticism.

Alternative therapies may be used by these groups to induce belief, thus strengthening the religious dimension (which can qualify for charitable status with resulting tax benefits). Illness may be proclaimed as being a 'punishment' for lack of faith or other misdemeanour.

A major area for the development and growth of these movements has been the United States where some of their activities in the field of health have been shown to be actively dangerous. It has been reported that one group has been linked to a substantial number of deaths, and that perinatal mortality for members of the organization is substantially higher than for that of the general population.[2]

In the context of this discussion, it is not our intention to dwell upon such organizations in any great detail. Indeed, little is known about many of them. But we do believe that, subject to the necessity to maintain the principle of freedom of religion in this country, they should be carefully and continuously monitored in order to ensure that they do not become a threat to the health and well-being of those who enter into association with them.

ALTERNATIVE THERAPIES IN PERSPECTIVE

What now follows is a review of those alternative therapies which, in our opinion, are of relevance to medical practice in this country. There is a wide variety of reasons for their importance, ranging from scientific validity (manipulation, for example) to simple widespread public support.

Homoeopathy

As the background to medicine makes clear, rational developments in medical treatment began in the early part of the nineteenth century. However, Hahnemann originated the ideas underlying homoeopathy at the end of the eighteenth century

---

[2] *Washington Post* (2 Oct. 1984).

when allopathic 'cures' probably aided the demise of more patients than were helped by the treatment. By the end of the nineteenth century homoeopathy had become a static philosophy remaining more or less unchanged, while mainstream medical practice continued to refine its understanding of the pathology of disease and extend its methods of treatment. The value of homoeopathic techniques in 1800 lay in the provision of an alternative therapy for patients who might otherwise have consulted an allopathic practitioner.

In the course of evidence given to us we were told that medically qualified homoeopaths nowadays treat medical and surgical emergencies, together with serious diseases, with the full resources of modern therapeutics and surgery. In addition, the acute diseases of infancy and old age are similarly treated. Homoeopathic remedies may be used for those acute illnesses that normally resolve without drug intervention, and also for the treatment of symptoms which continue to cause distress after diagnosis has eliminated any pathology susceptible to intervention using orthodox techniques.

No pharmacological basis for homoeopathic therapeutics could be found in the administration of a few drops of concentrations of remedies so dilute that a concentration of 12C, for example, may no longer contain one molecule of the original remedy, but will contain many different molecules of the fluids or powders used to dilute the original remedy. Nor indeed was any pharmacological basis claimed by individuals who discussed homoeopathy with the Working Party. What was claimed by the originator and is still claimed today, is that the process of dilution and 'succussion' effects an 'immaterial and vital' force and that this force is therapeutic. We have found no evidence for this belief.

However, in the homoeopathic physician's belief in the reality of the 'immaterial force' derived from the dilution and succussion of the medicines he prescribes, and in its transference to the patient we do detect a potent and valuable component of the self-healing induced effect, familiar to all who practise the craft of medicine. In identifying this transferred belief the patient is reinforced in its reality by the unique appearance of the medicine and its special dosage regimen. These are all factors likely to invest the 'medicine' with special properties. Since belief in the diagnosis and craft of the physician when allied to belief in the efficacy of orthodox medicines are potent components of the placebo phenomenon, commonly identified and randomized in clinical trials, it appears that a placebo effect is the explanation of the belief, shared by homoeopaths and their patients, in the efficacy of homoeopathic therapeutics.

In considering the propriety of applying homoeopathic remedies to accurately diagnosed conditions that ordinarily resolve without medical intervention we are satisfied that withholding unnecessary medication in these circumstances is advantageous.

Manipulation, osteopathy, and chiropractic

Medical manipulation, osteopathy, and chiropractic treatments are currently available to patients with musculo-skeletal disorders. Orthodox medicine looks on manipulation as but one of a range of approved treatments that include analgesia, anti-inflammatory techniques, physiotherapy, injection therapy, and surgery, and would restrict manipulation to the treatment of pain arising from spinal disorders.

In contrast, a specific concept of diseases arising from 'subluxations' is common to chiropractic and osteopathy, with the distinction that chiropractic defines subluxations as almost the exclusive cause. Though their methods of detection differ, their treatment is essentially similar.

Of the practising osteopaths who described their methods to us, all emphasized the anatomical and physiological basis of the training for the registrable qualification. Yet, most held organic diseases and vertebral problems to be causally related. We could detect no physio-pathological basis for these theories.

Turning to the reports we cite of the internationally recognized authorities on the place of manipulation in orthodox medicine, and its relation to lay practice, we find there is unanimous agreement on its value, agreement about its dangers, emphasis on the necessity for a prior medical diagnosis, and total agreement about the contra-indications and how they can be avoided. Significantly, there is agreement in restricting its use to pain arising from mechanical or degenerative causes originating in the vertebrae.

In attempting a perspective of the varying methods by which

pain is treated, the Working Party found it necessary to review shortly the known ways in which pain is sensed and how relieved. There is long-established physiological knowledge about the two kinds of sensor involved: one, because it senses pain and inflammation, is called the nociceptor; the other, because it senses movement, is called the mechanoceptor. Because the mechanoceptors share the additional valuable property of modifying pain, these are the ones activated by the manipulators, using differing methods.

Recent research has concerned itself with the ways in which the signals from the mechanoceptors modify pain, and there now exists acceptable experimental evidence that the release of peptide modulators, notably met-enkephalin and dynorphin, are involved at two distinct 'gating' sites, one locally in the spinal cord, the other centrally, in the brain. These peptides fall into the group now called endorphins.

These considerations offer an explanation for the relief of pain that follows stimulation of mechanoceptors, and for the effect of the established methods of chiropractors and osteopaths. It provides a rationale for the modern approach of the recently established British Association of Manipulative Medicine (BAMM) as well as for the traditional use of massage and of acupuncture. The techniques used by all these groups are aimed at the selective stimulation of mechanoceptors while sparing the nociceptors.

As to the current research directed to developing a more effective method to achieve this aim, the Working Party was made aware of non-intrusive and less vigorous methods using vibrators, electrical low-impedence, low-output stimulation, and low-frequency transcutaneous nerve stimulation aimed at the large diameter nerve fibres.

The perception of pain, 'gated' locally and again centrally, is further modified by previous experiences stored in the brain. This bedevils the objective judgement of patient and manipulator, makes diagnosis difficult, limits prognosis, and complicates the measurement of effect. Only with the emergence of the new generation of medical manipulators will this change. Only properly designed clinical trials will justify the choice of altern-ative treatments.

At a time when current research is identifying a growing range of endogenous peptides, and other putative transmitters in cerebrospinal fluid, it would be unwise to assume that no substance other than the analgesic endorphins may be involved in the gating of pain. However, we wish to emphasize that we have uncovered no evidence that manipulation has effects other than the relief of pain. For this reason we can detect no substance in the theory that advances manipulation as a system of healing.

The core of the problem of the part to be played by the lay osteopathic manipulator rests in the knowledge that only some hundreds of the estimated 2,000 in practice are registered as having had formal instruction. There are fewer chiropractors and these subscribe to the outworn concept of manipulation as a system of healing. The medical manipulator (MBAMM) with qualifications in orthopaedics or rheumatology and with osteo-articular neurological practice may be expected to train and instruct medical manipulators and physiotherapists in the developing modern techniques, but this will take time.

The registered lay practitioner may be regarded as providing a generally safe and helpful service, provided that a medical diagnosis is first made, and in addition, the known contra-indications to certain manipulations are respected.

Acupuncture

Two sorts of acupuncture therapy were described to us. One related to the traditional points of stimulation and their meridians, one for each day of the solar year, to traditional Chinese 'treatment descriptions', and not to symptoms. Practitioners of this art sometimes used moxibustion in which the dried leaves of the common mugwort were burned on the site of insertion. A wide range of conditions were treated: these included acute appendicitis, dysentery, stroke, deafness, and paraplegia for which only anecdotal accounts were available.

The second kind, adopted by doctors trained in orthodox medicine, described the use of a restricted number of stimulation points and referred these to dermatomal sensory distribution. Often electrical stimulation of needles was preferred, and some used transcutaneous nerve stimulation.

There was acceptable evidence for its use in certain musculo-skeletal diseases like low backache, frozen joint syndrome, osteoarthritis, and some forms of facial pain and headaches in patients presenting to conventional pain clinics in this country. Of these, some 10 to 15 per cent claim to have subjective relief from their pain. One-third of these, or some five in every hundred do without analgesics, while the rest do not have objective evidence of reduced analgesic intake. It seems that acupuncture has but a small part to play in the armamentarium of pain clinics.

For many years the gate control theory provided a physiological explanation for the pain-modulating effect. More recently, acceptable experimental evidence, and in addition measurements in man, allow the conclusion that different frequencies of electro-acupuncture release two kinds of opiate peptides within the central nervous system. With manual and with low-frequency stimulation beta-endorphin is released in the brain, where it modulates pain. With high-frequency stimulation a precursor of endorphin, called dynorphin is set free in the spinal cord. Here it has a gating effect on the transmission of the pain signal.

These observations provide a basis for the application of acupuncture for the modulation of pain, and explain its intervention in the management of opiate abuse withdrawal effects. Yet one must keep an open mind to the likelihood that peptides, amino acids, and other modulators of central nervous tissue origin may also be released. Some may prove advantageous, others a hazard.

Little imagination is needed to appreciate the potential dangers of careless insertion of needles. The 365 traditional points run near, some perilously so, to vital structures, and complications ranging from the minor to the serious and the fatal have been reported. The public should not be exposed to acupuncturists who have not been trained to understand the relationships between acupuncture points and anatomical structures, and also the physiology of organ function.

The potential dangers of local and systemic infection following an invasive technique such as acupuncture are real and well documented. While strict asepsis and sterile needles are self-evident requirements, we were led to believe it was an aim rather neglected in practice. Yet the transmission of infectious hepatitis has been reported and the increasing incidence of the AIDS virus infection makes the possibility of transmission by contaminated acupuncture needles a reality.

There is a third potential danger in the inappropriate use of acupuncture. The central analgesic effects are now well-known, but less well appreciated are the opioid-like central effects on mood and behaviour, affecting in turn the patient's responses to disease. Again, the balance of steroid control of the inflammatory process has been observed to change. The temporary abolition, or attenuation of signals of underlying disease may mask symptoms and so lead to delay in diagnosis. Thus a situation may arise in which what was patently amenable to conventional therapy becomes irremediable because of the delay.

The above considerations led the Working Party to conclude that the practice of acupuncture should conform to the same ethical and technical standards as does medical practice.

Hypnotherapy

Hypnotherapy is now being used by a substantial number of doctors to provide techniques of relaxation to patients with anxiety states, to help conditions such as asthma if there is a psychological element, and to provide an alternative to the use of drug therapy in conditions such as hyperemesis gravidarum. Having studied the literature and evidence submitted to us, we have no doubt that hypnotherapy can benefit some patients.

The precise nature of the hypnotic state remains to be elucidated, but we think that this should not lead to neglect of the technique. Material provided to the Working Party demonstrated that the value of hypnotherapy can be quantified using acceptable research methodology, and we think that there is a case for increased research to provide a better understanding of hypnotherapy.

However, those therapists and doctors who discussed the matter with the Working Party stressed that hypnotherapy should be undertaken only after a diagnosis has been made, unless it is itself part of the diagnostic procedure. While it is a useful tool for the treatment of illness, it can have no separate function as a panacea for ill health.

The Working Party was therefore concerned by evidence of the use of hypnotherapy by people with no medical or psychological training, some of whom reject the need to make a diagnosis before hypnotizing their clients. Like any other therapy, it is our opinion that hypnotherapy should only be employed as part of the planned management of a condition, and the making of a proper diagnosis is a fundamental first step towards an acceptable system of management.

It is the view of the Working Party that the use of hypnotherapy should be restricted to medical practitioners, dentists, and trained and qualified clinical psychologists.

MISCELLANEOUS SYSTEMS OF HEALING

As we have already commented, there are many other alternative therapies, with generally much smaller numbers of devotees in this country than the therapies to which we have just turned our attention, and with little in common between them except that they pay little or no regard to the scientific principles of modern medicine. As a group, they have much in common with the 'folk healers' of primitive societies. They may have roots in sacred or in secular philosophies, and may now exist in traditional or modern forms. . . . Such literature as does exist on the efficacy of these assorted methods suggests that patients often feel better after therapy, but that there are limits to its effects, and that while unwanted effects are unusual, they do occur. Such therapists may help people deal with their experience of illness, but they are not effective in the treatment of disease. While they may be sensitive to people's needs, practitioners of these alternative therapies do not necessarily respond in a systematic manner to organic, psychiatric, or psychosocial problems.

While these systems of therapy are diverse there are nevertheless some common features.

Many of the 'sacred' systems depend on spiritual faith in one way or the other, and 'healers' who use them (with the exception of those involved with the potentially dangerous cults to which we have drawn attention) do generally understand that the advice of a doctor will be required for the diagnosis and treatment of organic disease. Beyond that, the techniques of the faith healers, divine healers, and others in associated groups are safe and non-invasive, and offer the prospect of increased well-being for many sufferers. Why such 'healing' is more effective for some ills than others is not known. It certainly cannot be a panacea.

Another trait shared by groups of alternative therapies is belief in a notion of 'energy', which flows and forms linkages both within the body and outside it. Hahnemann's 'vital force' is related to such a concept. So is 'chi' of the Chinese, 'tai' of the Japanese, and 'prana' of yogis. Polarity theory, to take a more recent example, postulates that there are five major centres in the body, and that energy flows between these various centres. Health, it is claimed, is attained through the free flow of energy between perfectly balanced centres. Taking a different but related view, practitioners of reflexology divide the body into ten equal vertical zones ending in the fingers and the toes, with parts of the body lying in any one zone being related by energy links to each other, and through energy connections to given segments of the foot.

'Energy patterns' are also fundamental to the belief of those who practise radionics, who do not even have to see the whole person in order to direct the therapeutic process. Only the instruments used by the practitioners are able to measure and direct the relevant energy patterns.

In our view, reliance on descriptions of energy flows to account for the effect of alternative therapies, in the absence of precise definitions or an explicit (let alone systematic) theoretical framework, is no more than dogmatic metaphysics. Even some chiropractors have fallen back on 'energy flows' to explain the mechanism by which subluxations can affect the health of internal organs. We understand the appeal of such concepts to those who wish to reject what they see as the materialism of scientific medicine, but we do not believe that these methods are of therapeutic value in themselves. . . .

MEDICAL PRACTICE IN PERSPECTIVE

The Royal College of General Practitioners has defined health as 'a satisfactory adaptation of the individual to his environment— physical, psychological and socio-cultural'. It will be clear from the earlier section of this Report which gave an overview of modern medical practice that in many respects therapeutic methods, as currently employed, give results which fall short of such an ideal.

For many disorders, modern medical treatment is demonstrably effective. Some of the procedures and remedies appear to be overly 'technological', even distressing, and for some diseases such as cancer the cure may seem as horrifying as the disease, but of course for many other conditions it is not applicable. Medicine appears to be making little headway with the chronic illnesses which contribute so much, especially among the elderly, to mortality and morbidity in Western industrialized societies.

Further, the increased strength of the armamentarium of technological techniques and medicines used to diagnose and treat illness has raised the risk of iatrogenic disorders, that is, disease or disability brought about by the medical intervention itself. However, any effective treatment is likely to have unwanted effects. It is not true to say that alternative therapies are completely free of unwanted outcomes. We have already drawn attention to the potential dangers of manipulation, and of cultish faith, to take two widely different examples. Acupuncture is far from free of risk, let alone discomfort. Some Chinese 'herbal' remedies actually contain powerful drugs, in quantities neither assessed nor labelled.

safety

The fact remains that the perception of many lay people is that alternative therapies can offer something that orthodox medicine cannot, that they can do so with safety, and that they take more account of the individual than the disease. To many patients, the theories of disease held by alternative practitioners are highly persuasive. Furthermore, patients who are afraid of organic disease, especially of a malignant nature, may prefer to go to an alternative therapist rather than a medical practitioner because they are afraid of what the orthodox diagnostic process might reveal. Medicine must address these issues. It is the nature of the relationship between practitioner and patient that lies at the core of the matter, and it is a relationship which is now under enormous pressure at a time when so many other authority-based relationships are also being brought into question.

'Illness' is not simply a pathological condition which responds to a particular therapeutic tool. It is a condition which affects an individual human being, who in turn is in relationship with other human beings, who has a unique experience of previous illness as well as good health, and who has unique desires, responses, ambitions, and responsibilities. Asthma, for example, is not simply bronchospasm brought about by allergenic or other triggers. For the individual patient, already influenced by genetic and environmental factors about which he can do nothing, it may be a terrifying experience which wakes him, breathless, from sleep, or brings about an abrupt and wheezy termination to a bout of exercise or laughter. That person's otherwise normal activities may be severely curtailed. Accordingly, the treatment of asthma must take into account not only the choice, dosage, and administration of drugs, but also the individual's response to the feeling of breathlessness and the way that breathlessness affects relationships with other people. In other words, this is just a simple example of how a doctor should take the whole person into account when treating a given illness.

When it comes to the relationship of orthodox medicine to alternative therapies, there appear to be two groups of patients whose conditions are of special relevance. On the one hand, there are those in whom the doctor can find no pathological condition which might be responsive to conventional treatment. On the other hand, there are those for whom a diagnosis of a pathological condition can be made, but for whom no successful treatment currently exists for the illness diagnosed by the doctor.

Patients in both these groups may well feel that they have reached the limits of the benefits offered by orthodox medicine. Accordingly, they may suggest that their best next course of action is to consult an unorthodox practitioner.

It is at this point that the doctor's reaction is at its most critical. The fundamental aim must be that the patient receives maximum benefit overall, and that can only be brought about by a continuation of an ongoing process of diagnosis, review, and (as far as possible) treatment. The doctor must continue to see the patient because this relationship is critical to diagnosis and treatment, especially if the patient develops new and potentially more serious signs and symptoms.

We believe that the patient must be assisted by the doctor to understand this process if the patient does decide to seek the non-specific help offered by, for example, an aromatherapist in order to alleviate distress, hopelessness, or despair. The patient should also be helped to understand that consultation with the practitioners of some alternative therapies may be attended by the risk of great harm. This may occur through delaying or denying access to effective medical care by persistence with alternative therapies which are without a beneficial effect on the developing disease process at a time when orthodox medical treatment is urgently needed, or through the unwanted effects of unwarranted or untested remedies.

There are many features of good medical practice that are entirely consistent with the view of a patient as a whole person with a disability, rather than as a living disease process, and that minimize the adverse consequences of the use of modern medical technology. To the extent that consideration of alternative therapies draws attention to these features, it has real value; and it is to some of them that, finally, we now turn.

TIME, TOUCH, AND COMPASSION

Time, touch, and compassion are all features of good medical practice. Alternative therapists do not have a unique claim on these aspects of healing, or a monopoly on their use. Especially when medicine can promise neither relief nor cure, the relationship between doctor and patient becomes ever more important. The pressures of a busy practice may tend to limit the extent to which a medical practitioner can apply appropriate skills, but the importance of what might once have been called the 'bedside manner' should never be forgotten, and medical students must always be taught it. An intimate bond between physician and patient has always been a hallmark of good medical practice, and the quality of the individual physician is crucial when it is the profession as a whole which is under question.

The role of the therapist in treatment is well understood by those concerned with alternative approaches. For example, the therapist can powerfully reinforce belief in the special properties of a homoeopathic medicine, or in the use of massage allied to reflexology. The homoeopathic physician who is identified by both parties as a 'healer' can firmly establish the need for self-healing to occur, through a well-considered approach to the patient. A similar mechanism exists through the faith of those, practitioners and patients alike, who believe that a patient's own healing power can be linked with the healing power of God.

The development of such a relationship between practitioner and patient takes time; the process of assessment by a homoeopathic physician requires, in the terms of his own dogma, a longer and more detailed examination of the patient than is allowed by the time usually available to a physician in orthodox medical practice. Further, [it has been noted] . . . that the average alternative therapist spends eight times longer over a consultation than an average general practitioner. There can be little doubt of the appreciation and gratitude of most patients for a long, detailed, and sympathetic examination by the physician. Many patients feel that the time available to their general practitioner or hospital doctor is too brief to discuss the peculiarities of their illness, yet all good doctors appreciate the importance of an accurae and detailed history as part of the diagnostic process.

Physical contact plays an important part in human communication. Parents 'kiss away the pain' of their injured children. The way a therapist uses the touch of hands on a patient can reinforce a sick person's confidence, and reinforce the will to recover full health. A particular example of the use of deliberate techniques of this kind is given by aromatherapy, which seems almost entirely to be based on the caring, reassuring, and pleasing effects of touch. Reflexology is another example of a therapy which makes use of such benefits.

To the extent to which the individual is treated as a whole, and that the mind and the body are considered as inseparable components of the sufferer from a disease, good medicine has always been 'holistic'. Yet some doctors feel uncomfortable when faced by vague somatic complaints which are actually expressions of emotional tensions, and they are happier when dealing with physical illness that can be diagnosed and cured. The current teaching of medical students, however, now reflects as far as possible the admonition of Dr William Osler, that it is the patient who has the disease who needs the treatment, not just the disease the patient has. The great success of hospices in the management of terminal malignant disease is a good example of such medical care.

Family practitioners have become advocates for viewing ill health in the broad context of a family and social network, viewing the maintenance of health and the prevention of disease as desirable goals, with counselling and the use of the behavioural scientists as essential adjuncts. The same concerns are widespread in medicine generally.

'Cures' for diseases, or the alleviation of troublesome and

chronic conditions, spring from many sources, through ideas and development guaranteed by a wide assortment of disciplines. The development of modern medical practice has been assisted over the years by concepts and techniques originally developed by groups outside the mainstream of medicine, methods which may indeed have been viewed with scepticism by some orthodox practitioners. The essence of logical development, however, is that new and unconventional techniques should be evaluated with the same scientific methods as have been applied to therapeutic methods now known, through the results of careful evaluation, to be effective. In the results of such studies does progress lie.

17

Response to the British Medical Association Report

British Holistic Medical Association

The British Medical Association Report fails to understand medicine both in relationship to society and in a historical context. The concept of disease reflected in the document belongs to a limited scientific model which characterizes constellations of physical symptoms and the biological conditions which underlie them, and ignores social factors, psychological correlates, and illness behaviour.

SOCIAL FACTORS

We cannot ignore the social correlates of personal distress. If, as practitioners, we consider the plight of children then we must take heed of the influence of the emotional milieu in which they live and the socio-economic climate in which those emotional relationships are located. Research and practice cannot be founded solely on the premises of biology and physiology. The medical problems which children experience occur as part of a pattern of stress, symptoms, and relational difficulties. These are often woven into a fabric of parental unemployment and poverty.[1]

The poor live in a situation of increased vulnerability, with a

[1] D. Black, *Inequalities in Health*, Report of a Research Working Group (London: Department of Health and Social Security, 1980); S. Curtis, 'Community Health Survey of Victoria District', Final Report, Queen Mary College, University of London, 1985; B. Jarman, 'A Survey of Primary Care in London', Royal College of General Practitioners, Occasional Paper No. 16, 1981; id., 'Identification of Underprivileged Areas', *British Medical Journal*, 286 (1983), 1705–9; id., 'Under-privileged Areas: Validation and Distribution of Scores', *British Medical Journal*, 289 (1984), 1587–92; id., 'London: A Unique Problem', *The Physician* (Nov. 1985), 482–4; A. H. McFarlane, G. Norman, D. C. Streiner, and R. G. Roy, 'The Process of Social Stress: Stable, Reciprocating and Mediating Relationships', *Journal of Health and Social Behaviour*, 24 (1983), 160–73.

continued anxiety about regular income. They have few reserves for responding to adverse conditions. When we speak of the poor we are speaking of the frail, the sick, the elderly, the young, and the handicapped.[2] It is to these sections of the community that we are asked to direct our health care concerns. The experience of poverty cannot solely be expressed and measured in discrete units, and mocks our current research in its inability to recognize the needs of the poor and to exercise compassion.

ILLNESS BEHAVIOUR

The concept of 'illness behaviour' describes the ways in which people respond to bodily indications, and the conditions under which they view those indications as 'abnormal'.[3] Illness behaviour takes into account the realms of psychological and social interaction. What happens to a person's body is interpreted, monitored, adjusted, and responded to, utilizing a variety of resources which can be personal, relational, familial, or cultural. This process continues before and beyond any medical treatment.[4] When we come to consider doing research we have to accept that the events which we extract from a person's stream of life then become distorted by the very act of extraction.

The implication of illness behaviour for both health care practice and research is that longitudinal data are important for establishing causal links and for demonstrating the patterning of recurrent events. The cross-sectional multi-variated analyses used in orthodox medicine ignore these dynamic features of illness. By sacrificing such interactive factors on the altar of tradition we lose those vital understandings necessary for meeting the needs of primary health care.

CULTURAL FACTORS

There are differences in the perception of illness among cultures both for the characterization of illness, how illness is caused, and

---

[2] D. Aldridge, 'Children in Distress', *Crucible* (Apr.–June 1985), 67–76.

[3] D. Mechanic, 'The Concept of Illness Behaviour: Culture, Situation and Personal Predisposition', *Psychological Medicine*, 16 (1986), 1–7.

[4] D. Robinson, *The Process of Becoming Ill* (London: Routledge & Kegan Paul, 1971).

how it is responded to.[5] In our local populations people respond with a mixture of scientific ideas and folkloric knowledge learned from their peers and families. While orthodox science may have its own consistent epistemology, the people whom we treat and research are informed by differing world-views. Unless we take time to discover those views then our endeavours will flounder.[6] This does not mean that we discard 'science', rather that we respond imaginatively and creatively as scientists to discover the construction of health and disease as a social process.

A recommendation of the British Medical Association Report is that in our research we concentrate on intractable symptoms and work back to situations where those symptoms are less severe. To take such a position ignores the variety of processes whereby people adapt to circumstance. People experience many difficulties and tensions which culminate in various adaptations expressed in differing forms of disorder; i.e. physical illness, psychological disorder, and spiritual malaise. [Yet] . . . clinical entities are not homogeneous, it is only our particular perspective which lumps them all together as if they were one thing. These clinical entities, as viewed by modern medicine, appear to be the end-process of a variety of singular pathways. This is patently untrue. As clinicians we know that there are alternative pathways to the same clinical problem. Simply put, there are more ways than one of becoming asthmatic, diabetic, or depressed.

We can also use the perspective of continuing change. People are not wholly 'asthmatic' or 'diabetic'; they are persons, not 'clinical entities'. Sometimes they behave by exhibiting the symptoms of asthma and diabetes but these symptoms are not their total existence. Furthermore, by aggregating clinical entities and defining their distribution in a population, all we demonstrate is a statistical description. We say nothing about the process of changing from the status of 'being sick' to that of 'becoming healthy'. As there are alternative pathways to sickness then there are also alternative pathways to health.

This Report ignores the process of becoming ill. We have known for some time that the contact between patient and

[5] C. G. Helmann, 'Feed a Cold, Starve a Fever', *Culture, Medicine and Psychiatry*, 2 (1978), 107–37.

[6] J. Hasler, 'The Very Stuff of General Practice', *Journal of the Royal College of General Practitioners*, 35 (1985), 121–7.

doctor involves symptoms and illnesses that are widely distributed in the population and that are more frequently untreated than treated.[7] When a person seeks help there is a constellation of contingencies which surrounds the perception of those symptoms. The symbolic aspect of illness at a time of personal threat, or the use of symptoms as justification at a time of failure, is of paramount importance for treatment decisions yet we cannot submit symbolic meaning to the same sort of measurement techniques as determining blood pressure. The British Medical Association Report fails to address this aspect of measurement by ignoring the realm of illness behaviour.

Similarly, the political implications of symptoms for a marital or family relationship have been widely discussed in the literature.[8] To ignore these implications is to limit our scientific knowledge. Of course such differing levels of analysis make understanding complex, but surely science can rise to this level of complexity. That is the challenge we face as scientists today. A central tenet of science has been to make things as elegantly simple as possible using the principle of Occam's razor. Unless we are careful, in our blinkered pursuit of the simple, we will be in danger of wielding Occam's machete, and degenerate into a reduced simplicity.

PERSONAL CONSTRUCTIONS OF ILLNESS

People vary in their knowledge and understanding of illness, and in their tolerance of discomfort. While we may categorize a

---

[7] J. Horder and E. Horder, 'Illness in General Practice', *The Practitioner*, 173 (1954), 177–85; K. L. White, T. F. Williams, and B. G. Greenberg, 'The Ecology of Medical Care', *New England Journal of Medicine*, 265 (1961), 885–992.

[8] D. Aldridge, 'Suicidal Behaviour and Family Interaction: A Brief Review', *Journal of Family Therapy*, 6 (1984), 309–22; M. H. Banks, S. A. Beresford, D. C. Morrell, J. J. Waller, and C. J. Watkins, 'Factors Influencing Demand for Primary Care in Women Aged 20–44 Years: A Preliminary Report', *International Journal of Epidemiology*, 4 (1975), 189–95; J. Dominian, 'Marital Breakdown and Health', *Update* (1985), 809–16; J. Haley, *Leaving Home* (New York: McGraw-Hill, 1980); D. Jackson, 'Family Rules: Marital Quid Pro Quo', *Archives of General Psychiatry*, 12 (1965), 589–94; C. Madanes, *Strategic Family Therapy* (San Francisco: Jossey-Bass, 1981); S. Minuchin, *Families and Family Therapy* (Cambridge, Mass.: Harvard University Press, 1974); M. Selvini-Palazzoli, *Paradox and Counter Paradox* (New York: Jason Aronson, 1978); J. T. M. Van Eijk, 'Serious Illness and Family Dynamics 1', *Family Practice*, 2 (1985) 61–9; id., 'Serious Illness and Family Dynamics 2', *Family Practice*, 2 (1985) 70–5.

variety of symptoms into a clinical entity we can miss personal psychological orientations and predispositions.

Although physical thresholds may appear to be similar from one person to another, subjective responses may vary a great deal. The personal implications of illness, how symptoms are perceived and responded to, how they have been handled in the past, and the personality of the patient, all influence illness behaviour.[9] Yet the discussion section of the British Medical Association Report fails to include any of these aspects. To do so is grossly to distort our understanding of health and illness. By neglecting these areas of personal, social, political, and cultural influence the Report fails to grasp the importance of some 'alternative' practices, and why people are turning to those practices.

A HISTORICAL CONTEXT

The issues in the document do not exist separately from both current events, or outside the context of history. The dilemma of whom to consult, doctor, priest, herbalist, folk healer, or shaman, has been around for a very long time. Anthropological studies show that a universal factor of illness behaviour is that where more than one 'healer' exists within a culture there is a hierarchy of resort.[10]

First, there are family traditions of managing illness. We turn to those in our family, or amongst our peers, whom we recognize through experience or expertise, for advice about the meaning of symptoms and what to do about them.[11] Secondly, we consult an agent who is outside the family. This is usually a practitioner chosen according to our perception of the problem and our expectations of resolution.[12] The more we support and promote

[9] G. Kelly, *The Psychology of Personal Constructs*, i and ii (New York: W. W. Norton and Co., 1955); D. Bannister and F. Fransella, *Inquiring Man* (Harmondsworth: Penguin, 1971); J. Murray, 'The Use of Health Diaries in the Field of Psychiatric Illness in General Practice', *Psychological Medicine*, 2 (1985), 551–60; R. Pill and N. Stott, 'Concepts of Illness Causation and Responsibility', *Social Science and Medicine*, 16 (1982), 43–52.

[10] A. Kleinman, *Patients and Healers in the Context of Culture* (Berkeley, Calif.: University of California Press, 1980).

[11] E. M. Russell and F. Iljon-Foreman, 'Self-Care in Illness: A Review', *Family Practice*, 2 (1985), 108–21.

[12] E. Freidson, *Profession of Medicine* (New York: Dodd, Mead and Co., 1975).

particular health initiatives and deny others, the more we promote their use without questioning the premises on which they are founded. However, we live in a time when people are questioning the premises of orthodox medicine, challenging the efficacy of medical practice in the context of chronic disease, and demanding a greater say in health issues.

The division of health practice and the seeds of the medical monopoly of health care were sown in the early nineteenth century. The Medical Act of 1858 allowed medical schools to increase their emphasis in natural science, notably physiology. This promoted an orthodoxy of knowledge and belief which could easily be replicated. With the emphasis on natural science explanations and their proofs and unified theories, homoeopathy and folk-healing techniques, which relied upon empirical evidence, were displaced. Cogent explanations routed clinical results. It is those explanations which are being questioned today. The questioning of such explanations is a political act and a threat to the status quo, to the monopoly of decision-making by a powerful minority, and to their restrictive licensing practices.

We have all been part of a process which has reified science and curative technology above the need for holistic considerations for health. There is no blame attached to orthodoxy. However, for this Report to deny both the influence of culture and history by omission is deceiving the general population. Readers of this document are directed away from holistic understandings by omission. What is far more sinister is the misdirection and scurrilous implication that alternative practice is 'cultish'. Although a direct link is not made, by putting the ideas together within the concluding section of the Report a link is made by innuendo.

THE POLITICS OF SCIENCE

In the discussion section of the British Medical Association Report, scientific methodology is described as 'generally held to be an acceptable basis on which to set reliable judgements, free from overriding social values and political bias'. This is not true. When science is used to validate what is acceptable in terms of practice, to grant funding for research, and maintain institutional dominance, then it is political and subject to bias. Science is not an objective reality, it is constructed as a social entity by persons. To say that science is true and value free is rather like saying that Islam is true because everyone subscribes to the faith in Iran. To object to the truth of Islam would be dangerous in Tehran, but for an outsider a different view is possible. Islam is seen as a faith and a matter of belief. So too with medicine and 'natural science'. What appear to be 'natural' laws in the eyes of the faithful can appear to be distinctly shaky from the relativist perspective of modern physics. All systems of belief, whether clinical medicine, theology, or acupuncture, have a rationale. The difficulty is that of discovering another person's rationale from the standpoint of our own rationale. Sometimes, in our scientific endeavour, we have to leave what we know and to learn that which is new. This is not abandoning our knowledge, but gaining greater understanding. Unfortunately the British Medical Association has failed to grasp this point by its inability to see it.

Certainly medical science has led to many benefits. However, we face a current situation where medical science is being faced with many challenges and is found wanting. Chronic disease, asthma, diabetes, stress disorders, psychological disorder, and arthritis, are not tractable to orthodox medicine.[13] Similarly, medicine is under attack for the side-effects of its reductionist approach. The over-prescribing of medication, the ramifications of iatrogeny, the alienation of patients and the failure to provide access to health care for the poor are all factors which indicate the limitations of orthodox medicine. While secondary care may well be successful in dealing with trauma, it is in the areas of primary health care, preventive practice, and chronic illness that orthodox medicine is being questioned. It is simply not good enough that the British Medical Association say to alternative practitioners that they cannot carry out the medical and surgical procedures performed in hospitals. Alternative practice does not set out to do this. First, some alternative practices attempt to avoid the need for such referral by preventive practice. Secondly, the intention is to practise complementarity. The idea of alternative practice is to complement and inform orthodox medicine, such that the opportunities for health care are extended by *working together.*

---

[13] A. T. Rose, 'Chronic Illness in General Practice', *Family Practice*, 1 (1984), 162–7; W. R. Arney and B. J. Bergen, 'The Anomaly, the Chronic Patient and the Play of Medical Power', *Sociology of Health and Illness*, 5 (1983), 1–24.

THE WAY FORWARD

Health care in the twenty-first century, involving practice, education, and research, will have to incorporate within its understanding of the human condition the following concepts:

1. The human organism is a multidimensional being—body, mind, and spirit—and exists within the context of a social structure (family and community) which in turn derives its existence from its relationship with the environment.
2. There is an interconnectedness between all things, micro-scopic–macroscopic, living–non-living. The whole is greater than the sum of its parts and the part contains the whole.
3. Health and disease lie along a continuum and represent the organism's intrinsic state of harmony with the universe.
4. The linear model of cause and effect is only partly applicable to disease and health.
5. Consciousness plays a role in the physical universe, i.e. we each possess a powerful and innate capacity for altering both our internal and external environment.
6. Matter and energy are interchangeable.
7. One of the primary tasks of someone entrusted to heal, be he a doctor, priest, or acupuncturist, is to encourage the innate capacity of the individual in distress and help restore and state of balance and harmony.

The concepts will need to underpin practice, education, and research in the following manner:

Practice

(*a*) It will be necessary to expand our primary health care service and finance it adequately.
(*b*) Primary health care based around general practice will need to move towards multidisciplinary team work which will include complementary practitioners.
(*c*) Health education, promotion, and anticipation should become a central feature of all primary health care activities.
(*d*) Self-help and self-care activities should become a regular feature of treatment.

Education

(a) The education of doctors should no longer be carried out exclusively in hospitals.
(b) Multidisciplinary undergraduate teaching should involve doctors, nurses, and social workers, as well as students from complementary therapies.
(c) Health care practitioners should be provided with a support system that enables them to examine their own health care needs, both from a personal as well as a professional base.
(d) The focus on the scientific and technological base to disease should be balanced by a focus on the human aspects, including the importance of good communication skills.

Research

(a) Research studies should no longer be the major factor determining promotion and preferment.
(b) Research studies on patients should be replaced by research studies with patients.
(c) Research studies should pay due cognizance to the moral, ethical, and financial consequences of their outcome.
(d) Research studies out of context to the social and cultural needs should be deemed of low priority.

18

Brussels Post-1992: Protector or Persecutor?

Tom Huggon and Alan Trench

There are two questions which affect the legal status of practitioners in the United Kingdom: Who may lawfully practise medicine? And how can patients obtain treatment—that is, whether a particular therapy is available through the National Health Service?

DOCTORS AND LAY PRACTITIONERS

Under English common law, anyone has the right to practise therapy or medicine subject to the consent of the patient (and the position under Scottish law is comparable). However, this freedom is considerably restricted by statute law and in particular by the Medical Act 1956. Those who are registered as practitioners under it—meaning apothecaries and doctors with medical degrees or comparable qualifications conferred on them by one of the Royal Colleges—are at a considerable advantage over those who are not registered.

Without registration people may not use any title or description implying that they are registered; they may not take posts reserved for those who are registered; they may not recover charges for their attendance or advice through the courts; and they may not possess or supply controlled drugs, directly or by prescription.

Qualification as a practitioner also involves acceptance of a code of professional behaviour. This may restrict the practitioners but it also provides protection if he or she is accused of misconduct as well as giving patients a guarantee of the practitioner's behaviour. For doctors, this is implemented through the General Medical Council, a statutory body first established in 1858 and now regulated by the Medical Act 1978.

There are certain other restrictions on what a practitioner may do if unregistered. The Venereal Disease Act of 1917 prohibits anyone treating venereal disease in certain localities. No one may practise as an apothecary if not specifically registered to do so. (Apothecaries formerly both treated patients and dispensed medicines, but now apothecaries are treated as registered practitioners and are permitted to use the title of 'doctor' so this has become rather academic.)

Anthroposophical medicine is exceptional in that it is a principle of the Steiner movement that all its practitioners should have orthodox medical qualifications as well as learning the anthroposophical approach. In general, however, natural medicine in Britain is legally practised by a mixture of registered and unregistered practitioners.

This state of affairs enjoys the protection of English common law, based on court judgments over many years and an ancient safeguard of the rights and freedoms of the inhabitants of these islands. The choice of practitioner this grants has helped to ensure the survival of natural medicine in the face of the suspicion or hostility of the medical profession—which often has regarded natural medicine as old wives' cures.

This system has many advantages for all involved. It enables patients to choose the sort of care they wish. Holistic health care, as it is becoming known and used in Britain, depends on this freedom of choice, a freedom which means that patients can benefit from the different skills and outlooks of both doctors and other practitioners.

The status of doctors creates the irony that doctors may practise natural medicine with little or no formal training, while many 'lay' practitioners with considerable knowledge and experience are at a disadvantage to them, if only because all their patients must come to them privately. It is essential for all to recognize the distinctive skills of doctors, particularly in diagnosing patients' problems, and of lay practitioners. Each has its place in treating patients and each complements the other.

Homoeopathy is the school of natural medicine with arguably most recognition from registered practitioners. Medical doctors who practise homoeopathy are often members of the Faculty of Homoeopathy, which shares the premises of the Royal London Homoeopathic Hospital. The Faculty provides the system of training and examination in homoeopathy for doctors with orthodox medical qualifications, together with a forum for research, and the discussion of matters which affect homoeopathic doctors.

Practitioners of other schools of natural medicine have their own institutions, the status of which varies. Herbalists are represented mainly by the National Institute of Medical Herbalists, lay homoeopaths mainly by the Society of Homoeopaths, aromatherapists mainly by the International Federation of Aromatherapists, and so forth.

In fact, herbal practitioners have a special legal status under the Medicines Act 1968. Herbalists who use these powers must notify the enforcement authority (which is the Secretary of State and the Pharmaceutical Society) of their intentions. They may prepare remedies for particular patients who ask them in person to do so, provided that these remedies consist only of crushed, dried, and mixed herbs with no ingredient added other than water or another inert substance. The herbs which may be used, and the quantities of them, are prescribed by the Act, and this list includes herbs usually considered toxic, such as belladonna (deadly nightshade).

[margin handwritten note: legal standing]

ACCESS TO NATURAL HEALTH CARE

Besides the question of who may practise medicine, there is the question of how accessible it is to patients. Many people rely on the National Health Service for their health care, and this makes it much harder for them to obtain treatment using natural medicines.

The National Health Service . . . has a considerable bias towards allopathic medicine. There is *no statutory basis for this*. The 1946 National Health Act does not specify what sort of treatment should be available on the National Health Service. It guarantees the independence of doctors to prescribe what treatment they see fit for their patients.

The parliamentary debates about the National Health Bill— before it finally became law (in 1946)—make interesting reading. An amendment to the Bill was tabled which would have given people the right to receive the care they chose under the National Health Service. But the then Minister of Health, Aneurin Bevan, rejected this, calling it 'an impossible suggestion' and adding that 'any Tom, Dick or Harry would be able to prey upon the credulity of any citizen and could call upon the state to provide the money for that service'.[1]

In the same debate Mr Bevan justified the reliance on qualified doctors, 'who are people who have passed the examinations and acquired the right to give whatever form of treatment they conceive to be necessary'.[2] He described conventional medicine as being scientifically ascertainable, in contrast to natural medicine, which would become an accepted form of medicinal therapy 'if it was capable of systematisation, codification or verification'.[3]

None the less, homoeopathic treatment remained available on the National Health Service, perhaps because of the well-known use of it by the Royal Family. The National Health Service continues to support the Royal London Homoeopathic Hospital, and treatment at the homoeopathic hospitals in London, Liverpool, Bristol, and Glasgow is covered by the National Health Service. But to benefit from it you first have to find a homoeopathic doctor, or one who is sympathetic to homoeopathy.

It is the reliance of the National Health Service on doctors which places lay practitioners at such disadvantage. Natural medicine is not presently taught in any British medical school, though [it is planned to open] a department specializing in it . . . at Glasgow University. Few doctors are introduced to natural medicine during their training and it is hard for many to accept it by the standards they are taught.

As a result it is often difficult to obtain non-allopathic treatment on the National Health Service. Administrators of the service are often reluctant to support unorthodox schemes for treating patients. Even Dr Dixon's holistic cardiology clinic at the Charing Cross Hospital in London relies heavily on donations of money and time from outside the health service.

Doctors may prescribe any treatment or medicines they see fit for their patients. This includes medicines which do not have product licences for use in the United Kingdom, but which

[1] See Hansard, 23 July 1946, col. 1902.   [2] Ibid.
[3] Ibid., cols. 1903–4.

manufacturers or pharmacists are able to supply or obtain on request. However, the facilities of the National Health Service are only available to registered practitioners, that is, doctors. There is no way others can use the service except through a doctor. This creates great problems for others to use the service and prevents patients enjoying the freedom of choice of therapy they are supposed to enjoy.

Despite this, holistic clinics have enjoyed great growth in recent years, even though individuals have to pay for much if not all of the treatment they receive through them. Examples of such places are the Hale Clinic or the Marylebone Healing Centre in London.

The impending reforms of the National Health Service offer the opportunity to improve this situation. Natural medicines and therapies are often cheaper than allopathic ones, as well as gentler. They also avoid the dangers of drug-induced, or iatrogenic, disease. They are frequently used by many people, and limiting their use to those who can afford to pay for them directly out of their pockets, rather than financing them out of taxes, is manifestly unfair. The Government and Members of Parliament should be lobbied and encouraged to recognize natural medicines formally as part of the National Health Service when the service is reformed.

THE CONTINENTAL SITUATION

In other European countries the situation is rather different to Britain. In general, only doctors may practise medicine or treat patients. There is therefore a great contrast with British practice. Doctors often have a broad range of skills which they publicize, and patients may consult specialists in whatever sort of medicine they choose.

There are some exceptions to the doctors' monopoly, of which the best known are probably the German *Heilpraktikeren* (health practitioners). There is, moreover, great reluctance among doctors generally, especially among those from Latin countries, to accept the credentials of those without formal medical training.

The situation is made worse by the great variety of sorts of practitioners that exist. Some of the German *Heilpraktikeren* specialize in certain sorts of therapy, others do not. There are also differences in the quality of training they receive. It is consequently very hard to demonstrate the value of these sorts of practitioners to the policy-makers who will have to be convinced— and to whose ears doctors have easier access.

The reluctance to accept properly trained lay practitioners as having comparable status to doctors has been a problem with the formation of a European doctors' body for natural medicines, the . . . European Council for Therapeutic Plurality in Medicine. This formally came into being in October [1989] . . . It aims at ensuring plurality of choice in therapy, rather than representing the interests of any particular school of medicine. Many Continental doctors and their organizations have been reluctant to accept lay practitioners, such as members of the British Society of Homoeopaths.

Another problem with this body has been the divisions among doctors. They have had difficulty accepting that the only successful way to deal with the European Community is to form a single European body to represent their interests. The European Council for Integrated Medicine was formed early in 1989 and is based on the Dutch and Belgian Akademien voor Integrerende Geneesswijzen (AIG).

The main aim of the European Council for Integrated Medicine is to share information with the aim of promoting integrated health care. While this is an admirable goal, there are more pressing matters which require the existence of a doctors' body— of which representation to the European Community, and in particular to the European Commission, is the most important.

Although Britain is somewhat unusual in the freedom which exists for unregistered practitioners, it is not unique. The Society of Homoeopaths is well aware of the dangers in its present situation. To deal with this it is forming links with similarly placed groups elsewhere in Europe, particularly in West Germany and The Netherlands. It is even helping to establish such groups where necessary.

The question of the availability of natural medicines is also important on the Continent. The situation there is somewhat different from Britain because other European Community countries have insurance-based reimbursement systems rather than an all-encompassing health service. Reimbursement for natural medicines takes place in most countries to some extent but nowhere is this coverage complete and this makes it hard for many people to be treated as they wish. Britain therefore has an opportunity to lead Europe in its recognition of natural medicines— if the opportunities of the National Health Service Reform Bill are used to the full.

EUROPEAN COMMUNITY LAW AND MEDICAL
PRACTITIONERS

The European Community is based on its own 'four freedoms'. Two of these are the free movement of goods and capital. The others are the free movement of people and services, which also covers the right of establishment. These are covered by Articles 48–66 of the European Economic Community Treaty.

The 'right of establishment' means the freedom of a business or individual to carry on their business or professional activity (which is usually classed as a 'service') in another member state without hindrance. There should be nothing to prevent, say, a shopkeeper moving to France and trading there. On the contrary, various Community rules have been introduced to guarantee this right and to ensure that anyone moving for this purpose may take with them their family and other dependants.

These rights are better established for workers than they are for professionals or the self-employed. Community legislation exists to ensure that in practice doctors and other medical professions may move about the Community. The main concern of European Community legislation has been the mutual recognition of diplomas and other formal qualifications, and directives to ensure this have been approved for doctors, dentists, nurses, midwives, veterinary surgeons, and pharmacists.

Provision has already been made for the removal of many of the legal obstacles to free movement of people. Few measures connected with this have therefore been included in the single market programme but some connected with it have taken place. In particular, there have been persistent rumours of a directive concerning those who may practise medicine or therapy, and what qualifications they will need. . . . [Our] attempts to discover whether this actually exists or what it might involve have indicated that the European Commission *has no such plans at present* (and with the single market it has a great deal of work already).

Ultimately some action at European Community level is, however, likely. The different standards are inconvenient in themselves, but that does not give the basis to act. What are more likely to force it to act are the way these different standards distort economic activity in the Community, and the effects of uneven standards on consumer protection. Consumer protection has become a major force in European Community law and policy,[4] and this concern is likely to force the Community to act at some point.

The question, therefore, is how to ensure that natural medicines and holistic therapies continue to be available while satisfying the needs of European Community policy. The easiest and, overall, the most satisfactory way is to ensure that all non-registered practitioners belong to organizations which have strict codes of conduct and high standards of membership. This means they can protect themselves and their members from accusations of malpractice and can demonstrate to the European Community (and, in particular, to the Commission) that there is no need for intrusive regulation from outside. The code of practice of the Society of Homoeopaths is an admirable example of the sort of standards which are necessary to achieve this.

CONCLUSION

The arrival of the single market heralds great changes for the future of natural medicines in Britain. Policy for Britain in very many areas now comes from Brussels rather than London. Increasingly what happens in the Commission's Berlaymont building is more important than what happens in Westminster or Whitehall.

This alarms many, but it does not necessarily threaten natural or alternative medicines as much as some fear. It is necessary to adapt to the new situation and to accept the ways of thinking which are common in the European Community. The opportunities that the present situation creates—both in Europe

---

[4] See, for example, R. Eccles and J. Maitland-Walkers, 'The European Community and the Consumer', *The Law Society's Gazette* (15 Nov. 1989).

through the single market programme and associated changes, and in Britain through the reform of the National Health Service—are considerable. It would be appalling if these were to be lost because of reluctance to adapt to these circumstances or an assumption that changes in either direction were necessarily harmful because of their source.

To be able to do this, above all, it is necessary to organize. Only groups which are organized on a European level can hope to influence European Community policy. This is not easy to achieve and requires considerable tact and willingness to compromise. However it brings considerable rewards and is well worth the effort. Avoiding such action will unquestionably lead to the interests of alternative medicine being neglected and leave both users and practitioners out in the cold.

INDEX

Index